Statelessness and Citizenship

The idea for this book emerged from a study commissioned by the Geneva Academy for International and Humanitarian Law to commemorate the 60th Anniversary of the Universal Declaration of Human Rights. This volume develops some of the findings from that study but is based on much original material, including new country chapters. We are grateful to our Swiss colleagues for the intellectual and financial support which they gave to enable the initial research. This book has however been produced independently. In recognition of the human rights challenges that stateless people everywhere face – and in the knowledge that the Universal Declaration of Human Rights remains the cornerstone for their protection – we would like to affirm its importance by reprinting the commemorative logo designed by the Geneva Academy, alongside the logos of our institutions.

Statelessness and Citizenship

A Comparative Study on the Benefits of Nationality

Edited by

Brad K. Blitz

Professor of Human and Political Geography, Kingston University, London, UK

Maureen Lynch

Refugees International, Washington, DC, USA

Edward Elgar

Cheltenham, UK • Northampton, MA, USA

Published by
Edward Elgar Publishing Limited
The Lypiatts
15 Lansdown Road
Cheltenham
Glos GL50 2JA
UK

Edward Elgar Publishing, Inc.
William Pratt House
9 Dewey Court
Northampton
Massachusetts 01060
USA

A catalogue record for this book
is available from the British Library

Library of Congress Control Number: 2010927661

MIX
Paper from
responsible sources
FSC
www.fsc.org   FSC® C013604

ISBN   978 1 84980 067 9 (cased)
        978 1 78195 215 3 (paperback)

Contents

Contributors

Rustem Ablyatifov is a Political Analyst with the Crimean News Agency in Simferopol, Crimea and a Lecturer in Law at the Crimean Law Institute, Odessa State University. He received a BA in Law and an MA in Public Administration from the National Academy of Public Administration and has held several advisory appointments with human rights bodies and non-governmental organizations (NGOs) dealing with the naturalization of the returning Crimean Tatars. From 2002–06, he served as a governmental official in the State Committee of Ukraine for Nationalities and Migration as both Chief of the International Relations division and Deputy Chief of the Department for Nationalities. From 2006–07, he was Senior Legal Adviser to the Office of the Permanent Representative of the President of Ukraine in the Autonomous Republic of Crimea. A former Fellow of the Kennan Institute, Woodrow Wilson International Center for Scholars and Visiting Fellow at Carleton University, Ottawa, he has led training programmes and workshops on public administration reform and minority rights in the Autonomous Republic of Crimea and has worked with the Open Society Institute-Budapest and Konrad Adenauer Foundation to develop curricula and deliver training for local government officials. He is the author of several papers on minority rights, national self-government in Ukraine, the adaptation and integration of Crimean Tatars, as well as developments in multiculturalism and Ukraine's prospects of European integration.

Brad K. Blitz received his Ph.D. from Stanford University and currently is Director of Graduate Research Programmes and Professor of Human and Political Geography at Kingston University, London. He is a former Jean Monnet Chair at Oxford Brookes University and Research Associate in the Department of International Development at the University of Oxford. In 2007, he founded the International Observatory on Statelessness, a global web-based initiative which seeks to draw together academics, policy-makers, activists and others concerned about the human rights of stateless people. He has served as a consultant to international agencies including UNICEF, UNDP, the UN Office of the High Commissioner for Human Rights, the World Bank, Council of Europe, Organisation for Security and Cooperation in Europe, as well as several governments. He has published several studies on citizenship, statelessness, post-conflict development and minorities and human rights. Publications include *Statelessness in the European Union: Displaced, Undocumented, Unwanted* (with Caroline Sawyer) (Cambridge University Press, 2011), *War and Change in the Balkans: Nationalism, Conflict and Cooperation* (Cambridge University Press, 2006) and a multi-country study on the benefits of citizenship (with Maureen Lynch), a project funded by the Swiss and Norwegian Ministries of Foreign Affairs to support the 60th Anniversary of the Universal Declaration of Human Rights. Recent articles have appeared in *Mobilities, Europe-Asia Studies, Politics, Contemporary European History, Journal of Human Rights, Citizenship Studies, International Journal on Multicultural Societies, Journal of Refugee Studies, Political Studies, Journal of South East European and Black Sea Studies, International Studies Online, Journal of European Social Policy, Journal of Ethnic and Migration Studies,* and *Human Rights Review.* He is currently completing a book on citizenship and mobility and is directing a comparative study of the livelihoods of stateless and formerly stateless people in Bangladesh, Kenya, Slovenia, and Sri Lanka, funded by the US Department of State.

Greg Constantine is an award-winning Photojournalist who has created a multimedia resource around his project 'Nowhere People', a comparative investigation on the struggles of stateless ethnic minority groups in Asia. His work has been exhibited at the National Academy of Art in Bangladesh, the Angkor Photo Festival in Cambodia, the Foreign Correspondents Club of Thailand in Bangkok and the US House of Congress. His work on stateless people led to two nominations for the United Nations Children's (Emergency) Fund (UNICEF). Photographer of the Year in 2006 and 2007. In February 2007, his work on the Rohingya and Bihari was recognized in the 64th Pictures of the Year International (POYi) photojournalism contest with two awards. In 2008, he was named the winner of the Award for Excellence in Feature Photography in the 2008 Society of Publishers of Asia Awards. Most recently he received the Osborn Elliott Prize for Excellence in Journalism on Asia for his photographs on Cyclone Nargis in Burma which were published in the *International Herald Tribune* and *New York Times* in autumn 2008 (see http://www.gregconstantine.com).

James A. Goldston is the founding Executive Director of the Open Society Justice Initiative, an operational program of the Open Society Institute (OSI) that promotes rights-based law reform and the development of legal capacity worldwide. A leading practitioner of international human rights and criminal law, Goldston has litigated several groundbreaking cases before the European Court of Human Rights and the United Nations treaty bodies, and has served as Coordinator of

Prosecutions and Senior Trial Attorney in the Office of the Prosecutor at the International Criminal Court. Prior to his tenure with OSI, Goldston served as Legal Director of the Budapest-based European Roma Rights Center; Director General for Human Rights of the Mission to Bosnia-Herzegovina of the Organization for Security and Cooperation in Europe; and Prosecutor in the office of the US Attorney for the Southern District of New York, where he specialized in the prosecution of organized crime. He previously worked for Human Rights Watch. A graduate of Columbia College and Harvard Law School, Goldston has engaged in law reform fieldwork and investigated rights abuses in more than 30 countries in Africa, Asia, Europe and Latin America. He has taught at Columbia Law School and Central European University.

Julia Harrington Reddy is Head of the Equality and Citizenship programme of the Open Society Justice Initiative. After graduation from law school, she worked as a Legal Officer at the African Commission on Human and Peoples' Rights in the Gambia, developing the individual complaints procedure. In 1997, she co-founded and became Executive Director of the Institute for Human Rights and Development in Africa, also based in the Gambia, now a leading organization in African regional human rights litigation. Among the Institute's significant early victories was a decision against Mauritania, in which the Institute acted as counsel. She joined the Justice Initiative in 2003 upon the founding of the Justice Initiative, and has developed the Equality and Citizenship programme's focus on the link between ethnic discrimination and statelessness.

Maureen Lynch is Senior Advocate for Statelessness Initiatives at Refugees International (RI), an independent Washington-based refugee and humanitarian advocacy organization. Her current efforts on the global issue of statelessness are based on RI's 2005 report *Lives on Hold: the Human Cost of Statelessness* and the 2009 report *Nationality Rights for All: Progress Report and Global Survey on Statelessness*. This work follows an earlier study *Forced Back: International Refugee Protection in Theory and Practice* (2004). Since joining RI in 1999, Maureen has conducted assessment missions to more than 25 countries including Azerbaijan, Bangladesh, Cote d'Ivoire, Ethiopia, Haiti, Ingushetia, Kosovo, Kyrgyz Republic, the Occupied Palestinian Territories, Syria and Zimbabwe. Prior to RI, she worked for the United Nations High Commissioner for Refugees. Maureen holds a PhD in Human Development and Family Science from Oregon State University.

Abbas Shiblak is a specialist on the status of refugee and stateless communities, with particular interest in the Arab region. He has been a Research Associate at the University of Oxford Refugee Studies Centre (RSC) since 1992 and formerly worked as a Journalist and Senior

Information Officer at the Arab League in Cairo. He is the author of a book on Iraqi Jews, *The Lure of Zion* (1986), and has been leading a major research project on *de jure* and *de facto* statelessness communities including Palestinian, Kurdish and Bidoon peoples in the Middle East. He has also carried out work for the European Union on the status of refugees as part of the Middle East multilateral peace talks and participated in the United Nations Committee for the Elimination of Racial Discrimination (CERD) special session on discrimination against non-citizens. He holds an MPhil in Sociology from Kingston University and an LLM from the University of Cairo.

Abraham Korir Sing'Oei is currently the Conflict and Rule of Law Specialist at the US Agency for International Development in Nairobi, Kenya. Previously, he was the Legal and Strategy Director of the Centre for Minority Rights Development (CEMIRIDE), a non-profit organization he co-founded and for which he served as Executive Director for seven years. CEMIRIDE seeks the legal and political recognition of minorities and indigenous communities in Kenya and Greater Africa through strategic litigation, research and frontline advocacy. Mr Sing'Oei has also served as a Research Fellow at the Advocates for Human Rights in Minneapolis and at the Center for Justice and International Law in Washington DC. Mr Sing'Oei is an advocate of the High Court of Kenya and holds an LLB degree from the University of Nairobi and LLM degrees from the University of Pretoria, South Africa and the University of Minnesota Law School. He serves as Advisor to the African Commission on Human and Peoples' Rights Working Group on Indigenous Peoples' Rights and has extensive experience using international and regional human rights mechanisms to secure group rights, including the right to nationality and citizenship, for communities in Africa.

P.P. Sivapragasam (Siva) is President of the Human Development Organization of Sri Lanka, an NGO that works on behalf of minorities, internally displaced persons and other marginalized groups. He also serves as Honorary Secretary and Board Director of the Asia Committee of the International Movement Against Discrimination and Racism (IMADR), one of the leading NGOs lobbying and advocating on behalf of minorities. He received his BCom Hons in Management from the University of Peradeniya, and Postgraduate Dip in Human Rights and Masters in Human Rights from the University of Colombo. He has published several studies on plantation issues and human rights. He has worked extensively in the issues of minority rights in the context of non-discrimination policies, participation in public decision making, equality and justice. He has considerable experience in citizenship rights, political participation, language and educational policies with particular respect to the Plantation Tamils in Sri Lanka, as well as other minority groups in Sri Lanka.

Katherine Southwick is a Program Manager at the American Bar Association Rule of Law Initiative, but the views reflected in her chapter are her own. As the Robert L. Bernstein Fellow at Refugees International, her research and advocacy focused on statelessness worldwide, and included field visits to Bangladesh and Africa. She co-authored *Nationality Rights for All: A Progress Report and Global Survey on Statelessness* (2009) and other reports and articles on statelessness. She has also served as a federal judicial clerk in the Eastern District of New York, worked in private practice and lived in New Delhi, India for a year working with the South Asia Human Rights Documentation Centre. Ms Southwick mostly grew up in Africa, and has commented on conflict in Uganda and other human rights issues in major news media and scholarly publications. She holds a JD from Yale Law School.

Laura van Waas holds a PhD in International Law from Tilburg University, the Netherlands. Her doctoral thesis, entitled 'Nationality Matters – Statelessness under International Law' (2008), is an in-depth analysis of the international normative framework for the prevention of statelessness and the protection of stateless persons. She is currently working with the Regional Protection Hub for the Asia-Pacific department of the United Nation High Commissioner for Refugees (UNHCR) on a project that looks at gaps and good practices in the field of statelessness in the ASEAN region. She has previously assisted UNHCR with a similar research and consultation process for the Middle East and North Africa, helped to compile a number of training materials on statelessness and worked directly with UNHCR Beirut to build capacity to address statelessness in Lebanon and has also conducted research on behalf of Plan International on the link between irregular migration, birth registration and statelessness.

Raivo Vetik is Professor of Comparative Politics and former Director of the Institute of International and Social Studies at the University of Tallinn. He received his PhD in Political Science from the University of Tampere and has written extensively on inter-ethnic relations and identity, national integration policy, democratic processes and cultural semiotics in Estonia. In addition to numerous articles on nationality issues in Estonia and the Baltic states, he is the author of the *Estonian Sustainable Development Report* (2002) – the Estonian Official Report to the United Nations Johannesburg Summit on Sustainable Development, and *Perspectives on Democratic Consolidation in Central and Eastern Europe* (2001).

Jelka Zorn trained as a Social Worker and Social Anthropologist before receiving her PhD in Sociology from the University of Ljubljana. She is a Senior Lecturer in the Faculty of Social Work at the University of Ljubljana and former Visiting Fellow at the University of Stirling. She is a concerned activist and one the authors of *the Erased: Organized Innocence and the Politics of Exclusion* (2003), the first full account in English of the situation of denationalized persons who were rendered stateless by Slovenia during the first stages of independence. She has published several articles on the 'erased' in scholarly journals, including *Citizenship Studies, Nations and Nationalism, European Journal of Social Work*, and has edited several books and Slovene scientific journals.

Acknowledgements

Many people assisted in the production of this book. We are especially grateful to Tim Williams and Georgiana Applegate at Edward Elgar Publishing for soliciting this study and for their professional assistance throughout the publication process. It has been a pleasure to work with them both. We would also like to thank Professor Andrew Clapham, Aline Baumgartner and Annyssa Bellal of the Geneva Academy of International Humanitarian Law and Human Rights for their early encouragement of this work. The Academy was instrumental in the development of this comparative study and kindly recommended us to Edward Elgar Publishing. We are also grateful to our colleagues in UNHCR's Statelessness Unit, in particular Mark Manly, who has consistently supported our work and has championed efforts to reduce statelessness.

This was a complicated research project, which involved a team spread across several corners of the world. Colleagues at Oxford Brookes University facilitated an earlier study, which gave rise to this book and then helped us secure permission to reuse some material from the initial study in this volume. We are especially grateful to Brian Rivers, Lucinda Frew, Jennie Cripps and Kevin Henderson. Tempe Lautze of *Midnight Express Edits* carefully read every word of this document and provided helpful recommendations as she prepared the manuscript. Emily Hirst of Oxford Brookes University assisted with proofreading and Emily Kenny at the Open Society Justice Initiative helped in securing permissions.

Sections of this book first appeared in Brad K. Blitz and Maureen Lynch (eds) (2009), *Statelessness and the Benefits of Citizenship: A Comparative Study* (Oxford: Oxford Brookes University and International Observatory on Statelessness) (ISBN 978-0-9563275-0-5/ISBN 978-0-9563275). They are reproduced with permission from Oxford Brookes University. Sections of Chapter 12, Epilogue, appeared in James A. Goldston (2006), 'Holes in the Rights Framework: Racial Discrimination, Citizenship, and the Rights of Noncitizens', *Ethics and International Affairs*, 20, 321–4. They are reproduced with permission from Wiley-Blackwell.

A number of colleagues provided comments and insights on both earlier versions of this study and public presentations of our research at the 2009 Nicosia Conference of the International Association for the Study for Forced Migration. Colleagues at the Refugee Studies Centre, University of Oxford and at the University of Kingston also helped to guide the final product with probing questions during the autumn conference and CEESR Seminar Series, respectively. Finally, a note of thanks to Joel Charny and Dawn Calabia at Refugees International and to Hayley Blitz for their insightful comments throughout the course of this project and for their constant encouragement of our research.

Perhaps most importantly we want to thank each one of the individuals who willingly gave their time and shared their experiences with the researchers. Without them, it would not be possible to identify the hardships or to witness the beneficial impact that enjoying one's human rights can have on everyday life.

This volume is dedicated to the memory of Kenneth H. Bacon, President of Refugees International (2001–09), a man who stood up for stateless people.

Brad K. Blitz and Maureen Lynch

1. Statelessness and the deprivation of nationality

Brad K. Blitz and Maureen Lynch

Source: © Greg Constantine 2010.

Figure 1.1   In southern Nepal, a Dalit man and his grandson rest in the morning. The man's family has lived in the Terai for over five generations, yet he is still without Nepalese citizenship.

Under the 1954 *Convention relating to the Status of Stateless Persons*, a stateless person is an individual not considered as a national by any state under the operation of its law.[1] Although statelessness is prohibited under international instruments, the United Nations High Commissioner for Refugees (UNHCR) estimates, that there may be as many as 12 million stateless people in the world.[2] The existence of stateless populations challenges some of the central tenets of international law and the human

1

rights discourse that have developed over the past 60 years. Most importantly, the reality of statelessness is at odds with the right to nationality, which is explicitly recorded in the *Universal Declaration of Human Rights* (UDHR). Article 15 of the UDHR implicitly acknowledges the principle whereby an individual's nationality is linked to his or her identity, and it states, 'no one shall be arbitrarily deprived of his nationality nor denied the right to change his nationality'.[3]

The right to nationality has been further elaborated in two key international conventions which have brought the concept of statelessness into the United Nations framework and will be explored in greater detail in Chapter 2: the 1954 *Convention relating to the Status of Stateless Persons* and the 1961 *Convention on the Reduction of Statelessness*. The 1954 *Convention relating to the Status of Stateless Persons* was initially conceived as a protocol on stateless persons that was to be included as an addendum to the 1951 *Convention relating to the Status of Refugees* but was later made into a convention in its own right and is now the primary international instrument that aims to regulate and improve the status of stateless persons. A second convention was introduced in 1961 with provisions to avoid statelessness. While the 1961 *Convention on the Reduction of Statelessness* reiterates the main concerns of the 1954 instrument, in practice it defers to states and asserts that nationality shall be granted by 'operation of law to a person born in the State's territory' to anyone who would otherwise be stateless .[4] One important failing of this convention is that it does not prohibit the possibility of revocation of nationality under certain circumstances nor does it address the subject of retroactively granting citizenship to currently stateless persons; hence, the problem of statelessness has not been resolved.

Few states have ratified the stateless conventions, and the problem of disenfranchised groups and individuals being left without nationality has multiplied.[5] Some advocates have described the plight of stateless people as a matter of 'human security'[6] since while stateless people enjoy many human rights under international law[7], in practice, those who lack nationality have great difficulty in exercising their rights and therefore enjoy a precarious existence.[8] Research by Refugees International has highlighted the innumerable barriers which stateless people contend with, including the denial of opportunities to: establish a legal residence, travel, work in the formal economy, send children to school, access basic health services, purchase or own property, vote, hold elected office, and enjoy the protection and security of a country.[9] All too often the births, marriages and deaths of stateless people are not certified and, as a result, many stateless persons lack even basic documentation. This lack of identification means that they are often powerless to seek redress through the courts.[10]

Significant numbers of stateless people therefore face extortion from state and non-state agents as well as arbitrary taxation.

While the 1954 Convention focuses on *de jure* stateless persons, there are also countless others who cannot call upon their rights to nationality for their protection and are effectively stateless or *de facto* stateless persons. It should be noted that the convention includes a non-binding recommendation that calls upon states to 'consider sympathetically' the possibility of according *de facto* stateless persons the treatment which it offers to *de jure* stateless people, but often *de facto* stateless people are unable to obtain proof of their national identity, residency or other means of qualifying for citizenship and as a result are excluded from the formal state. Most governmental reporting on this issue concentrates on *de jure* stateless populations although there is a growing awareness that *de facto* stateless people are unable to realize their human rights and may be equally vulnerable for lack of effective protection from the state to which they have a formal connection.[11]

Until recently, statelessness remained a minor interest within UNHCR, which is principally a field organization. However, over the past five years, influential international NGOs and monitoring bodies have actively campaigned to raise the profile of stateless populations and have supported the expansion of UNHCR's efforts in this area.[12] To this end, they have been encouraged by United Nations (UN) committees, including the Committee on the Elimination of Racial Discrimination and other UN agencies, such as the Office of the High Commissioner for Human Rights (OHCHR).

During Kofi Annan's first term as UN Secretary-General, there was considerable examination of the scope of the Committee on the Elimination of Racial Discrimination and the exploration of ways in which the protection of human rights could be achieved through collaborative actions. These highlighted the relevance of social and economic factors for development, safety and security. One consequence of this activity was the 2003 report on the Rights of Non-Citizens drafted by the UN Special Rapporteur on the rights of non-citizens.[13] While non-citizens and stateless people are not coterminous, the report affirmed that non-citizens – and in this instance also stateless people – enjoy universal human rights and concluded that international law grants non-citizens virtually all rights to which citizens are entitled, except the rights to vote, hold public office and to exit and enter at will.[14] However, Weissbrodt also identified a 'large gap between the rights that international human rights law guarantees to non-citizens and the realities they must face' and noted that in many countries there were institutional and endemic problems confronting non-citizens.[15] The report served to set an agenda for reform that was later picked up by US-based activists and human rights monitoring organizations working closely with UNHCR, such as the Open Society Institute's (OSI) Justice Initiative, Amnesty International, Equal Rights Trust and Human Rights Watch as well as the UN Independent Expert on Minorities.[16]

For academics and practitioners, the issue of statelessness raises several concerns. First, the subject has received infrequent attention from scholars and there is relatively little comparative research on the causes, patterns and consequences of statelessness in the international system. Even less attention has been paid to the value of acquiring or reacquiring citizenship.

Second, for development agencies, the concept of statelessness introduces an essential power dynamic which is particularly challenging for the design and delivery of effective pro-poor social development programmes.[17] Most stateless people are the victims of ineffective governance, political restructuring or discrimination by the states in which they live; yet these national governments remain key interlocutors for multilateral agencies and non-governmental bodies, which are tasked with delivering aid. Arguably, stateless groups are not prioritized in social assistance programmes and are further disadvantaged as a result of aid policies which do not succeed in reaching them.[18]

Third, there is an inherent problem in the recourse to international law as a means of reigning in states that violate human rights. It is a long recognized norm of international law that states have the sovereign right to determine how nationality, and hence citizenship, is acquired.[19] However, in the case of stateless people, the state's prerogative of determining formal membership is often at odds with the protection of human rights in practice.[20] Indeed, the very notion of statelessness exposes the essential weaknesses of the global political system, which relies on the state to act as the principal guarantor of human rights. As Hannah Arendt noted more than 50 years ago, those who are left outside the state are vulnerable to abuse, poverty, and marginalization in all its forms.[21]

In light of the problems associated with statelessness, the right to nationality and citizenship takes on added significance, especially when one considers how those who lack citizenship live and what effect their disenfranchisement has on society at large. It is an irrefutable fact that discriminatory practices that may give rise to statelessness undermine the promotion of human security understood in the broadest sense as not only violence directed against individuals but also in the context of vulnerabilities caused by poverty, lack of state capacity and various forms of socioeconomic and political inequity.[22]

The negative effects of denying people their rights to nationality and citizenship are illustrated across the globe where by disenfranchising significant populations, states have sown the seeds for underdevelopment and unrest as, for instance, in Palestine, Israel and the surrounding states, Bangladesh and the Great Lakes region of Africa. As Bronwen Manby records:

> Those who have never been deprived of official papers may find it hard to imagine the powerlessness which results: powerlessness that can and does lead people to take up arms. Even in the poorest countries, a passport or identity card does not just provide the right to travel, but forms the basis of the right to almost everything else.[23]

Under conditions where large numbers of people are disenfranchised, states also lose in terms of lower economic output and a reduced fiscal base. The greatest losers, however, remain the individuals who are unable to pursue their daily existence free from interference and who have difficulties actualizing their rights, including the rights to work, to educate their children and to access health care services.

Arguably, the granting of citizenship may undo many of the harmful acts associated with the denial and deprivation of citizenship as described above. Yet, surprisingly, in spite of the significance of this area of investigation, few scholars have sought to uncover concrete evidence of the benefits of citizenship as a means of countering human rights violations and social, economic and political instability. It is precisely this gap that the proposed research seeks to address.

The central premise of this research is that elements of discrimination and inequality are common to all forms of statelessness, and it is therefore necessary to develop an understanding of the mechanisms that not only create statelessness but also perpetuate deprivation as well as those common elements found in solving statelessness and restoring nationality.

CAUSES OF STATELESSNESS

Statelessness persists due to political restructuring and changes in law triggered by state succession; discrimination or the arbitrary deprivation of nationality; technical and administrative gaps; and causes linked to climate change.[24]

State Succession

In many contemporary situations, statelessness has been linked to political restructuring following state succession. The transfer of territory or sovereignty in particular affects those living under new jurisdictions and may be subject to new citizenship laws and new administrative procedures.

Individuals may become stateless in these situations if they fail to acquire nationality under the new legislation or under new administrative procedures, or if they are denied nationality because of a reinterpretation of previously applicable laws and practices.[25]

State succession is often though not necessarily a consequence of war, and is frequently associated with discriminatory treatment of people who find themselves living under a different jurisdiction to one formerly known to them. An historical example of the effects of state succession can be found following the break-up of the Austro-Hungarian and Ottoman Empires and, later, the Soviet Union. The dissolution of these political structures fomented numerous nationality contests that left millions stateless and forced them to live as minorities in new political contexts. Since 1992, the de-federation and division of Czechoslovakia has left thousands of Roma in a precarious situation while their citizenship status was initially challenged and questioned by both successor states, often because individuals lacked documentation and proof of nationality.

State restoration can also create statelessness. In the case of the ethnic Russians in Estonia and Latvia, individuals of Slavic origin moved to the country during the Soviet occupation and were not given automatic citizenship (nor were their descendents) when these countries regained their sovereignty in 1991. In Latvia, citizenship was granted only to those who were Latvian citizens before 17 June 1940 and to their descendants. As a result, 30 per cent of the population was left without nationality. The government has since only recognized as 'stateless' fewer than 1000 individuals who do not have a claim to foreign citizenship and are not eligible to apply for naturalization in Latvia; the rest of the non-Latvian population, approximately 350 000–400 000, have been considered as non-citizens and presumed members of another state.[26]

Discrimination and the Arbitrary Deprivation of Nationality

Although international law prohibits discrimination on the grounds of race, colour, descent, or national or ethnic origin in the determination of nationality,[27] in practice many individuals are victims of discrimination and as a result find themselves unable to acquire the nationality of a particular state despite having strong ties to it. Discrimination can be either overt or created inadvertently in the laws or as they are implemented.[28]

Denial or deprivation of citizenship takes place as a result of a specific state action. This may include the introduction of discriminatory laws that target specific communities, the carrying out of a census of selected populations, or the introduction of onerous provisions that make it virtually impossible for certain groups and individuals to access their rights to citizenship, including establishing a legal identity by means of formal registration of births, marriages and voting.

One of the central concerns for the prevention and reduction of statelessness is the degree to which race and ethnicity are prioritized over civic criteria, or vice versa, in the design of exclusive nationality and citizenship laws. In practice, nationality policies built on the principle of blood origin (*jus sanguinis*) rather than birth on the territory (*jus soli*) have made the incorporation of minorities, especially children of migrants, particularly difficult. In several parts of the world from Cote d'Ivoire to the Dominican Republic to the former Soviet Union to Germany and Italy, the principle of membership on the basis of blood origin has locked many minority groups out of the right to citizenship in their place of birth and habitual state of residence.

During periods of national homogenization, ethnic membership may be associated with loyalty. This has been be a major factor in the denial and granting of citizenship; for example, in the 1990s, Croatia introduced several barriers that prevented ethnic Serbs from obtaining citizenship even though they had resided on Croatian territory prior to Croatia's independence and met the criteria for nationality. The discrimination against ethnic Serbs born in Croatia was compounded by the policy of granting citizenship to ethnic Croats from Bosnia who had recently been invited to settle in parts of Croatia.[29]

For more than 30 years, the Bihari community in Bangladesh has been segregated from the major Bengali population amid accusations that the Bihari were collectively disloyal and favoured the regime based in Islamabad during Bangladesh's break from Pakistan. Similarly, in parts of Central and East Africa, minority populations have been denied citizenship because they have been identified with colonial powers or historic 'enemy' groups, notably the Nubian population in Kenya and the ethnic Rwandese Banyamulenge in the eastern provinces of the Democratic Republic of Congo. In some instances, the persistent denial of citizenship may relate to both a positive action by the state and the lack of infrastructure to implement the action, as illustrated by the case of Kazakhstan where, in the 1990s, returning ethnic Kazaks ('Oralman') were encouraged to settle in large numbers before they had received any nationality status.[30]

Gender-based discrimination in matters of nationality is also a major problem and source of statelessness. In many countries where nationality is determined exclusively by patrilineal descent, women are not permitted to pass their nationality on to their children. Moreover, some states automatically change a woman's nationality status when she marries a non-national. A woman may then become stateless if she does not automatically receive the nationality of her husband or if her husband has no nationality. She can also become stateless if, after she receives her husband's nationality, the marriage is dissolved and she loses the nationality acquired through marriage, but her original nationality is not automatically restored. In several Arab states, children of mixed parentage – especially in cases where the mother is married to a non-national – may be denied nationality in their country of residence and may be left stateless.[31] Another gender-related category is orphaned and abandoned children who often do not have a confirmed nationality. In some contexts, illegitimate children may also be prevented from acquiring nationality.

Statelessness may result from the withdrawal of nationality. Denationalization occurs when a state deprives an individual of citizenship, usually because the state is engaging in discriminatory practices that may have exclusive and ideological roots. During and shortly after the First World War, foreign-born citizens who had been naturalized were stripped of their citizenship by France, Belgium, Turkey and the Soviet Union. Racist laws have similarly been used to advance denationalization campaigns, most famous of which is the 1935 *Nazi Law on the Retraction of Naturalizations and the De-recognition of German Citizenship*, which stripped Jews in Germany of their citizenship. More recently, former migrants from West Africa who had settled in Cote d'Ivoire were denaturalized during a programme of ethnic homogenization and intense xenophobia. Other groups have also been singled out such as the Bidoon in Kuwait and Banyamulenge in the Democratic Republic of Congo.

Migration and the failure to integrate minorities are also contributing factors that have influenced states' actions in both the active and accidental creation of stateless populations. While the process of exclusion often occurs during periods of state creation or state transformation, it should be noted that the ways in which states determine membership and access is fluid and migration may simply be one link in the causal chain that gives rise to statelessness. For example, as P.P. Sivapragasam discusses in this volume large numbers of Tamils who were brought to work in Sri Lanka in the late nineteenth century and kept isolated on plantations where they were later denied citizenship in Sri Lanka post-independence. More recent migrations have similarly created nationality problems, which, if left unaddressed, could also give rise to situations of statelessness. One case of reform is Germany, a country that for more than 40 years has played host to hundreds of thousands of people of Turkish origin, mostly guest workers and their descendants, who had settled there but few acquired the right to German citizenship until the law was amended in 2000.

In the former Soviet Union, forced migration generated new minority groups, which decades later led to problems of ineffective nationality. Indeed, many citizenship issues in Russia and Central Asia are directly related to former Soviet policies: mass deportations conducted in the 1940s created large minorities whose citizenship status is still uncertain; for example, Ossetians in Georgia, Crimean Tatars in Uzbekistan and Kazakhstan, Ingushetians and Meskhetian Turks in Southern Russia, to name a few.[32]

Laws Affecting Children and the Issue of Birth Registration

Other ways in which people become stateless include the application of laws and practices that particularly affect children. Although international law records that all children have a right to acquire a nationality, nationality is the prerogative of the state, and hence the nationality of a child is determined according to the laws of the states involved. While lack of birth registration does not equate to statelessness, lack of documentation has been used to deny people access to citizenship and state services. For many vulnerable people, the first hurdle to overcome is the registration of their child's birth. The *United Nations Convention on the Rights of the Child* (CRC) calls upon states to register children at birth (Article 7) but, according to Plan International, approximately 51 million births per year are not registered. The most affected regions are South Asia and Sub-Saharan Africa where approximately 23 million births (66 per cent) were not registered in 2006.[33] Children's advocates claim that birth registration provides the first legal recognition of the child. It is generally required for the child to obtain a birth certificate, which provides permanent, official and visible evidence of a state's legal recognition of his or her existence as a member of society. Birth registration is central to the campaign to reduce statelessness and inequality since states rely on birth registration and other means of documentation to grant access to basic services vital for the promotion of human security.[34]

Technical Failings

The application and enforcement of international law regarding non-discrimination in matters of nationality requires coordination between states. Problems may arise when nationality legislation in one state conflicts with that of another state. In such situations, individuals may be left without the nationality of either state. The situation known as conflict of laws explains, in part, the pervasiveness of statelessness around the world. In addition, it is important to note that conflicts between national legal systems may also be linked to the deliberate renunciation of nationality. Some states allow individuals to renounce their nationality without having first acquired, or been guaranteed the acquisition of, another nationality. Hence, the act of renouncing one's nationality may render a person stateless. Further, some states automatically revoke the nationality of an individual who has left his or her country or who resides abroad for an extended period of time.

There are also countless administrative practices that may result in the loss of nationality. Even if an individual is eligible for citizenship, excessive fees, red tape, insufficient documentary proof and the everyday challenges associated with living in poor developing country contexts may disadvantage the individual from acquiring citizenship.

Other Causes and Sources of Statelessness

At the 2009 UN Conference on Climate Change, the Intergovernmental Panel on Climate Change (IPCC) report identified the Netherlands, Guyana, Bangladesh and a number of oceanic islands as being especially threatened by a rising sea level (IPCC 2008). Press reports, however, publicized the claim that approximately 600 million people could be affected by the effects of rising sea levels before the end of the twenty-first century and might be forced to leave their countries of origin, suggesting that statelessness might be caused as a result of the physical disintegration of the state.[35] More recently, the UNHCR has addressed this challenge in a policy document on statelessness and climate change in which he noted that should statehood cease, the population of the former state could be considered *de facto* stateless.[36]

THE LITERATURE ON STATELESSNESS

General Themes

There is an emerging body of research that is related to the problem of statelessness and which has several intellectual sources. Some of the most widely cited publications include reports and articles on human security and specifically the rights of non-citizens.[37] Within the world of academia, one of the most influential writers on human security, Amartya Sen, has drawn attention to the problems associated with the lack of citizenship for personal and social development.[38] Sen (2001) argues that citizenship is integrally connected with the possible enhancement of human capabilities; hence, the granting of citizenship removes some of the 'unfreedoms' that place people at risk from want and fear. Others, however, challenge Sen's claims and note that human security is often undermined by other domestic factors that operate at the sub-national level. One important counter argument is that in both weak and strong states where political divisions are defined by gender, ethno-national, religious, tribal and party affiliations, there are many layers of discrimination that dilute the potency of citizenship by reinforcing discriminatory structures.[39] Thus, rather than consider citizenship to be a unifying force, one may speak of several classes of citizenship and a range of entitlements.[40]

The vast majority of writing on statelessness and related issues, however, has not introduced theoretical considerations but has taken the form of descriptive reports that have sought to set an agenda at critical times. In the late 1990s, a precursor to the discourse on statelessness – primarily a discourse on the rights of non-citizens who were not necessarily stateless – centred on issues of equality and were justified on the grounds that exclusion fosters inequality and hence insecurity. Indeed, this was one of the central premises of the United Nations Development Programme (UNDP) 1994 Human Development Report and the more influential Human Security Commission report entitled *Human Security Now: Protecting and Empowering People* (2003).[41] The reasons why this discourse was important to the emergence of a new and explicit discourse on statelessness lie in the fact that through these publications the UN had identified a causal connection between developmental concerns such as poverty and deprivation, the protection of human rights and problems of governance – all of which directly relate to statelessness:

> In the final analysis, human security is a child who did not die, a disease that did not spread, a job that was not cut, an ethnic tension that did not explode in violence, a dissident who was not silenced. Human security is not a concern with weapons – it is a concern with human life and dignity.[42]

Over the past five years, the policy language has shifted from a development focus to a rights-based theme and, in addition to UNHCR, a number of UN monitoring bodies and NGOs have drawn particular attention to the practice of denying and revoking rights to citizenship and the related problem of linking minority rights, namely the rights to enjoy and practice one's culture, language or religion, to citizenship status.[43] In 2008, the UN Independent Expert on Minorities devoted a section of her annual report to the arbitrary denial and deprivation of citizenship.[44] The United Nations Human Rights Council recently adopted a resolution on the human rights and arbitrary deprivation of nationality, which named statelessness as a human rights issue and reaffirmed that the right to a nationality of every human person is a fundamental human right.[45]

To date, the most comprehensive studies on statelessness include the 2008 publication, *Nationality Matters: Statelessness under International Law* by Laura van Waas and the 2009 report by Katherine Southwick and Maureen Lynch on behalf of Refugees International, 'Nationality Rights for All: A Progress Report and Global Survey on Statelessness'.[46] Van Waas dissects the two statelessness conventions and related international instruments and examines the legal provisions for stateless people and the need for reform in key areas including conflict of laws, state succession, and arbitrary deprivation of nationality, birth registration and migration. The report, 'Nationality Rights for All: A Progress Report and Global Survey', like the 2005 Refugees International study 'Lives on Hold: The Human Cost of Statelessness',[47] provides a wide-ranging overview of the political and human rights challenges that stem from the lack of nationality and offers a useful global survey of the problem on a country-by-country basis. The publications produced by Refugees International include inter-view data gathered during field visits to the region. The value added of the reports and field studies by Refugees International lies in the inclusion of historical details and micro-level descriptions of the way in which repression and the denial of human rights affects individuals on the ground.

Another influential publication is James Goldston's 2006 article in *Ethics and International Affairs*.[48] Goldston acknowledges that while there is growing consensus that nationality laws and practice must be consistent with general principles of international law above all human rights law, there is a clear protection gap. He then illustrates how the denial of citizenship excludes people from the enjoyment of rights and pays particular attention to 'indirect discrimination' which occurs when 'a practice, rule, requirement, or condition is neutral on its face but impacts particular groups disproportionately, absent objective and reasonable justification'.[49] He concludes that the growing divide between citizens and non-citizens in practice is 'primarily a problem of lapsed enforcement of existing norms'[50] and offers a set of useful recommendations to remedy this situation.

In addition to the above experts, several academics have touched on the issue of statelessness in their philosophical and sociological studies; inter-pretations of international law; examinations of regional conventions and treaty systems; research on children, gender issues and birth registration; and most recently, through their investigations of the effects of the war on terror, for individuals held in detention. These are briefly discussed below.

Philosophical and Sociological Studies

Within the fields of social and political theory, there has been a growing interest in Hannah Arendt's work, which has led to a re-examination of her brief writings on statelessness included in *The Origins of Totalitarianism*.[51] In Arendt's account, statelessness was symptomatic of the hollowness of human rights that could only be guaranteed by states. However, only a few scholars have linked Arendt's work to the failure of the human rights regime to provide protection for today's stateless populations.[52] One notable exception is Richard Bernstein, a peer and colleague of Arendt.[53] In general, one may observe that the issue of statelessness has not been addressed squarely among contemporary authors – only indirectly in the context of alienage.[54] For example, Gillian Brock and Harry Brighouse (2005) make an important contribution to contemporary political theory and cosmopolitan claims to citizenship by bringing together scholars who examine the moral obligations to foreigner residents on the basis of national identity; but the authors do not single out those who are excluded from participating on account of their nationality status.[55] More influential is the work of Seyla Benhabib (2004) who goes further than Brock and Brighouse in her condemnation of the denial of access to aliens, a term which is open to both foreign non-citizens and *de facto* stateless persons.[56]

Others who have approached the issue of nationality have often addressed the subject not from the perspective of rights per se but from a pragmatic problem of the politics of integration, which has implicitly drawn attention to *de facto* stateless persons. For example, Rainer Bauböck (2006) records in his study on acquisition and loss of nationality that political pressure from pro- or anti-immigrant forces has been especially significant in helping to define the situation for non-citizens, some of whom have been regularized as a result of activist campaigns.[57] Arguably, the primary contribution of scholars' writing on citizenship has not been in defining the problem of statelessness but rather in pushing some of the boundaries of liberal political theory and articulating challenges to realist constants of sovereignty, fixed notions of membership and the conceptual division of state responsibility between domestic and external arenas as recorded in the literature on cosmopolitanism.

Legal Analyses

Within the field of international law, some older texts provide an interesting historical account of the development of UN legislation on statelessness and the impact of the conflict of nationality laws on the creation of stateless populations.[58] While these publications are set in the context of Cold War divisions and have been supplemented by more recent writings that reflect contemporary geo-political realities in newly independent states,[59] one of the most comprehensive treatments of this subject from a rights-based perspective remains Paul Weis's 1979 *Nationality and Statelessness in International Law*.[60] Weis's book addresses the conceptual challenge of placing nationality in the context of international law and examines conditions under which it may be withdrawn, and multiple nationalities granted. Among the most useful chapters is his study of nationality in composite states and dependencies, which pays particular attention to the operations of the British Commonwealth in the context of nationality rights; the chapter on conflict rules also offers an initial attempt to set out typologies of statelessness.

Several well-known legal experts have further evaluated the right to nationality and the principle of non-discrimination within international human rights law.[61] Most important of these is David Weissbrodt's *The Human Rights of Non-citizens.*[62] Weissbrodt reiterates his conclusion from his 2003 report and argues that regardless of their citizenship status, non-citizens should enjoy all human rights just as formal citizens unless exceptional distinctions serve a legitimate state objective. Further relevant studies have appeared as a result of examinations of related international instruments including the *Convention on the Rights of the Child.*[63] Many of these studies are cited by van Waas and Weissbrodt who also include a detailed review of the literature on the above-mentioned aspects of law.[64]

One central theme, which links the studies on international instruments to the broader problem of human security and the practical aspects of protection, is the issue of implementation and the identification of a gap between the rights that international human rights law guarantees to non-citizens and the realities they face.[65] Also relevant is the distinction between the treatment of refugees and stateless people under law and the human rights obligations of states to both populations.[66] In recognition of these obligations, some practitioners have sought to examine the possibility of transforming international legal principles into law.[67] For example, van Waas presents an interpretation of the existing international framework to explore the scope of the civil and political as well as the economic, social and cultural rights of stateless populations under international human rights laws.

Regional Studies

There have been some notable studies of regional conventions and the commitments of regional treaty bodies with respect to stateless persons and non-citizens. Several have focused in particular on the European region with an emphasis on the European Union[68] and the Council of Europe's Convention on Nationality; others have examined the problems of dual nationality and the challenges of state succession, most notably in the Baltic states and former Soviet Union.[69] Other regions have featured as well, for example, the OSI has published the influential *Africa Citizenship and Discrimination Audit.*[70] Most international legal studies that do not focus on either the development of international instruments or the expansion of European-specific jurisprudence tend to focus on selected regions. These are briefly described below.

Africa

While Africa has been the the site of considerable international advocacy on issues of nationality,[71] until recently relatively few academics have written on the subject. Two important publications are the result of research and advocacy carried by the Bronwen Manby, the OSI's Africa Governance Monitoring and Advocacy Project (AfriMap) and Justice Initiative.[72] In *Struggles for Citizenship in Africa,* Manby (2009b) explores the history of nationality policies, identifies some of the most egregious examples of citizenship discrimination in Africa and makes the case for urgent reform of the law. The second OSI publication, *Citizenship Law in Africa* is a comparative report on the arbitrary, discriminatory and contradictory citizenship laws that exist in African states. The report covers topics such as citizenship by descent, citizenship by naturalization, gender discrimination in citizenship law, dual citizenship and the right to identity documents and passports. It describes how stateless Africans are systematically exposed to human rights abuses: they can neither vote nor stand for

Source:　© UNHCR/Greg Constantine 2010.

Figure 1.2　*The Galjeel, numbering 3500 to 4000 people, is a sub-clan of Somali descent and has lived in Kenya since the late 1930s. A Galjeel boy rests in an abandoned classroom. In the late 1980s and early 1990s, the Galjeel were stripped of their Kenyan status and evicted from their land.*

public office; they cannot enroll their children in school, travel freely or own property; they cannot work for the government. It also recommends ways that African countries can bring their citizenship laws in line with international legal norms.[73]

Elsewhere the most widely reported writings on nationality in Africa include articles on state failure and related country-specific reports on the conflict between Ethiopia and Eritrea[74] and the internal conflict and state collapse in Somalia.[75] These publications describe the context in which nationality laws were designed and focus on issues of governance alongside discrimination and citizenship. For example, the 2003 report by Human Rights Watch documents how the expulsion of people from Ethiopia, who had not taken up Eritrean citizenship, led to multiple instances of statelessness. Also relevant are writings on specific communities which highlight particular problems of citizenship in Kenya where stateless people are included among refugees[76] and Southern Africa where there are large populations of *de facto* stateless people.[77]

Americas

Historically, in the Americas where most states operate on the basis of *jus soli*, nationality issues have been less contested than in other regions. Nonetheless, certain human rights issues have attracted attention. These include important writings on racial discrimination and denial of citizenship in the Dominican Republic.[78] The USA has also come under scrutiny for its historical and current treatment of non-citizens.[79] In other parts of the Americas, contemporary flows of asylum seekers from the conflict in Colombia have also been the subject of academic investigation.[80]

Asia

There have been several important studies on stateless populations in Asia. Most of them relate to protracted situations. For example, the Biharis[81] and Rohingya in Bangladesh and Myanmar have featured in major investigative reports;[82] the Estate Tamils in Sri Lanka have also been the subject of research.[83] The expulsion of ethnic Nepalese from Bhutan has also been noted[84] as has the fate of Tibetans.[85] Some studies have also highlighted the relationship between trafficking and statelessness in South Asia[86] in addition to the particular vulnerability of women, children and other forced migrants from Burma, many of whom are Rohingya who have been coerced at the hands of criminal organizations to transit through Thailand and the neighbouring states.[87] Recently some parliamentarians have drawn attention to the several hundred ethnic minorities in Hong Kong who hold British Nationals overseas passports but have been unable to register themselves in Hong Kong and now remain *de facto* stateless.[88]

Europe

Within the field of European studies, there has been renewed interest in the problems of nationality and the incorporation of non-nationals. One major tendency within a number of these studies has been their primary emphasis on legal residents[89] and established ethno-national minorities.[90] That said, the fate of undocumented migrants and the revision of nationality laws has featured in some excellent work. This includes reports on the resettlement of deported persons, principally Crimean Tatars, and evaluations of the Ukrainian government's efforts to reduce statelessness,[91] as well as critical studies on the barriers which Roma have faced as a result of discriminatory naturalization requirements in the Czech and Slovak Republics.[92] In addition, it is important to highlight some comparative studies[93] and work on nationality issues in advanced states such as Germany,[94] Hungary[95] and, in particular, Bauböck's research on ethnic Turks, the descendants of former guest workers in Germany and Austria and recent pan-European investigations of membership rights in Europe.[96] Research on the problem of refused asylum seekers in the UK is also serving to fill an important gap.[97]

The most relevant studies that relate to the problem of statelessness tend to highlight the nationality problems associated with state restoration and the treatment of ethnic Russians in Estonia and Latvia.[98] Studies also discuss the case of the 'erased' in Slovenia – the non-ethnic Slovenes who saw their residency rights cancelled shortly after Slovenia declared independence from the Socialist Federal Republic of Yugoslavia.[99] Recently Jelka Zorn has further examined the plight of the 'erased' in the context of the right to remain and the freedom from deportation.[100]

Middle East

Research on statelessness in the Middle East has identified some important instances of discrimination on the basis of nationality. Curtis Doebbler (2002) and Abbas Shiblak (2009) argue that there has been a systematic failure to apply international human rights instruments to alleviate the plight of stateless people in the Middle East.[101] The most widely researched groups include the Bidoon[102] and, to a much lesser extent, the denationalized Kurds of Syria.[103] The issue of Palestinian rights to nationality features prominently, not only in regard to Israel and international law[104] but also to a much lesser extent in the context of historic discrimination by Arab host states.[105] In January 2010, Human Rights Watch published an alarming study regarding the denationalization of Palestinian-born citizens in Jordan.[106]

New Dimensions of Statelessness

Global issues and challenges have given rise to important publications that have increased understanding not only about some of the causes of statelessness but also previously under-researched populations. For example, trafficking and children have recently featured in important studies by academics and advocacy organizations such as Refugees International and Youth Advocate Program International (YAP).[107] An additional global issue concerns the war on terror. Since 2001, the relationship between statelessness and the war on terror has attracted the attention of some notable scholars and journalists on both sides of the Atlantic, not least because of the practice of placing foreign nationals in indefinite detention.[108]

RESEARCH DESIGN AND RATIONALE

The above literature review highlights some important gaps and provides a useful context for further investigation. The study in this volume explores the above themes to investigate the practical benefits of citizenship and the degree to which basic human rights are currently enjoyed by formerly stateless populations. It is motivated by three main research questions:

1. Has the granting of citizenship enabled individuals to access rights and resources?
2. How has the granting of citizenship enabled individuals to enhance the quality of their lives?
3. What barriers prevent people who have been granted citizenship the full enjoyment of their rights?

The empirical basis for this study is derived from semi-structured interviews ($n = 120$) conducted with formerly stateless individuals and a small number of policy and human rights experts as well as representatives of social service organizations in eight countries: Bangladesh, Estonia, Kenya, Kuwait (and neighbouring Gulf states), Mauritania, Slovenia, Sri Lanka and Ukraine. Reaching vulnerable populations is notoriously difficult, and, therefore, the research team relied upon community bodies, NGOs and social service organizations to gain access to individuals who might have been classified as effectively stateless. In order to build up a network of potential research participants, team members drew upon personal contacts in social service organizations where they were able to establish personal relationships and build up trust with potential participants, some of whom then agreed to take part in the research.

Interviewees were asked to assess the changes that the granting of citizenship brought to formerly stateless individuals. The eight countries were selected as a set of diverse illustrations of sites where both domestic and geo-political considerations have shaped national policies regarding the granting of citizenship to non-citizens. In each of the eight countries, indicative interviews were primarily conducted with selected individuals who had received citizenship. The purpose of the interviews was exploratory, and the questions simply sought to identify obstacles that participants had faced and to highlight what provisions might increase their sense of security.

In Kenya, the research focused on the treatment of the longstanding Nubian population in and around Nairobi. In the Gulf states, principally Kuwait, research focused on the Bidoon population. In Slovenia, interviews were conducted with the 'erased', some of the thousands of former Yugoslav nationals who did not opt for Slovene citizenship in 1992 and lost their residency rights and, with them, other essential rights following their removal from the Register of Permanent Residents. In Sri Lanka and Ukraine, the emphasis was placed on populations that have had many of their rights restored and these states have been hailed as success stories by the UNHCR.

In the Sri Lankan context, the communities concerned include some of the lower caste Dalit who are known as plantation Tamils, the descendants of former Indian labour migrants who had been brought in to Sri Lanka during colonial rule to work on the tea plantations in the centre and north of the country. In the case of Ukraine, the focus was on the return and repatriation of Crimean Tatars from Central Asia, above all Uzbekistan, to Ukraine during the 1990s. Individuals included the descendants of those who had been deported to Central Asia in the 1940s and whose nationality status was left in question following the demise of the Soviet Union.

In Mauritania, the research focused on the black Mauritanian refugees, exiled since 1989 in Senegal, who recently returned to their country under the terms of a tripartite agreement between the UNHCR and the Senegalese and Mauritanian governments. In Bangladesh, the research concentrated on the Urdu-speaking minority, also known as Biharis or 'stranded Pakistanis', whose situation has been linked to geo-political tensions between Pakistan and Bangladesh over the past four decades and whose fortunes were changed following the 2008 ruling of the Bangladesh High Court to grant citizenship to the disenfranchised population.

The final case study on Estonia focused on the Russian-language speakers who had acquired Estonian citizenship. The situation of this specific group was investigated by means of selected interviews and by analysing data gathered through the Integration Monitoring exercise, a statewide poll conducted four times over the past decade (2000, 2002, 2005 and 2008).

This study proceeds through three sections: a critical review of the development of international law and the establishment of human rights instruments to prevent and reduce statelessness followed by an analysis of the gaps in the international legal framework relating to the protection of stateless persons; a presentation of eight case studies; an evaluation of the benefits of citizenship with concrete recommendations to help ensure that the human right to a nationality and associated social and economic rights can be enjoyed by all.

NOTES

1. See UN General Assembly (1954).
2. UNHCR (2009c).
3. UN General Assembly (1948).
4. Ibid; UN General Assembly (1975). See also UN General Assembly (1961).
5. To date, 63 countries have become party to the 1954 *Convention relating to the Status of Stateless Persons*, and 35 countries have acceded to the 1961 *Convention on the Reduction of Statelessness*.
6. UNDP (1994).
7. The term 'Human security' appeared in mainstream development circles as a result of the 1994 global *Human Development Report*. It was the subject of a 2003 Global Commission study co-chaired by Sadako Ogata and Amartya Sen who popularized the concept through his writings, above all the Nobel Prize winning book *Development as Freedom* (2001).
8. Blitz (2009b); Lynch (2005).
9. Southwick and Lynch (2009).
10. Goldston (2006).
11. van Waas (2008).
12. UNHCR (2007).
13. See Weissbrodt (2003).
14. Ibid.
15. Ibid.
16. See also the report on denial of citizenship for the Advisory Board on Human Security and European Policy Centre, Sokoloff (2005).
17. Farzana (2008); Weissbrodt (2003).
18. Blitz (2009b).
19. League of Nations (1930).
20. Lynch (2005); van Waas (2008); Weis (1979); Weissbrodt and Collins (2006); Weissbrodt (2008).
21. The most frequently cited theoretical discussion of statelessness can be found in Arendt (2004).
22. Human Security Commission (2003); Sokoloff (2005); UN General Assembly (2008); UNDP (1994).
23. See Manby (2009a).
24. For a good discussion on causes of statelessness, see: Inter-Parliamentary Union (2005).
25. Ibid.
26. Southwick and Lynch (2009).

27. Weissbrodt (2003).
28. Inter-Parliamentary Union (2005).
29. See Blitz (2005, 2008).
30. UNDP (2006).
31. Southwick and Lynch (2009).
32. See Ginsburgs (1966); Helton (1996).
33. See UNICEF (2008).
34. Other means of documentation are also increasingly important and may act as substitutes in some developing country contexts. See Vandenabeele (2007).
35. Adam (2009).
36. UNHCR (2009a).
37. See Aurescu (2007); Bhabha (1998); Frelick and Lynch (2005); Goldston (2006), Human Security Commission (2003), Lynch (2005); Weissbrodt (2003); Sokoloff and Lewis (2005); Southwick and Lynch (2009).
38. Sen (2001).
39. See, for example, Elman (2001).
40. See the widely cited Cohen (1989).
41. UN (2003).
42. Ibid., p. 22.
43. See Goldston (2006); Open Society Justice Initiative (2006); UN (2009); UNHCR (2007).
44. UN General Assembly (2008).
45. UN Human Rights Council (2009).
46. See van Waas (2008); Southwick and Lynch (2009).
47. Lynch (2005).
48. See Goldston (2006).
49. Ibid., p. 238.
50. Ibid., p. 341.
51. See Arendt (2004), Chapter 9.
52. Leibovici (2006); Parekh (2004); Tubb (2006).
53. Bernstein (2005, 2008).
54. Benhabib (2004); Carens (2005)
55. See Brock and Brighouse (2005).
56. Benhabib (2004).
57. Bauböck (2006).
58. Aleinikoff (1986); Brownlie (1963); Ginsburgs (1996); Loewenfeld (1943); Samore (1951).
59. Bowring (2008b); Craven (2000).
60. Weis (1979).
61. Aurescu (2007); Doek (2006); Donner (1994); Goldston (2006); Weissbrodt (2003, 2008).
62. Weissbrodt (2008).
63. Buck (2005); Detrick (1999).
64. van Waas (2008); Weissbrodt (2008).
65. Batchelor (1995); Gyulai (2007); Hodgson (1993).
66. Anderson (2005); Batchelor (1995); Boyden and Hart (2007); Grant (2007); Weissbrodt and Collins (2006); Weissbrodt (2008).
67. Batchelor (2006); Gyulai (2007); van Waas (2008).
68. Batchelor (2006); Dell'Olio (2005); Shaw (2007).
69. See Barrington (1995); Bowring (2008b); Fehervary (1993); Ginsburgs (2000); Hughes (2005); Kionka and Vetik (1996); Vetik (2001); Wiegandt (1995).
70. Open Society Institute (2004).
71. Blitz (2009b).
72. See Manby (2009b).
73. Open Society Justice Initiative and Afrimap (2009).

74. Human Rights Watch (2003).
75. Menkhaus (1998); Menkhaus and Prendergast (1995).
76. Bartolomei et al. (2003).
77. Crush and Pendleton (2007).
78. Baluarte (2006); Human Rights Watch (2002); Wooding (2008).
79. Aleinikoff and Klusmeyer (2000); Ansley (2005); Camerota (2005); Kerber (2005, 2007).
80. Korovkin (2008).
81. Farzana (2008); Lynch and Cook (2006); Paulsen (2006); Sen (2001).
82. Amnesty International (2004); Arakan Project (2008); Refugees International (2008a).
83. Phadnis (1967); van Waas (2008).
84. Amnesty International (2000).
85. Hess (2006).
86. Lee (2005).
87. Anderson (2005); Arakan Project (2008); Mydans (2009); Nyo (2001); Refugees International (2004).
88. Avebury (2009).
89. Beckman (2006); Dell'Olio (2005); Pattie et al. (2004); Shaw (2007); Soysal (1995).
90. Minahan (2002).
91. Ablyatifov (2004); Uehling (2004, 2008).
92. Linde (2006); Perić (2003); Struharova (1999).
93. Hansen and Weil (2000).
94. Green (2000); Groenendijk and Hart (2007).
95. Magocsi (1997).
96. Bauböck (2006).
97. See Blitz and Otero-Iglesias (2010, forthcoming); London Detainee Support Group (2007, 2009); see also Sawyer and Turpin (2005).
98. Barrington (1995); Bowring (2008b); Fehervary (1993); Ginsburgs (2000); Hughes (2005); Kionka and Vetik (1996); Vetik (1993, 2001, 2002); Wiegandt (1995).
99. Andreev (2003); Blitz (2006); Dedić et al. (2003); Jalušič and Dedić (2008); Zorn (2005, 2009c).
100. See Zorn (2009c).
101. Doebbler (2002); Shiblak (2009).
102. Ali (2006); Barbieri (2007); Rizzo et al. (2007).
103. Bryce and Toynbee (2000); Lynch and Ali (2006).
104. Feldman (2008); Peled (2005, 2008); Takkenberg (1988).
105. Knudsen (2009); Mavroudi (2008); Shiblak (2006, 2009).
106. See Human Rights Watch (2010).
107. Berezina (2004); Bhabha (2003); Lynch (2008).
108. Bowring (2008, 2008b); Brouwer (2003); Equal Rights Trust (2009a); Hegland (2007); London Detainee Support Group (2007, 2008, 2009); Stevens (2006); Wright (2009).

2. Nationality and rights

Laura van Waas

In the autumn of 2003, a law was passed by the Sri Lankan parliament that promised to change the lives of several hundred thousand of the country's inhabitants: the *Grant of Citizenship to Persons of Indian Origin Act*. This impressive piece of legislation aspired to bring an end to the marginalization, disenfranchisement and exclusion of the 'Hill Tamils' who had lived in a condition of statelessness for many decades by granting them Sri Lankan nationality.[1] In time, reports came in of people who had benefited from the new law and who explained in their own words what this policy meant:

> I was really thankful when my national identity card arrived because it allowed me to travel to Colombo and find work here. I am earning much more than I would have if I stayed on the estate.[2]

The resolution of cases of statelessness through the reinstatement of the bond of nationality with a state can evidently have a positive impact upon the individual's enjoyment of rights and quality of life; it can put an end to years, even a lifetime, of exclusion and abuse. But is this always the case? And to what extent does the formal acquisition of a nationality put an end to the difficulties experienced by previously stateless persons? These are the questions that guide the case studies in the chapters to come, where the situation of these new citizens of Sri Lanka and that of other populations whose statelessness has been addressed is investigated in detail.

However, another question underlies those that are presented above; a more fundamental question about nationality and rights: in the contemporary human rights environment, to what extent is nationality still relevant to the enjoyment of rights? In order to better understand the findings of the case studies that are presented later in this book, it is important to be aware of the role that international law actually attributes to nationality today – the extent to which the stateless fall into a 'protection gap' that is, or should be, remedied by the acquisition of a nationality. This subject is the focus of the present chapter which looks at the trend towards the denationalization of protection that is apparent in the development of modern human rights law, analyses how this same international legal framework addresses the specific plight of the stateless and discusses those areas in which the stateless may, indeed, find themselves excluded from the enjoyment of rights until their actual statelessness is resolved.

THE DEVELOPMENT OF HUMAN RIGHTS LAWS AND THE DENATIONALIZATION OF RIGHTS

Following the atrocities of the Second World War, the newly formed United Nations determined that the responsibility for the protection of people's rights and freedoms could no longer be wholly entrusted to domestic legislation and institutions. Historically, states have bestowed certain privileges – as well as duties – upon their citizens.[3] Until the Second World War, it was generally left to each state to delineate and guarantee such rights through their own domestic arrangements.[4] However, the acts committed by the Nazi government in Germany were proof that municipal law could all too readily be manipulated to become a weapon of persecution and that state authorities could become the agents of such persecution. The United Nations therefore set itself an international agenda for protection, committing time and resources to the agreement of a catalogue of rights that were to be respected by all governments alike. This marked the birth of the contemporary human rights framework.

The earliest instrument to be promulgated was the *Universal Declaration of Human Rights*, which continues to inspire the contours of universal and regional human rights regimes to this day. The Declaration opens with the important proclamation that 'all human beings are born free and equal in dignity and rights'.[5] While this powerful sentiment is not new, its inclusion in the Declaration is an affirmation that this philosophy lies at the heart of international human rights protection. This means that the Declaration is not only a compilation of rights that all governments pledge to respect, it also houses rights to which we are all entitled on the grounds of our membership in the 'human family'.[6] For instance, no one shall be held in slavery or servitude; no one shall be subjected to arbitrary arrest, detention or exile; everyone has the right to freedom of thought, conscience and religion; and everyone has the right to a standard of living adequate for the health and wellbeing of himself and his family.[7] These are just some examples of how, from the starting point of 'all human beings are born free and equal in dignity and rights', the international community elaborated a catalogue of standards to be enjoyed by everyone everywhere on the basis of the simple fact that they are human beings.

In other words, the development of human rights law heralded both a

move towards universally recognized rights as well as the possible denationalization of rights. Previously, states were largely concerned with the
enjoyment of rights by their own citizens be it through domestic legal
arrangements or the exercise of diplomatic protection abroad. The advent
of human rights law initiated an uncoupling of nationality and rights.
Instead of citizenship being the basis for the enjoyment of rights, 'the
principles of human rights would maintain that being human is the right
to have human rights'.[8]

The diminished relevance of nationality and the broad notion that
citizen's rights have made way for human rights is reflected across the
full spectrum of human rights instruments. Thus, the UN Human Rights
Committee commented that:

> the rights set forth in the [International Covenant on Civil and Political Rights]
> apply to everyone, irrespective of reciprocity, and irrespective of his or her
> nationality or statelessness.[9]

Other bodies have echoed this observation in their own statements on
the application of human rights instruments. The UN Committee on the
Rights of the Child, for instance, has declared that:

> the enjoyment of rights stipulated in the [Convention on the Rights of the Child]
> is not limited to children who are citizens of a State party and must therefore,
> if not explicitly stated otherwise in the Convention, also be available to all chil-
> dren . . . irrespective of their nationality, immigration status or statelessness.[10]

Herein lie the first signs that, thanks to the influence modern human
rights law has had on the relationship between nationality and rights, the
position of those individuals who lack any nationality, the stateless, is far
less precarious than it once was.

Indeed, there is now case law confirming this development. For example,
over the past decade the European Court of Human Rights has had
numerous complaints brought before it by stateless persons. In each case,
the Court opens the description of the facts by noting that the applicant
is stateless. This finding has no subsequent impact on the admissibility of
the claim since the Court need only determine that the violation occurred
within the jurisdiction of a state party to the European Convention on
Human Rights. The nationality of the applicant is not deemed relevant.[11]
Thus, in the case of *Al-Nashif v. Bulgaria,* the stateless Mr Al-Nashif
makes a successful appeal against the violation of his right to be free
from arbitrary detention, his right to the enjoyment of family life and his
right to an effective remedy.[12] Moreover, alongside such opportunities
for stateless persons to access individual complaints procedures in order

to effectuate their rights, human rights supervisory bodies have taken an active interest in monitoring the treatment of stateless persons in countries across the globe. There are countless examples in which the enjoyment of rights by non-nationals generally, as well as stateless persons specifically, has been subjected to scrutiny and commented upon, for instance, in the context of periodic reporting by states to the UN treaty bodies and other human rights supervisory apparatus.[13] In summary, the protection of the stateless has become an integral part of overall human rights protection and stateless individuals can rely on the international legal framework in the same way as persons who do hold a nationality.

STATELESSNESS AND THE 'HUMAN' IN HUMAN RIGHTS

So far in this chapter, a very positive picture has been painted of the human rights framework as a tool for the protection of the rights of state-less persons. However, as suggested in the introduction, this is not the full story. While the majority of human rights are, indeed, guaranteed under law to everyone regardless of nationality, this is not the case across the board. There are a number of standards that have been formulated in such a way as to call into question the inclusiveness of the term 'human rights', suggesting that the denationalization of rights remains an incomplete process. There are, in fact, still a number of citizens rights dressed up as human rights.

The first and most evident example of this phenomenon is the right to participate in government. For instance, in Article 21 of the Universal Declaration, this political right, which includes the right to vote, to stand for election and to work in public service, is formulated as follows: 'everyone has the right to take part in the government of his own country'. While the norm addresses itself to 'everyone', this provision still stands out from other human rights standards because it is only guaranteed with respect to one's 'own country'. And since the notion of 'own country' is generally deemed to refer to the country of nationality, this proviso that pretends to be merely a jurisdictional technicality actually operates as an exclusion clause for those who have no country, the stateless.[14] Thus, human rights law as it stands today does not provide the stateless with any claim to the right to participate in government.

The human rights regime admits a similar limitation of the enjoyment of rights by the stateless in relation to the freedom of movement, which includes the right to leave, the right to enter/re-enter and the right to remain in a state. In a number of human rights instruments, such as the

European and American conventions, the right to enter/re-enter and the right to remain are granted to everyone with respect to the territory of 'the state of which he is a national'.[15] Elsewhere, individuals are guaranteed the right to re-enter and remain in their 'own country', which is again understood in principle to refer to the country of citizenship. So, while citizens enjoy the right to enter/re-enter and remain in their country of nationality, states remain free to 'set the conditions for entry and residence of aliens [and retain] the right to expel them'.[16] An individual may, therefore, be refused admittance to or be expelled from a state of which he is not a national.[17] Where the stateless are concerned, that is, every state. The stateless are, once more, the victims of a hidden exclusion clause and find themselves without any automatic and unqualified right to enter/re-enter or remain on the soil of any state. Moreover, in the absence of a right of entry/re-entry, the third component of the freedom of movement, the right to leave, also becomes a practical impossibility. The stateless are left without the ability to travel internationally as well as without a country that they can rightfully call home.

A third area in which human rights law plainly allows for restrictions to be placed on the enjoyment of rights by the stateless is that comprised of 'economic rights'. In one of its opening articles, the *International Covenant on Economic, Social and Cultural Rights* (ICESCR) proclaims that developing countries with due regard to human rights and their national economy may determine to what extent they would guarantee the economic rights recognized in the present Covenant to non-nationals.[18]

Developing states are hereby expressly permitted to restrict the economic rights of non-citizens, including stateless persons, on their territory. Neither the expression 'developing country' nor the phrase 'economic rights' are explained elsewhere in the Covenant nor do they appear in the comments and jurisprudence of the Committee on Economic, Social and Cultural Rights. This leaves questions about the scope and application of the article. Nevertheless, this provision is another example of how, in spite of the overall trend towards denationalization of rights under human rights law, there are areas in which the stateless may still be excluded from the full enjoyment of rights.

Furthermore, even where the human rights framework does espouse rights that can and must be enjoyed by everyone, including the stateless, there is no guarantee that nationals, non-nationals and stateless persons will always enjoy such rights on equal terms. Indeed, although the general principles of non-discrimination, equality before the law and equal protection of the law are absolutely central to the human rights system as a whole, distinctions between citizens and non-citizens are not necessarily outlawed under these standards. On the one hand, for instance, the

Convention on the Elimination of Racial Discrimination does not cover 'distinctions, exclusions, restrictions or preferences . . . between citizens and non-citizens'.[19] On the other hand, the Committee charged with overseeing the Convention has declared that:

> under the Convention, differential treatment based on citizenship . . . *will* constitute discrimination if the criteria for such differentiation, judged in the light of the objectives and purposes of the Convention, are not applied pursuant to a legitimate aim, and are not proportional to the achievement of that aim.[20]

Whether a distinction based on citizenship would pass muster or not therefore depends on the specific circumstances at hand; which instrument, which right, which facts? Such distinctions are not by definition prohibited, and the leeway that is thereby left to states may have a far-reaching impact on the equal enjoyment of rights by stateless persons.

In view of the foregoing observations, it is fair to conclude that the notion of human rights as rights belonging to all human beings regardless of nationality or statelessness is not beyond question when the human rights framework is subjected to a more thorough analysis. In particular, the situation of the stateless, the lack of a bond of nationality with any state, places some doubt on the inclusiveness of the term 'human' in human rights. Interestingly, the human rights framework itself recognizes this apparent flaw and attempts to remedy it by promulgating, among the rights to be enjoyed by everyone, the right to a nationality.[21] This is, in itself, a confirmation of the enduring role of nationality in the exercise of rights, even in the contemporary human rights era. If the right to a nationality were fully realized, then no one would be without this legal bond and unable to access the related rights. Yet statelessness is an enduring – if not growing – phenomenon, afflicting many millions of individuals worldwide. For them, the incomplete denationalization of rights under the human rights framework as presented above may pose a serious threat to the enjoyment of the full range of human rights. Thus, the acquisition/reacquisition of a nationality, putting an end to their actual statelessness, may indeed be the only real remedy to their vulnerability.

STATELESS-SPECIFIC PROTECTION UNDER INTERNATIONAL LAW

Fortunately, the fact that even under current human rights law, the stateless are in an anomalous and potentially highly vulnerable position has not escaped the attention of the international community. On the contrary, the UN has long taken an interest in statelessness and developed a pair of specialized instruments to address the issue.[22] One of these documents, the 1954 *Convention relating to the Status of Stateless Persons*, is devoted in its entirety to improving the standard of living of individuals who find themselves without any nationality. The other instrument, the 1961 *Convention on the Reduction of Statelessness*, attempts to definitively resolve the issue of the stateless as a vulnerable group by laying down concrete rules for the realization of the right to a nationality and thereby the prevention of statelessness. In the present chapter, the 1954 Convention will be the main focus of discussion as the analysis of the relationship between nationality and rights continues.[23]

The 1954 *Convention relating to the Status of Stateless Persons* introduces the concept of 'stateless person' as an internationally acknowledged legal status. Thus, in its Article 1, the convention determines that a stateless person is 'a person who is not considered as a national by any state under the operation of its law'. If an individual meets this definition – and is not disqualified from protection by one of the exclusion clauses included in the convention[24] – he is entitled to the enjoyment of the rights and freedoms set forth in the instrument. A total of 30 successive articles cover a wide variety of concerns from the freedom of religion to the right to work; from the right to housing to the protection of intellectual property. In other words, this document touches upon a large number of human rights issues. It provides in each case tailor-made guarantees for the stateless.

However, it is important to be aware that in delineating the rights to be enjoyed by stateless persons, the 1954 Convention adopts a very particular technique. The convention recognizes five different 'levels of attachment' that a stateless person may attain, noted here in order of strengthening attachment to the state: subject to the state's jurisdiction, physical presence, lawful presence, lawful stay and durable residence. With increasing attachment comes access to more rights. Thus, stateless persons who enjoy the weakest form of attachment to a contracting state and are simply subject to that state's jurisdiction are accorded among other things certain entitlements relating to access to courts and to education. The enjoyment of freedom of religion is guaranteed as soon as a person is physically present but only when such presence is also lawful is the freedom of movement within the state protected. Once lawful stay or even durable residence is achieved, the stateless person will gain access to additional rights; for example, those relating to wage-earning employment and travel documents. The enjoyment of rights therefore varies according to the relationship between the stateless person and the state in question.

A second distinctive and noteworthy characteristic of the 1954 Convention relates to the formulation of the substantive rights themselves.

The standard of protection offered also differs from one right to another. The convention employs three different standards, the weakest of which is treatment at least as favourable as that accorded to non-nationals generally. This is in fact the minimum standard of treatment that is always to be enjoyed by stateless persons under the 1954 Convention:

> except where this Convention contains more favorable provisions, a Contract State shall accord to stateless persons the same treatment as is accorded to aliens generally.[25]

This means that even in areas in which the convention does not provide for specific protection stateless persons can always invoke this minimum standard. Importantly though, many of the rights that are explicitly outlined in the 1954 Convention are offered at a higher standard of treatment by either providing for treatment on a par with nationals or in the form of absolute rights rather than a contingent standard. For instance, stateless persons are to enjoy the right to public relief on the same terms as nationals, and they are to enjoy an absolute right to legal personhood. In some cases then, the 1954 Convention resolves any potential difficulties that the stateless may experience as a result of their lack of nationality by placing them on a par with nationals or by directly attributing them certain rights.

Meanwhile, one of the other absolute rights elaborated in the 1954 *Convention relating to the Status of Stateless Persons* is also one of the instrument's most significant provisions. Article 27 determines that identity papers are to be issued to any stateless person in the territory of a state party who does not possess a valid identity document. Such papers are envisaged to fulfil two vital purposes: to establish certain facts relating to the identity of the individual and to vouch for his status as a stateless person. By providing for the documentation of identity and status in this way, the 1954 Convention ensures that stateless individuals are able to prove their eligibility to the entitlements bestowed upon them by virtue of their stateless person status (as well as their personal status). This is a critical factor in the enjoyment of rights in practice. Moreover, in the subsequent provision, Article 28, the convention also provides for the issuance of travel documents, this time to stateless persons who are lawfully staying in the territory of a contracting state. The so-called Convention Travel Document (CTD) is designed to function in lieu of a passport, a document that is generally unavailable to stateless persons since it is usually issued by the country of nationality. The CTD also offers proof of the stateless individual's identity and status, but it may additionally entitle the holder to enter/re-enter the issuing state.[26] In providing for the issuance of CTDs and the recognition of such papers by other state parties the 1954

Convention takes an important step towards the facilitation of travel by stateless persons as well as helping to ensure access to the privileges that accompany the status of the stateless person when he is abroad.

It is clear that the establishment, on the periphery of the human rights framework, of a convention to deal specifically with the rights of stateless persons is further confirmation of their position as a vulnerable group. As discussed above, the development of human rights law brought about a progressive denationalization of rights but stopped short of rendering nationality entirely irrelevant for the enjoyment of rights. With this in mind, the international community set out specific protective measures for stateless persons in the 1954 *Convention relating to the Status of Stateless Persons*. The hope is that the traditional human rights framework and the specialized regime of the 1954 Convention will together provide an adequate legal foundation for the full and effective enjoyment of rights by stateless individuals across the globe. And indeed, with this initial perusal of the 1954 Convention, it quickly becomes apparent that the instrument covers a wide array of substantive issues and boasts a number of provisions that are absolutely key to effectively protecting the rights of the stateless. However, concerns also surface as to the adequacy of many of the substantive guarantees especially in view of the very particular way in which these rights have been formulated. To what extent the overall international legal framework relating to the protection of stateless persons still exhibits gaps is a question that will be discussed in greater detail below.

GAPS IN THE INTERNATIONAL LEGAL FRAMEWORK RELATING TO THE PROTECTION OF STATELESS PERSONS

The preceding sections highlighted two parallel developments within international law: the denationalization of rights under human rights law to the effect that stateless persons are to a large extent able to rely on this regime in the same way as those who do hold a nationality and the establishment of stateless-specific guarantees to further promote the enjoyment of rights by the stateless. Laying these two components of the international legal framework relating to the protection of stateless persons alongside one another, it becomes possible to identify gaps that remain and thereby pinpoint those areas in which nationality continues to play a part in access to rights today.

In particular, there are the three concrete, problematic issues raised in the discussion of the contemporary human rights framework. According to that analysis, there is no guarantee that stateless persons will have the

opportunity to participate in government, enjoy freedom of movement –
that is, the right to re-enter and remain in a state – and be entitled to economic rights in developing countries. It is time to consider whether each
of these questions is resolved by the stateless-specific protection offered
under the 1954 *Convention relating to the Status of Stateless Persons* and,
if not, whether there are any other relevant developments pointing the way
forward.

The enjoyment by stateless persons of political rights is one of the topics
that came up for discussion during the drafting of the 1954 *Convention
relating to the Status of Stateless Persons*. However, rather than being
focused on ensuring that stateless persons are not rendered at a disadvantage due to their lack of any nationality and coming to some agreement
on an appropriate mode of political participation for the stateless, the
state delegations deliberately chose not to include political rights in the
convention. Indeed, not only were rights relating directly to participation
in government absent from the draft, but all attempts to codify even the
freedom of opinion and expression or the freedom of political assembly –
rights that can be exercised to the benefit of political activity in the broadest sense and are critical to individual empowerment – were also beaten
back. States were instead keen to retain the right to restrict the political
activity of stateless persons.[27] But this stance no longer seems tenable in the
contemporary human rights environment. The possession of a nationality
is certainly not a condition for the enjoyment of the freedom of opinion,
expression and of political assembly. These rights are all attributed to
everyone and, although the political activities of both nationals and non-
nationals may be subject to restrictions in order to protect other esteemed
values such as the rights of others or national security, a blanket denial
of these rights to stateless persons could not be legitimated under these
limitation clauses.[28]

Moreover, there are a number of persuasive arguments for giving
renewed thought to finding a suitable way to offer stateless persons the
right to participate in government, including the fact that the lack of
empowerment and denial of an opportunity to effect political processes
through regular channels creates a breeding ground for dissent that may
take a more destructive form.[29] Plus, the traditional view that allowing
non-nationals to participate in government would constitute a threat to
national security because of their conflicting allegiance is no longer defensible because the stateless do not owe allegiance to another state because
they lack any nationality and because the dislocation of political rights
from citizenship is a trend already in evidence in a number of countries
around the world.[30] Nevertheless, although the human rights community is receptive to the development of what is commonly described as

denizenship,[31] as international law currently stands, the stateless cannot rely on a right to participate in government since nationality is still a central factor in the enjoyment of this right.

The failure to settle questions related to the freedom of movement for stateless persons in the 1954 *Convention relating to the Status of Stateless Persons* betrays an even greater weakness of the instrument. As discussed above, the 1954 Convention attributes different rights at different levels of attachment, such as physical presence, lawful presence, lawful stay and so on. The opportunity to lawfully gain access to a state's territory and to take up residence is therefore critical to the enjoyment of the full catalogue of rights housed in the 1954 Convention. Yet the convention omits any mention of the right to enter a state, leaving contracting parties free to refuse, detain or expel any stateless person seeking access to their soil without the proper authorization.[32] The convention does offer certain guarantees against expulsion, protecting the right to remain and to a limited extent also the right to enter/re-enter on the basis of a CTD, but only if the stateless person is in the country lawfully.[33] It would therefore seem that without any nationality and the associated automatic right of entry and residence in the country of citizenship the stateless may be passed from one state to another, kept in indefinite detention pending the possibility of deportation or be forever informally 'tolerated' without achieving a lawful status (the essential precondition for access to many of the rights housed in the 1954 Convention). In this also, there are signs of change – positive developments within the modern human rights framework that may offer a solution. The work of the UN Human Rights Committee to expand and come to a more appropriate interpretation of the notion of 'own country' when assessing a person's right to enter a state is of particular interest:

> the scope of 'his own country' is broader than the concept 'country of his nationality'. . . it embraces, at the very least, an individual who, because of his or her special ties to or claims in relation to a given country, cannot be considered a mere alien.[34]

The examples that are subsequently elaborated by the Human Rights Committee include various scenarios that may arise in the context of statelessness. Thus, in cases where nationality was lost through an act of denationalization that ran counter to a state's international obligations, where state succession created statelessness or where statelessness is prolonged due to the enduring denial of citizenship by the country of residence, the stateless person will be entitled to enter/re-enter or remain in that state regardless of the loss of citizenship. The main crux of the matter is establishing which state is 'responsible' for a person's prolonged statelessness. This task also requires a further clarification of the international legal framework for the prevention of statelessness since these rules are key to the identification of the 'responsible' state. By further crystallizing and applying this flexible interpretation of the concept of 'own country', the human rights framework can offer the answer to one of the major outstanding issues in the protection of stateless persons. This will, in turn, boost the enjoyment of other human rights guarantees and, more particularly, the effectiveness of the 1954 *Convention relating to the Status of Stateless Persons.*

Now to whether the 1954 *Convention relating to the Status of Stateless Persons* addresses concerns regarding the potential restriction of the economic rights of stateless persons by developing countries. The 1954 Convention does not decide the matter one way or the other. Developing countries do not receive any special attention under the convention, nor is a separate group of economic rights recognized. However, the convention does outline the minimum standard of treatment to be enjoyed by stateless persons with regard to a number of subjects that may be considered to fall within this category, namely the right to work, the freedom of association, the right to social security and other labour rights.[35] Of these provisions, the first two offer only the most basic standard of treatment. The stateless are to enjoy the right to work and the freedom of association on terms at least as favourable as those granted to non-nationals generally. In the event that a developing country has opted to limit the extent to which it bestows such rights on non-nationals, invoking the clause elaborated in the *International Covenant on Economic, Social and Cultural Rights*, the 1954 *Convention relating to the Status of Stateless Persons* does not stand in the way of the application of these restrictions to stateless persons.[36] However, with regards to the right to social security and a variety of other labour-related rights such as the minimum age of employment and the enjoyment of the benefits of collective bargaining, the stateless are to be accorded the same treatment as nationals provided that they are lawfully staying in the state. Again, it is unclear whether these are considered to be 'economic rights' and under which circumstances developing countries could invoke any limitations against non-nationals in their enjoyment. The 1954 Convention would seem to ensure that such restrictions are not imposed against stateless persons. In view of this mixed picture and the ambiguity of the relevant provision in the *International Covenant on Economic, Social and Cultural Rights*, an interpretative comment by the Committee on Economic, Social and Cultural Rights, including an explanation of the position of the stateless under this clause, is the best way to elucidate its terms and to ensure that it is not invoked to the detriment of stateless persons.

Lastly, it is necessary to consider whether the 1954 *Convention relating to the Status of Stateless Persons* offers clarity as to the extent to which stateless persons may be disadvantaged by a differentiation in treatment between nationals and non-nationals. Thanks to the technique adopted in the formulation of rights under the 1954 Convention, this instrument only provides some of the answers. Thus, where the 1954 Convention determines that stateless persons are to be treated on a par with nationals – for instance, with regard to the enjoyment of education, the freedom of religion and the protection of intellectual property – distinctions between nationals and stateless persons are clearly outlawed.[37] The 1954 Convention promulgates absolute rights, such as the right to identity papers, to recognition of legal personhood and to certain protections against expulsion, that are to be granted to stateless persons regardless of whether nationals enjoy the same protection. Distinctions between nationals and non-nationals in these areas are, therefore, not necessarily prohibited, but the 1954 Convention does demand that a certain substantive protection is offered to the stateless.[38] Finally, where the 1954 Convention provides for treatment at least as favourable as non-nationals generally – for example, in the case of property rights, the freedom of association and the right to work – the standard of treatment to be enjoyed by the stateless is contingent upon the overall treatment offered to non-nationals. Such guarantees have no impact on the margin of discretion that states are afforded to treat nationals and non-nationals differently. Nevertheless, it is important to recall that under human rights law, states may only distinguish between nationals and non-nationals when they have legitimate cause to do so. Thus, even where the 1954 *Convention relating to the Status of Stateless Persons* does not call for protection on a par with nationals, it may not always be easy for states to justify differential treatment. In correctly applying the principle of non-discrimination, states may in fact be required to take affirmative action in favour of stateless persons:

> in a State where the general conditions of a certain part of the population prevent or impair their enjoyment of human rights, the State should take specific action to correct those conditions. Such action may involve granting for a time to the part of the population concerned certain preferential treatment in specific matters as compared with the rest of the population.[39]

The uniquely vulnerable position of the stateless – as for non-nationals everywhere – may call for such positive measures. Therefore, whereas a distinction between nationals and non-nationals in the enjoyment of certain rights may generally be considered to be both legitimate and proportional, where this distinction affects stateless persons the reasonableness test may have a different outcome.[40] The specific circumstance of statelessness, as it differs from the situation of nationals and that of other non-nationals, must be taken into account in determining the standard of treatment owed to stateless persons. To date, human rights bodies have paid too little attention to the specific plight of the stateless when elaborating on the substance of rights. It would be helpful and appropriate if, for instance, the UN treaty bodies made an effort to clarify the treatment owed to stateless persons in their thematic comments. In the meantime, the aforementioned reasonableness test, taking into account the particularities of the situation of the stateless, presents a pragmatic, flexible and fair approach to questions regarding differential treatment of stateless persons in the enjoyment of rights.

It is clear that the 1954 *Convention relating to the Status of Stateless Persons* does not offer easy answers to the difficult questions that the human rights framework presents with regards to the enjoyment of rights by stateless persons. In fact, the 1954 Convention skirts around many of these issues, such as the problem of determining which country is to be deemed 'home' for a stateless individual, thereby ensuring a right to live somewhere and protection from the ping-pong effect of being passed from one state to another, indefinitely. There are then still a number of critical gaps in the normative regime for the protection of stateless persons. However, as discussed in this section, there are many clues within the overall human rights framework as to an appropriate way to resolve these issues. Until these are properly consolidated and further developed to ensure the full and effective enjoyment of rights by stateless persons, it seems that the stateless will remain significantly disadvantaged. Only the acquisition/reacquisition of a nationality guarantees access to the entire gamut of human rights.

IMPLEMENTATION AND ENFORCEMENT OF NORMS RELATING TO THE PROTECTION OF STATELESS PERSONS

The circumstances in which stateless persons live vary greatly from one country to another, yet an impaired ability to exercise an assortment of rights remains a common complaint. Stateless persons may be unable to go to school or university, work legally, own property, get married or travel. They may find it difficult to enter hospital, impossible to open a bank account and have no chance of receiving a pension. If someone robs them or rapes them, they may find they cannot lodge a complaint because legally they do not exist, and the police require proof that they do before they can open an investigation. They are extremely vulnerable to exploitation as cheap or bonded labour, especially in societies where they cannot work legally.[41]

This extensive range of problems that stateless persons have reportedly experienced is cause for serious concern because it does not just point to a few incidental gaps in the international legal framework where the specific protection needs that accompany statelessness have yet to be adequately addressed. Instead, it suggests a much more comprehensive crisis whereby the implementation and enforcement of the normative framework is failing. Obviously, finding ways to effectively implement and enforce human rights norms is a difficulty that is inherent in the system as a whole with violations continuing to occur – and going unresolved – every day. Yet, in meeting the challenge of implementation and enforcement of the rights of stateless persons, there are several additional issues that cannot be ignored.

Arguably, the most influential factor in problems of both implementation and enforcement of norms relating specifically to the protection of the stateless is the absence of agreement on the identification of individuals as 'stateless persons'. Neither the 1954 *Convention relating to the Status of Stateless Persons* nor any other international instrument contains guidelines for the task of identification. Yet, this task is undeniably complex. In order to establish that an individual is stateless, it is necessary to substantiate that he does not possess any nationality. He must, in effect, prove a negative. This, in turn, requires coming to some understanding about the procedures to be followed and the weighing of types of evidence that can be submitted. Without internationally agreed upon guidelines, states are left to devise procedures and principles unilaterally, leading to a wide diversity in identification practices. Indeed, states do not have any mechanism in place for determining an individual's status as a stateless person.[42] This is likely to seriously impede actual recognition of a stateless person and subsequently the enjoyment of any rights emanating from the 1954 Convention and other relevant areas of international law.[43] Moreover, when it comes to the enforcement of the rights of the stateless by international supervisory bodies, the lack of clear consensus on the identification of stateless persons will also present problems for the examination and appraisal of state practice.

There are a number of avenues that could be pursued in an effort to elaborate suitable tools for the identification of statelessness. For example, a few cases have already come before international bodies in which a determination of the nationality or statelessness of the applicant was necessary.[44] Although such jurisprudence is still limited, these cases offer a basic insight into how an independent authority is able to rule on the nationality status of an individual, including by looking at documentary evidence and at the content of the relevant nationality Acts. Furthermore, both UNHCR and individual states are conducting nationality determinations every day in the context of Refugee Status Determination under the 1951 *Convention relating to the Status of Refugees*.[45] Procedures and principles for the identification of stateless persons – Stateless Person Status Determination – could be extracted from existing guidelines and practices in the area of refugee protection. Thus, for instance, in the context of Refugee Status Determination, the burden of proof lies in principle with the applicant, but the duty to ascertain and evaluate all relevant facts is shared between the applicant and the examiner, and in some cases it may be necessary for the examiner to use all means at his disposal to produce the necessary evidence in support of the application.[46] A similar principle could be adopted in guidelines for the identification of stateless persons.

A third field of international law that may prove useful is that of international claims jurisprudence. In order to decide on the admissibility of an international claim, whereby a state exercises diplomatic protection and raises a complaint against another state on the basis of an injury sustained by one of its citizens, the court or commission must determine whether the so-called 'nationality of the claim' is satisfied. According to jurisprudence in this field, at least four types of evidence have been allowed in the determination of the nationality of the injured party. These include not only direct proof, that is, documentary evidence that the person is recognized as a national by the state in question, but also, for instance, proof of peripheral facts from which it can be inferred that the person is deemed to be a national by a competent state authority.[47] This existing international practice relating to the determination of nationality is another relevant source of information on how the identification of cases of statelessness could be regulated. Combined with the other areas mentioned above, and best practices derived from a study of current state mechanisms for the identification of stateless persons (where these do exist), guidelines could be extracted and laid down in an international handbook for the identification of statelessness. The elaboration and implementation of such a handbook would have a significant impact on the protection of stateless persons.

Another factor that is still seriously impeding the enjoyment of rights by stateless persons is the absence of a supervisory agency tasked with monitoring and enforcing the proper treatment of the stateless. Indeed, the specialized statelessness regime which emerged from the 1954 *Convention relating to the Status of Stateless Persons* has always led a somewhat isolated existence. Outside the general UN human rights system, it has not attracted the same type of supervisory apparatus. Whereas the *International*

Convention on the Rights of All Migrant Workers and Members of Their Families, for instance, has its own treaty body with a broad supervisory mandate,[48] the 1954 *Convention relating to the Status of Stateless Persons* has no equivalent. Each of the UN treaty bodies may consider situations of statelessness within their own substantive mandate, and many have actively promoted the enjoyment of rights by stateless populations where the opportunity has arisen, including by encouraging states to ratify the 1954 *Convention relating to the Status of Stateless Persons*. None, however, are tasked with focusing specifically on the treatment of the stateless. Meanwhile, UNHCR has been bestowed with a universal mandate on statelessness, allowing the agency to get involved wherever situations of statelessness threaten to arise around the world. The agency now has a four-dimensional mandate, working on the identification, prevention and reduction of statelessness as well as the protection of stateless persons.[49] Nevertheless, UNHCR's operational capacity to engage in promoting the rights of stateless persons is limited since it is primarily a field organization, and there is no formalized procedure in place for supervising the full and correct implementation of the 1954 Convention or for the receipt of individual complaints by stateless persons. The fact that jurisprudence already exists in which a determination of nationality status and statelessness was made,[50] as well as the existence of a plethora of mechanisms for monitoring and enforcing human rights law, is evidence that a supervisory body for the protection of the rights of stateless persons would fit in with overall developments under international law. Further consideration, therefore, evidently needs to be given to the question of international supervision of the norms relating to the protection of the stateless.

A final point to note with regard to the implementation and enforcement of the rights of the stateless relates to the doctrine of diplomatic protection. As briefly touched upon above, there is a body of international jurisprudence involving claims made by one state against another on the basis of an injury incurred by one of its nationals. Thus, if a national of country A suffers an injury to person or property at the hands of country B, then country A can bring an international claim against country B to seek some form of redress. Traditionally, the bond of nationality has formed the basis for the right of country A to exercise diplomatic protection in this manner. As a result, the stateless are typically unable to benefit from the doctrine of diplomatic protection because they can never satisfy the 'nationality of the claim' and the defendant state can call for a dismissal of the case on this jurisdictional technicality.[51] This situation is regrettable because the exercise of diplomatic protection by a state can contribute to the enforcement of international norms and thereby to the enjoyment of individual rights.[52]

One of the provisions in a series of Draft Articles on Diplomatic Protection that is currently being considered by the UN General Assembly would address this problem by establishing the legal basis for diplomatic protection of stateless persons to be exercised by the state in which the stateless individual is lawfully and habitually resident.[53] If these articles were adopted in their present form, either as a declaration or a convention, another opportunity would be created for the effective enforcement of the rights of the stateless. Until that time, it remains within the power of a defendant state to have a claim submitted on behalf of a stateless person declared inadmissible.

CONCLUDING OBSERVATIONS: NATIONALITY AND RIGHTS ACCORDING TO INTERNATIONAL LAW TODAY

As mentioned in the introduction to this chapter, when a new nationality Act was adopted in Sri Lanka with a view to ending the statelessness of a sizeable segment of the population, this was heralded as an affirmative measure that would bring an end to the marginalization and exclusion that had marked their years of statelessness. Many of the case studies presented in this book illustrate the harsh reality of statelessness, which has been summed up as follows:

> for many stateless people around the world, it is a corrosive, soul-destroying condition that colors almost every aspect of their lives.[54]

In practice then, the lack of any bond of citizenship can have a severe impact on the enjoyment of rights. As a corollary of this fact, the possession or reinstatement of a nationality brings with it the promise of improved access to rights and of an enhanced standard of living. But this study poses the question: in the contemporary human rights environment, to what extent is nationality still relevant to the enjoyment of rights? In other words, is statelessness the crux of the problem and what difference should the acquisition/reacquisition of a nationality make in the access to rights for those involved?

In the past, nationality has been described as the 'right to have rights' and statelessness as tantamount to the 'total destruction of an individual's status in organized society'.[55] In such a world, the resolution of statelessness through the attribution/reattribution of nationality is a decisive act that restores the 'right to have rights' and paves the way for full integration/reintegration into society through the exercise of these rights. However, with the advent of human rights law, the relationship between nationality and rights has grown in complexity. Indeed, the very concept of universally acknowledged human rights grew from the failings of national authorities to guarantee the rights of their own citizens. The denationalization of rights through the elaboration of human rights norms presents new opportunities for the stateless to access various rights, proving the traditional view of the stateless as rightless to be outdated.

Nevertheless, the foregoing analysis of the position of the stateless within the contemporary human rights framework has demonstrated that the stateless remain, in some respects, uniquely vulnerable. Indeed, the human rights system itself seems to abhor their very existence since it severely challenges the ambition of universal enjoyment of human rights: stateless persons are, by definition, unable to enjoy those rights that are presently accorded only in relation to the country of nationality, such as key political rights and the right to enter/re-enter and reside in a state. Moreover, although citizenship is no longer a precondition for the attribution of most human rights, in practice it is often still a practical requirement for the exercise of such rights, for example, due to the lack of any official 'home country' in which residence rights are guaranteed or as a result of problems relating to an overall lack of documentation. Thus, where states are failing either individually or collectively to ensure that everyone enjoys the bond of citizenship somewhere,[56] the human rights regime's assertion of universality begins to crumble unless special provision is made for those persons who find themselves excluded by the system: the stateless.

NOTES

1. The group is commonly referred to as 'Hill Tamils' or 'Estate Tamils' because the population is comprised largely of tea-pickers brought over by the British from India, when both countries were still ruled by the crown, to work on the plantations in Sri Lanka's hill country. Their statelessness – and that of their descendents – springs from the independence of Sri Lanka from India and a failure at the time to resolve their nationality status in the legislation enacted following partition. See UNHCR's dedicated website on Statelessness in Sri Lanka, available at http://www.unhcr.lk/protection/statelessness/.
2. Words of a formerly stateless 'Hill Tamil', as cited in Perara (2007).
3. Consider, for example, the concepts of freedom, equality and rights as laid down in the United States Declaration of Independence (1776) and the French Declaration of the Rights of Man and of the Citizen (1789).
4. In fact, the only circumstance in which the protection of an individual became a question of international concern was when an injury was considered to have been committed against that individual's person or property by a foreign state. In such cases, the

international legal regime relating to state responsibility allowed the state of nationality of the individual to exercise so-called 'diplomatic protection' and demand some form of redress for this injury. See Elles (1980).

5. UN General Assembly, *Universal Declaration of Human Rights* (1948).
6. Ibid.
7. Ibid, Articles 4, 9, 18 and 25.
8. Weissbrodt and Collins (2006).
9. UN Human Rights Committee (1986).
10. UN Committee on the Rights of the Child (2005a).
11. See European Court of Human Rights, *Slavov v. Sweden* (1999), *Okonkwo v. Austria* (2001), *Al-Nashif v. Bulgaria* (2002).
12. *Al-Nashif v. Bulgaria.*
13. For instance, the Committee on the Rights of the Child reminded Iran of its obligation to 'ensure that all children, including refugee children, have equal opportunities on all levels of the education system without discrimination based on gender, religion, ethnic origin, nationality or statelessness' in UN Committee on the Rights of the Child (2005b), paragraph 496. Another example can be found in a report by the UN Special Rapporteur on contemporary forms of racism where great concern is expressed at restrictions placed on the freedom of movement of stateless Rohingya in Myanmar. See Diène (2007), paragraph 126.
14. This interpretation is confirmed by the article on the right to political participation in the *International Covenant on Civil and Political Rights* (UN General Assembly, 1966b) which confers this right explicitly and exclusively to 'citizens'. See also UN Human Rights Committee (1986, 1996a).
15. See, for instance, Article 13 of the *Universal Declaration of Human Rights* (UN General Assembly, 1948) and UN General Assembly, *International Covenant on Economic, Social and Cultural Rights* UN General assembly, (1966a).
16. Kamto (2005).
17. Note that a number of other human rights norms may offer individuals a right to (re-) enter or remain, *Convention Relating to the Status of Stateless Persons* (UN General Assembly, 1954).
18. Article 2, paragraph 3 of the UN General Assembly, *International Covenant on Economic, Social and Cultural Rights.*
19. Article 1, paragraph 2 of the UN General Assembly, *International Convention on the Elimination of All Forms of Racial Discrimination* (1965).
20. Emphasis added. UN Committee on the Elimination of Racial Discrimination (2004), paragraph 4. See also UN Human Rights Committee (1986) and UN Human Rights Committee, *Guye et al. v. France*, (Comment No. 196/1985, Decision of the Human Rights Committee Under Article 5 (4) of the Optional Protocol to the International Covenant on Civil and Political Rights, Thirty-fifth Session Geneva, 1989).
21. See, for example, Article 15 of the *Universal Declaration of Human Rights.*
22. The UN's interest in statelessness can be traced back as far as the late 1940s when a study was conducted to assess the need to adopt measures to tackle the issue: UN (1949).
23. As mentioned in the previous section, statelessness remains a widespread problem – evidence that the 1961 *Convention on the Reduction of Statelessness* has not been fully effective. For a detailed analysis of the strengths and weaknesses of the 1961 *Convention on the Reduction of Statelessness*, as well as other sources of norms pertaining to the right to a nationality and the avoidance of statelessness, see Part 2 of van Waas (2008).
24. Similar to the 1951 *Convention relating to the Status of Refugees*, the 1954 *Convention relating to the Status of Stateless Persons* excludes, for example, persons who are already receiving protection from a UN agency other than UNHCR and persons that have committed one of a variety of serious crimes. Note that this is not the only parallel between the refugee and stateless person instruments – the two documents were developed together and adopt the same approach to the elaboration of rights. They are also substantively highly similar.

25. Article 7, paragraph 1 of the 1954 *Convention relating to the Status of Stateless Persons.* Note that states are free, even encouraged, to extend additional rights and protection to stateless persons beyond the terms of the minimum standard of treatment provided for in the 1954 Convention. See Article 5 of the 1954 *Convention relating to the Status of Stateless Persons.*

26. Paragraph 13, section 1 of the schedule to Article 28 of the 1954 *Convention relating to the Status of Stateless Persons.*

27. Note that Article 2 of the 1954 *Convention relating to the Status of Stateless Persons* – where the general obligations of stateless persons are set out – was also introduced with a particular view to affording states the opportunity to curtail the political activities of these individuals. See Robinson (1955).

28. See Article 19 of the *International Covenant on Civil and Political Rights* as well as, for instance, UN Human Rights Committee (1996b), paragraph 120.

29. See Walker (1981) and Sokoloff (2005), p. 20.

30. In reaction to increasing levels of international migration, and thereby an expanding population of non-nationals in many countries, a growing number of states grant non-national residents the right to vote or be elected in local elections. Examples include Israel, Paraguay and Argentina. Furthermore, within the European Union, political participation is, to a certain extent, now offered on the basis of EU rather than national citizenship. See Tiburcio (2001), pp. 181–2; Aleinikoff and Klusmeyer (2000), pp. 51–4.

31. See the concluding observations of the UN Committee on the Elimination of Racial Discrimination (1997), paragraph 499 and (2002a), paragraph 167 as well as those of the UN Human Rights Committee (1997), paragraphs 322–326 and (2002), paragraph 76. See also Article 42, paragraph 3 of the *International Convention on the Rights of all Migrant Workers and Members of their Families.*

32. This is one of the ways in which the protection offered by the 1951 *Convention relating to the Status of Refugees* was diluted when the text was adapted to create an instrument to deal with the rights of stateless persons. Whereas refugees enjoy protection from *refoulement*, which may create an avenue for refugees to enter or legalize their stay in a state, the stateless are not provided with an equivalent guarantee.

33. See *supra* note 26 as well as Article 31 of the 1954 *Convention relating to the Status of Stateless Persons.*

34. UN Human Rights Committee (1999), paragraph 20.

35. As mentioned earlier, there is no overall consensus on the categorization of rights as 'economic rights'. The opinion of scholars varies from a broad definition that includes all rights that are related to the process of earning a living, such as the right to work, to form trade unions, to social security and to an adequate standard of living. Others offer a narrower reading, which would include only rights related to investment or the taking part in profitable activities. See, for instance, Elles (1980), pp. 30–4; Dankwa (1987); Tiburcio (2001), Chapters VI and VII.

36. It is worth noting that in the formulation of the right to engage in wage-earning employment, the 1954 *Convention relating to the Status of Stateless Persons* differs significantly from its sister-convention, the 1951 *Convention relating to the Status of Refugees.* The latter requires states to lift restrictions on access to the labour market for refugees once certain conditions have been met. This useful and important clause was sadly dropped when the text was adapted to form the instrument on statelessness.

37. Although it should be noted that some of the rights, which offer protection on a par with nationals, can only be invoked by stateless persons lawfully staying in the contracting state.

38. Again, these rights are granted at different levels of attachment, which may have a significant impact on the ability of a stateless person to qualify for protection in practice.

39. UN Human Rights Committee (1989), paragraph 10.

40. A concrete example of this is the right to enter one's own country. Whereas it is generally considered reasonable to interpret the term 'own country' as the person's country of nationality and therefore to distinguish between citizens and non-citizens in the

enjoyment of this right, such an interpretation may be unreasonable when applied to the situation of the stateless who would then have no country with regards to which to exercise this right. The development of a broader interpretation of 'own country' along the lines suggested earlier is therefore an expression of the principle of non-discrimination, which includes the obligation to offer different treatment where cases are clearly different.

41. Leclerc and Colville (2007).
42. In a 2004 survey, half of respondent states reported having neither a specialized procedure for identifying cases of statelessness, nor even a mechanism for identifying stateless persons within the context of asylum procedures. It is highly unlikely that the percentage is any higher among states that failed to respond to the questionnaire. UNHCR (2004a), pp. 26–7.
43. In addition, the absence for a mechanism for identification of statelessness is also jeopardizing the implementation and enforcement of norms relating to the prevention of statelessness since the ability to determine whether an individual would otherwise be stateless is a necessary precursor to the application of special fall-back provisions to avoid statelessness.
44. For example, European Court of Human Rights, *Tatishvili v. Russia* (2007) and Inter-American Court of Human Rights, *Yean and Bosico v. Dominican Republic* (2005).
45. Indeed, the finding that an individual as stateless is also relevant in the context of Refugee Status Determination since, in such cases, the country of former habitual residence (rather than the country of nationality) must be identified in order to assess the risk of persecution.
46. UNHCR (1992), paragraph 196.
47. Weis (1979), p. 221.
48. The committee is authorized to receive complaints from states and individuals as well as to carry out a periodic review of the situation in state parties.
49. See, for instance, UNHCR (2006).
50. See *supra* note 44.
51. In the remarkable *Dickson Car Wheel Company* case, the international arbitration panel voiced the situation of the stateless with regard to diplomatic protection as follows: 'A state. . .does not commit an international delinquency in inflicting an injury upon an individual lacking nationality, and consequently, no State is empowered to intervene or complain on his behalf either before or after the injury.' UNRIAA, *Dickson Car Wheel Co. (USA) v. United Mexican States* (1931), p. 678.
52. For example, following the partition and independence of Eritrea from Ethiopia and the accompanying hostilities, property confiscations and expulsions, a claims commission was established to 'decide through binding arbitration all claims for loss, damage or injury by one government against the other, and by nationals. . .of one party against the government of the other party'. Article 5, paragraph 1 of the *Agreement between the Government of the Federal Democratic Republic of Ethiopia and the Government of the State of Eritrea* 12 December, 2000. According to the traditional doctrine of diplomatic protection, only nationals of the two countries would benefit from these arrangements, and those persons who were rendered stateless in the partition process would be without such protection.
53. Article 8, paragraph 1 of the International Law Commission (2006) 'Report of the Work of its 58th Session', p. 47.
54. Leclerc and Colville (2007), p. 6.
55. Most famously by Justice Earl Warren of the US Supreme Court in United States Supreme Court, *Trop v. Dulles, Secretary of State et al.* (1958).
56. Recall that the right to a nationality has been included in the catalogue of human rights guarantees.

3. Citizenship in Kenya: the Nubian case

Abraham Korir Sing'Oei

Source: © UNHCR/Greg Constantine 2010.

Figure 3.1 *Unemployed Nubian youth collect garbage to help clean up the Nubian sections of Kibera and earn extra money. Nubian youth must go through a vetting process and continue to have difficulties obtaining Kenyan national ID cards.*

To assess the benefits of citizenship to former stateless persons and communities in Kenya, this chapter addresses two interrelated questions. First, does the conferment of juridical citizenship make any difference to the human rights situation of individuals and groups in Kenya? To respond to this question, an analysis of citizenship from a historical, legal and policy context is undertaken. Second, how has the granting of juridical citizenship impacted a former stateless community? The case of the Nubian community in Kenya will be evaluated.

This chapter draws on analysis of legal and non-legal material in the field of migration, international law and human rights, specifically on the topic of citizenship and its related dimensions, statelessness and the rights of non-nationals. Media reports, which constitute important sources of information, reports by treaty bodies and the observations or conclusions of these institutions are also reviewed. This chapter makes use of information obtained from focus group discussions and selected unstructured interviews carried out by the author in 2008 and 2009. The aim of this approach was to ensure, in the light of resource constraints, that the largest possible number of representatives of all the interest groups among the Nubians – women, youth, men and elders – were able to share their individual experiences. As the Nubians remain a very structured community, the researcher additionally elected to solicit the views of the Nubian Council of Elders and the Kibera Land Commission (KLC).[1]

CITIZENSHIP IN KENYA: THE LEGAL, HISTORICAL AND POLICY DEBATE

Kenya attained political independence from Britain on 12 December 1963. Its constitution, whose provisions on the subject of this chapter have not changed to date, identified the specific requirements that would qualify persons to access Kenyan citizenship.[2] Celebrating the constitutive character of citizenship in the context of Kenya, Lonsdale and Odhiambo (2003) assert that:

> No nation has been born without having to face up to the question about who is to be included, whom excluded; about how equal the rights of citizenship can in practice be; what degree of privileged differentiation is tolerable between regions, languages and personal status; what, in any conflict of rights, it means to be subject to more than one rule of law, local and customary, national and statutory.[3]

While the authors above acknowledge the potentially exclusionary nature of citizenship, the non-discrimination norm in the constitution[4] prohibits differential treatment in the conduct of public affairs in Kenya, including the conferment of citizenship. The constitution therefore assures that Kenyan citizenship is based on universal and inclusive values as opposed to exclusivist notions of race, ethnicity, class or gender. Chapter six of the constitution, which deals with citizenship, has no preamble that lays out the key principles undergirding citizenship in Kenya. As such, a reading of this part of the constitution reveals only a complex architecture for the acquisition or deprivation of citizenship and its different classes. The following observations emerge from an analysis of the constitutional provisions pertaining to the acquisition and loss of citizenship in Kenya.

First, citizenship in Kenya is defined with reference to the departed colonial order. While deemed a transitional arrangement, the requirement that Kenyan citizenship by operation of law was to be accessible to citizens of the United Kingdom and colonies or British protected persons as defined under the 1948 British Nationality Act,[5] remains confusing for at least two reasons. In the first instance, it is not clear whether Africans could be deemed 'citizens of the United Kingdom and colonies' (CUKC).[6] Additionally, the designation British protected person (BPP) was and remains ambiguous with regard to the potential beneficiaries of such a status. It has been said though that:

> The cumulative effect of the (British Nationality Act, 1948) and the Order in Council which followed it was to confine the term (BPP) to persons who had specific connections with specified protectorates and trust territories, and those who, by virtue of local law, were subjects of named protectorates and protected states.[7]

Like CUKC, acquiring BPP status in the Kenyan context could perhaps be applicable to the Asian community, which like the Nubians were bonded labourers for the colonial government, having been forced out of their own country to construct the Kenya-Uganda railway.[8]

The laudable aims of the *British Nationality Act 1948*,[9] however, when incorporated into Kenya's state succession framework, were problematic for non-indigenous African groups such as the Nubians. Although Africans, Nubians were considered neither as CUKC nor as BPP nor did they satisfy the onerous *jus sanguinis* requirements in the constitution. They were thereby not qualified for automatic citizenship. Indeed, this is the position espoused by the Kenyan government, which has held out for the community an opportunity to register as citizens, though an inferior citizenship as will be evident below.[10]

Second, the *jus sanginis* and *jus soli* requirements combined in section 87 of the Kenyan constitution demand that in addition to being a CUKC or a BPP, a person must have been born in Kenya as of 12 December 1963, by a parent who was also born in Kenya. In other words, to qualify for automatic citizenship, one had to be a member of a family that had lived in Kenya for at least two generations prior to 1963 while also meeting the *jus soli* requirement of having been born in the territory.

While on paper the above requirement may appear sufficiently clear, particularly for Britons and for Asians to a lesser degree, in practice, the implementation of this provision has been quite challenging. This is especially true with regard to African populations in the country for whom birth registration at the time, as now, was extremely low, thereby rendering them unable to provide the documentation needed to prove multi-generational births in Kenya. In practice, it was therefore assumed that indigenous African communities in Kenya satisfied this requirement without proof while the rest of the population, including the Nubians, had to provide documentary evidence to satisfy the constitutional demand. As a result, a practice emerged by which membership in a group indigenous to Kenya is the *de facto* determinant for complying with the citizenship requirements in the constitution rather than a case-by-case individual determination. Without this automatic citizenship, a generational chain reaction resulted in which a parent who was unable to meet the requirements was rendered incompetent to transmit citizenship to their child, who, even if born in Kenya, would only be entitled to citizenship by registration or naturalization.

To ameliorate the lack of documentary proof of registration, vetting or screening conducted through the agency of security organs of the state was put in place but only for certain communities, including the Nubians.[11] Without clear rules of procedure or an evidentiary statute to govern its factual parameters for determining the value of individual statements, these screening committees relied on subjective considerations of the committee members. According to one Nubian elder, who together with representatives of the Provincial administration, constitutes the part of the district vetting committee, all Nubian applicants for identification cards (IDs) must be vetted because 'the government says we are refugees. Because many of the refugees coming into Kenya have Muslim names like the Nubians, the Nubians have to be sure they are not Somalis coming in with arms . . . . But we do not have Somalis pretending to be Nubians here'. The procedure for vetting requires a person to appear before a magistrate in court and to testify that they are Nubian from Eldama Ravine. The applicant then proceeds to the Chief and the District Officer for further certification before going back to the registration centre where a picture is taken and a waiting card is issued. The process takes at least six months.

In spite of claims justifying the use of vetting procedures, such committees have been accused of exacting brazen bribery and for a lack of accountability.[12] On the one hand, the burden of proof on a claim for citizenship in the case of a member of a minority group is heavily tilted against such a member since, prima facie, they must rebut the presumption that they are not citizens. On the other hand, a member of a politically dominant community in Kenya enjoys the presumption that they are nationals and are therefore better placed, even in the absence of documentary proof to demonstrate their legitimacy vis-à-vis the Kenyan state.[13]

Third, the 1963 constitution created a differentiated and hierarchical citizenship, with both citizenship by naturalization and registration being markedly inferior to citizenship by birth to the extent that the former could be revoked at the behest of administrative officials.[14] In addition, legislation designed to enable the implementation of the citizenship provisions in the constitution lacks clear procedural rules to guide the administrative decision-making process, rendering it purely a discretionary measure, often one of the easiest means towards statelessness.[15] Further, the weak protection afforded citizenship by registration or naturalization has produced a disincentive for those pursuing citizenship. Instead, there is more pressure to acquire an ancestry-based citizenship, hence further toughening the requirements to obtain nationality.

Fourth, the gendered nature of citizenship is most pronounced in the context of Kenya. For instance, a non-national spouse of a Kenyan male entitled to citizenship by operation of law can only acquire citizenship by registration,[16] a situation that is fraught with uncertainty. Moreover, in this case, a husband and his wife will have Kenyan citizenship of completely varying qualitative character, which may imperil the right to family unity.[17] Women who are Kenyan citizens and married to either foreign diplomats or non-citizen spouses are also incapable of transmitting their Kenyan citizenship to their children.[18] Similarly, women with Kenyan citizenship are unable to transmit their citizenship to their foreign-born children.[19] Clearly, paternity is the locus for the granting of citizenship in Kenya.

Lastly, the current Kenyan constitution does not articulate the ways to retain or recover lost citizenship or the specific instruments that certify one's citizenship, the latter being left to legislation.[20] What is clear, however, is that various laws adopted since independence grant special rights to citizens of Kenya. These include the right to work without a permit,[21] leave or enter the country,[22] vote,[23] own property,[24] carry out certain business[25] and serve in the country's security sector.[26] So, while citizenship in Kenya is an important ingredient for realizing basic rights, human security and sustainable development, some categories of persons – notably women and minorities – will access them only with difficulty.

CITIZENSHIP TODAY: POLICY AND PERCEPTION

The legal and political landscape of citizenship in Kenya is undergoing a muted metamorphosis. The constitution review process has provided a lens through which some of the changing conceptions of citizenship may be observed, even though these changes are yet to crystallize into law. For instance, in the Draft Constitution of 2004, the inferiority of citizenship by registration or naturalization is no longer apparent.[27] Similarly, the gender-based discrimination in the current constitution is eliminated, and women are not only allowed to transmit citizenship to their children[28] but non-national spouses of Kenyan men also retain citizenship even in the event of divorce.[29] The Draft Constitution also recognizes dual citizenship[30] but maintains the status quo in relation to providing blanket recognition to current citizenship holders.[31] They have not created a mechanism for mediating the challenges faced by communities whose citizenship is currently doubted by the state, such as the Nubians. Moreover, by delegating to parliament the responsibility for enacting a more detailed legislation to govern procedure for acquisition, loss or renunciation of citizenship,[32] the Draft creates real fear that the arbitrariness that bedevils the current citizenship regime may be reproduced.

The 2004 Draft provided explicitly for the right of citizens to a passport and other registration documents.[33] It removed the arbitrariness currently found in the registration processes that particularly disadvantage minority communities.[34] The Draft law does not, however, address the status of a child of a stateless person as such, unless such a child is abandoned, in which event the child acquires Kenyan citizenship.[35] Adoption of the Draft would have fallen short of international law's normative intent to avoid statelessness.[36]

A Harmonized Draft of the Constitution of Kenya, published on 17 December 2009,[37] borrows largely from the 2004 Draft on the issue of citizenship. Some important points of divergence are, however, discernible. Article 17 of the 2009 Draft provides for citizenship by birth in two ways: if one is born in Kenya to parents, one of whom is a citizen or if one is born abroad, again, with at least one parent of Kenyan citizenship. Clearly, the 2009 Draft de-emphasizes the place of birth in favour of blood kinship with a citizen. This strict *jus sanguinis* basis for citizenship could create challenges for minorities such as Nubians, Galjeel, Somali and some coastal Arabs, the same groups that presently complain of discrimination. The provision is, however, of great benefit to children of Kenyan citizens in the diaspora, who in the present constitutional dispensation would have to acquire citizenship by registration. The other innovation of the 2009 Draft relates to the introduction of the concept of responsibilities of a citizen in Article 24. The import of this approach is that while citizenship presents the bearer with rights, there is a concomitant set of responsibilities that is often ignored. This idea further seems to echo the language of duties in the African Charter on Human and Peoples Rights, which is seen as the apotheosis of the African conception of human rights.[38]

Citizenship implicates other rights, particularly political representation. It is in this respect that the Harmonized Draft falls short. Article 163 (1) (a) requires that the president shall be a citizen by birth. This requirement differentiates between political rights accessible to persons who are already Kenyan citizens and is contrary to Article 37 (1) of the same Draft that forbids direct and indirect discrimination on any ground as well as Article 36 that provides for equality of all citizens before the law. Such a provision, if maintained, will increase the demand for citizenship by birth and delegitimize other means for acquiring citizenship, the same problem as is present in the current constitution. In fact, even the much-discredited present constitution does not require of presidential aspirants to be Kenyan citizens by birth. In contrast, the Prime Minister, whom the Harmonized Draft vests with the responsibility of being 'head of government', only needs to be a citizen (presumably of any category) by virtue of Article 127 (1) (a). Given that the president is the 'symbol of national unity' in terms of Article 157 (3), the proposal that such an individual be a Kenyan citizen by birth may be defensible in a democratic society.[39]

CITIZENSHIP AND ITS BENEFITS: THE NUBIAN CASE

When the Nubians, a Moslim community of about 100 000 people which has resided in Kenya for well over a century, challenged its denial of citizenship before Kenyan courts in 2002 on the assertion that most of its members were being denied identity cards and passports,[40] they were making the bold statement that they could no longer stand by and accept systematic state discrimination. Originally from the Nuba Mountains in the Sudan, the Nubians in Kenya had been conscripted into the British colonial military machine, serving as guards and soldiers in the colonial conquest of local communities in East Africa; afterwards, they fought alongside the British army in the two world wars.[41] They were granted settlement in Kibera as a token of appreciation for their service to the British,[42] but also the convenience of Kibera served the British design to maintain the Nubians in indentured labour, particularly as personnel in its Kenyan African Rifles.

Before 1963, Nubians generally perceived themselves to be equal with the rest of the African communities eking out a living in the less than ideal suburbs of Nairobi. The first change they experienced in the decade after independence was the massive influx of other African communities into Kibera, which was apparently attractive because of the informality of property rights and the accommodative Nubian culture.[43] The

Source: © UNHCR/Greg Constantine 2010.

Figure 3.2   *While the Nubians have lived in Kenya for over 100 years, they face challenges in being fully recognized in Kenya. A Nubian woman holds a photograph of her grandfather with other Nubian officers who served for the British in the King's African Rifles.*

demographic changes in Kibera over the years have reduced Nubians to less than 10 per cent of the total population of the area. This change is dramatically demonstrated in the political context. From the late 1960s to early 1970s the Nubians were represented by their own member of parliament, Yunus Ali, but by 2003, the Nubians could not even elect one of their own to the local authority, the lowest unit of civic representation.

Demographic changes alone are not the single variable that can explain the increasingly vulnerable political position of the Nubians. The other significant factor was that the registration of persons programme of the independent Kenyan government gradually began to take its toll on the Nubians, as exposed by the interviewees' accounts presented below. Rather than grant recognition to the members of the community by issuing them birth certificates, identity cards or passports, the registration centres became avenues of exclusion, especially from the younger generation. Further migration of other communities into Kibera has taken place in the context of violence associated with multi-party politics,

Source: © UNHCR/Greg Constantine 2010.

Figure 3.3 *The Kibera Primary School opened in 1953 and was built specifically so that future generations of Nubians could go to school.*

which displaced large groups of Luo and Kikuyu communities from the Rift Valley and Coast provinces in 1992 and 1997.[44] Kibera then became a sanctuary for these displaced people, severely altering its demographics further, but more importantly, increasing the pressure on social amenities to a near breaking point. At the height of the coming into power of Mwai Kibaki in 2003, for instance, a classroom in a primary school in Kibera had a child to teacher ratio of 100 to 1.[45]

The other pressure faced by the Nubians emerged from the government's policy to provide low cost public housing in the Kibera district. Consequently, more than ten forced evictions took place in Kibera between 1963 and 1994. These displacements, aside from constituting serious human rights violations,[46] have altered the geographies of human settlement in Kibera. For instance, it has been asserted that 'as many as 1,200 people live on one square hectare, sometimes in shacks as small as nine square meters'.[47] Basic necessities such as a clean water supply, adequate sanitation and drainage are extremely rare or non-existent. The Nubians suffered the worst from the displacements; they never benefited from the state's housing programme.[48]

The stereotyping and 'othering' of Nubians in public processes has greatly hampered the community's quest for recognition.[49] For instance, in the Kenya National Housing and Population Census, the primary governmental statistical and planning instrument that is constitutionally mandated,[50] the Nubians, prior to the 2009 census were categorized as 'others' while the rest of Kenyan communities were specifically identified.[51] The United Nation's Committee on Economic Social and Cultural Rights has identified the socio-economic challenges of the Nubians in their non-recognition, hence recommending that Kenya should ensure that Nubians are given distinct recognition as an ethnic community with rights to ensure the 'preservation, protection and development of their cultural heritage and identity'.[52]

It is important to note, however, that the marginalization of the Nubian community seems to have registered slight improvement in the last five years. The reason for this shift may include, in part, the success of the legal advocacy on the Nubian case at the Kenya courts as well as at the African Commission.[53] More immediately though, the political recognition of the Nubians came in the context of the assurances of President Kibaki in the electoral campaigns of December 2007.[54] This move was designed to politically neutralize Raila Odinga, the Orange Democratic Movement's candidate who was seeking re-election as Member of Parliament for Lang'ata constituency, of which Kibera is part.[55] The Nubians were, for the first time, caught up within a high-stakes game of presidential electoral politics that became the most violent ever in the history of post-independent Kenya.[56]

In the aftermath of the promises made during the presidential elections, it became apparent that 'Government initiatives to accelerate issuance of Identity Cards to members of the Nubian community were more effective.'[57] At the international level, the government also took up the political recognition of the community as sufficient defence against the criticism directed against the Kenyan state. For instance, while affirming the government's recognition of the Nubians and rebutting the statement of the UN Independent expert on Minorities, Jeanette Mwangi, Kenya's representative at the United Nations, informed the UN Human Rights Council of the specific programmatic approach taken by the state to resolving the challenges of the Nubians, thus:

> In order to address their needs, an inter-ministerial committee had been set up to address, among other things, their nationality. This committee had begun its work through a visit all over the country, including where the Nubian communities resided. Nubians held Kenyan passports and, in some cases held public offices. It was erroneous to state that Nubians did not possess lands in Kenya.[58]

As observed by the UN Committee on Economic Social and Cultural Rights, however, the Kenyan government must go beyond the rhetoric of recognition and grant Nubians clear and unambiguous citizenship.

IMPACT OF CITIZENSHIP: CASE STUDIES OF INDIVIDUALS

The cases discussed in this section of the chapter typify the challenges faced by many Nubians in gaining access to identity documents and reaping the benefits of citizenship. In most cases, the problems that need to be surmounted by Nubians are one of four types: refusal by hospital authorities to register births of Nubian children, failure by the state to issue late registration of births, onerous documentary requirements to prove citizenship and inordinate delay.

Halima Ibrahim was born in 1978 and her sister, Habiba Ramadan Riziki, was born in June 1979 in Kibera, Nairobi. Their mother, Hawa Ibrahim, was born in Kibera in 1954. Hawa's parents were born in Kibera as well although her grandparents moved from Kibigori in Kisumu to Nairobi. In 1999, Halima and Habiba applied for national identity cards but were asked to produce documentary proof that their grandfather was born in Kenya. Having neither met their grandfather nor possessing his birth certificate, they were unable to obtain any identity documents. Because they lacked this document, Halima lost several job opportunities, including an offer to work at a three star hotel. Habiba, in spite of her training at the Christian Concern Tailoring School, was unable to retrieve her certificate from the school, resulting in a negative impact on her pursuit for employment. Both Habiba and Halima obtained their identity cards in late 2007 without further condition, but their acquired civic recognition has not impacted their economic status, which has yet to improve although they were both able to vote for the first time. Even without employment, both women are hopeful that they can imagine a future without fear of harassment by police.[59]

Sadik Mohammed is a 27-year-old man whose application for an identity card was rejected in 2001. He is the son of Mohammed Senusi and Amina Mohammed Medi. Both of Sadik's parents are third generation Nubians in Kenya. His two siblings, Gharib Mohammed and Zahra Mohammed, aged 24 and 21 years, respectively, were never allowed to apply for identity cards. All three were given identity cards in November 2007 but bemoan the lost opportunities. Their ability to vote during the elections of December 2007 represented to them their most important civic contribution.[60]

Hawa Hamis Barkit who was born in 1928 in Nairobi applied for a passport as a matter of urgency to travel to Mecca for Hajj on 26 January 2001, to fulfil her obligation as a Muslim. According to her, she planned to travel on 17 March 2001. She was granted the passport in late 2007. Now at age 80, she feels she may not survive the journey, dashing her hopes to satisfy a spiritual obligation.

A graduate of one of Kenya's leading public universities, Adam Hussein Adam secured an offer of employment in Saudi Arabia through Al-Najmayn, a Kenyan agency, to begin work in November 2000. He was to be paid an annual salary of US$36000. However, he could not secure a passport to proceed to Saudi Arabia. To facilitate the passport process, the Ministry of Labor and Human Resources had written to the Principle Immigration Officer, urging them to issue Adam a passport. Adam received his passport in 2002 with the intervention of the Centre for Minority Rights Development (CEMIRIDE), but his Saudi Arabian employment offer had already lapsed. Due to Adam's academic qualifications, which many Nubians do not have, he was able to secure work at CEMIRIDE. Last year, Adam was appointed a programme officer at a leading international NGO, a job that takes him to many parts of Africa and the world.[61] Adam feels secure in his legal status in Kenya, although weak social integration of the community still worries him.[62] Consequently, he has invested in property outside of Kibera. He has recently married and has two daughters whose births were registered without much complication.

Medina Ibrahim Asman applied for a passport in May 2002 to travel to a summer conference in Hawaii as a presenter. He had obtained a full scholarship and was to take up graduate studies at George Washington University in the USA during the fall semester. He was advised by the Immigration Department in Nairobi to wait. Five years later, Medina was granted the passport but the dream of higher education was effectively lost and with it more potential opportunities for personal development and service.[63] Medina is now married and is involved in a small-scale business.

When retired Central Bank of Kenya manager Ibrahim Adhuman Said lost his national identity card seven years ago, he thought it was not of much consequence since he believed he could get a replacement. He was wrong. When he presented himself at the Registrar of Persons office in Nairobi, Said was armed with a photocopy of his national identity card and passport. Overnight Said was transformed from a respected retired civil servant and community elder into an outlaw who had to defend his name and honour. 'I was shuffled and tossed from one office to the next. I moved from the chief's office in Kibera to the Central Bureau of Registration. In the end my application was rejected,' Said recalls. 'They wanted me to prove that I was born in Kenya. I could not even operate a bank account that I had opened when my papers were in order. . . . In the eyes of the State, I neither existed nor belonged in the country in which I was born.' It took him three and half years to extricate himself from his status as a nobody, despite having worked for the Central Bank for 25 years as an assistant manager.[64] Said's journey to the Kibera chief's office marked the beginning of a long and painful journey that would end in court.

Shafir Ali Hussein has not surmounted the administrative obstacles to obtain a birth certificate for his daughter born in 2005. He observes:

> I have one child. She is 1½ years old. She was born at home in Kibera. Because she was born at home I had to apply for a birth certificate independently. I have been trying to get her a birth certificate since late December 2006. I went to Sheria House where I was given a form to fill. I filled out the form and took it back. I was told to go to City Hall. At City Hall I was asked for my wife's clinic card and my daughter's clinic card. I brought these cards back but I was told that they were not stamped. I had to return to the hospital and get them stamped. I took the stamped cards back to City Hall but could not find the person I was dealing with. After some visits, I found the officer and he told me to fill in a form B3. The form asked the names of the child, the father, and the mother and the date of birth of the child. I filled out the form. I then had to take the form to the Chief and Sub-Chief for signatures. I returned the form to the City Hall on Tuesday 4 February 2006. I am waiting for a response. I do not feel good about this process. The reason they are giving me all these hurdles are because of the Muslim name.[65]

For others, even those who are young and have successfully obtained documents, the effects of the vetting and application process have provoked feelings of ostracism and further served to remove them from mainstream society. Sebit, who applied for an ID in 2005 when he was in high school at Kiptoin was, together with a Nubian classmate, refused an identity card after being told they were not Kenyans and were required to be vetted. Upon completing high school, Sebit reapplied for the ID and after going through a long vetting process was successful. During the year-long ordeal of seeking an ID, however, Sebit could neither apply for a job nor pursue any higher education opportunities. This experience of discrimination, according to his widowed mother Zenna, has affected Sebit's confidence and reduced his interaction with the neighbouring Kalenjin community.

The granting of identity documents has not altered the Nubians exclusion from their land and even those who now have a form of citizenship are arguably 'second class citizens'. The case of Zura Abdul Aziz, a 40-year-old woman who lives in Kibera with her two sons aged 10 and 12, respectively, illustrates the discriminatory effect that results from the land-less situation of so many Nubians and which contributes to their economic and social vulnerability.

Zura obtained her identity card in 2003 because of what she believes was a political consideration to increase voter numbers in Kibera. In 2007, her three-room property in Kibera, which she inherited from her grandparents and to which she had no legal title and which she rented out for Ksh. 800 a month, was burned down during the post-electoral violence. In order to rebuild it, Zura went through a protracted ordeal. To make repairs to their houses, including the construction of latrines, Nubians have to apply to the area Chief for a permit and submit photographs of the property. The Chief then comes to inspect the property, if satisfied that such repairs are needed, approves the request, and forwards it to the District Officer (DO). Zura obtained the Chief's and DO's consent to proceed with the house repairs but this process took well over three months by which time she had lost her tenants and the income from the house, her main source of liveli-hood. Zura says that other non-Nubians in Kibera do not go through this permit process, which she says is conducted in an arbitrary manner and is riddled with corruption.

IMPACT OF CITIZENSHIP ON THE COMMUNITY

Nubian community leaders now report that nearly one-half of adult Nubians have national identity cards, and the registration process is no longer as onerous as before.[66] The impact of legal recognition of individu-als as discussed above includes improvement in their personal security, as exemplified by the reduced number of arbitrary arrests of Nubian youth, enhanced enjoyment of political rights – especially the right to vote – and in a few cases, acquisition of employment. Such employment has mainly been realized in the private sector and rarely in government departments or in the military, a sector no Nubian has been able to integrate.[67] The his-torical marginality of the community that denied them opportunities for social development, notably access to education, still undermines the fuller participation of Nubian individuals in the affairs of the country.

In addition to the struggle to obtain documents, the exclusion faced by Nubians has had inter-generational effects and has confined many to the margins of society, doomed to unemployment, destitution and deepening poverty.

Mwajuma Bashir's story demonstrates how the cumulative effects of dis-crimination may undermine a family's sense of security over many genera-tions. Mwajuma, who was born in 1954, lives in the Nubian settlement of

Mlimani in Eldama Ravine town in the Rift Valley province. She does menial jobs such as cooking and cleaning other peoples' houses. She obtained her ID in 1991 prior to Kenya's first multi-party elections. Prior to that time, she had no ID, as she did not know the process for acquiring one. However, in 1992, since she wanted to vote and was informed that an ID was a requirement, she was forced to try to get one. She reported that she was vetted by community elders and the local administration and was also required to provide documentary proof that her parents were born in Kenya. The vetting process took close to one year, but she was given an ID just in time for the 1992 elections. She believes that she was given the ID because politicians in the region were interested in ensuring that every adult voted.

Mwajuma's two daughters born in 1967 and 1969 died two years ago and left her with the burden of caring for five orphans aged 13, 11, 10, 9 and 3. None of the children have birth certificates. Their grandmother has no food, particularly for the youngest child whom she has had to breast-feed since the child was a few months old. She lives in a three-room mud-walled house she inherited from her father. The plot on which the house was built measures 500 by 100 metres, and the only document of ownership in her possession is an allotment letter issued by the Commissioner of Lands. She has no title to the property since the letter merely confers her licence, and she needs to have the land surveyed and thereafter pay the required premiums (land tax) before she can be granted title. She has no funds to carry out this process and feels that the letter of allotment may be revoked at any time. She knows that her neighbours from other communities have titles to their land since they have the resources to ensure completion of the titling process.

Mwajuma says that while her grandchildren go to Kamelilo Primary School, which has benefited from a free education programme of the government since 2004, they and other children from the Nubian minority community in Eldama Ravine do not receive any bursaries (unlike their Kalenjin indigenous neighbours) to pursue secondary education. Their prospects are especially limited.

The marginalization of the Nubians is summed up by Youssef Abdalla, a community elder:

> The problem we have is that the young Nubian generation does not have jobs. They ask for it in the army and police but they do not get it . . . so there are many who are unemployed in Kibera for simply being Nubians . . . and we all know you need a job to survive. We have no land and cannot vote. We have no representation and no voice.[68]

Youssef's views are shared by many others who provided further accounts of complex deprivation resulting from their lack of formal status in Kenya.[69] Moreover, the racial structures that have frustrated Nubians in their pursuit for fairness – corruption, ethnic favouritism and poverty – still hold back personal upward progress, recently acquired paper citizenship notwithstanding. Nubian individuals are also caught up within the broader latent discrimination of Muslims in the country.[70] In this case, their extrication from one layer of domination only exposes the Nubians to the reality that a more insidious form of discrimination still stands between them and the realization of substantive equality.

The relationship between the Nubians and the land they occupy remains tenuous, a reflection of the inability of juridical citizenship to secure stronger recognition of property rights for a minority group[71] As suggested earlier, part of the request of the Nubian community to the Kenyan president during the campaign period was for him to exercise his authority under the law to grant 900 acres in Kibera to the Nubians. This request was accepted and assurances of quick implementation were made to the Nubians.[72] Nonetheless, this promise has not been implemented even though the Nubians have incorporated a Trust in anticipation.[73] According to Jamaldin Yahya, the Secretary KLC, the community lacks a common position on how to address the land question, making it difficult for government to resolve the issue.[74]

As a result of being issued national identity cards, more Nubians were empowered to vote during the last general election. Consequently, for the first time since the early 1970s, the Nubians have two elected councillors in the Nairobi city council.[75]

While civic involvement among the Nubians is on the increase, its hierarchical societal framework that placed primacy for participation on elders and minimized the participation of youth and women threatens the gains made. The frustration of Nubian youth in particular is increasingly rupturing the tranquil age-old systems that favoured community cohesion.[76] This less hierarchical sense of community organizing could present both opportunities and threats in the resolution of the Nubian question.

CONCLUSION

The bifurcated nature of citizenship in Africa[77] undermines its usefulness for groups like the Nubians. Since at least half of them have procured national identity documents, the Nubians are now recognized by the state. They are, however, still considered non-indigenous for purposes of social and political entitlements, including public sector employment, education grants or scholarships and land ownership.

The recognition of Nubian citizenship has become entangled within civic mistrust and breakdown as the Kenyan state itself faces the challenge of corruption, ethnic discord, and mobilization as it makes a fragile political transition from authoritarianism to democracy. The legitimacy of this conferment, namely the granting of nationality to excluded groups and individuals, must be seen in the context of domestic political restructuring. The dominant forces of the state sought the appropriation of minorities for political gain and enabled the above-mentioned nationality reforms to take place.

The integration of the Nubians into the political market is not sufficient without a corresponding integration into the labour market. In addition, without clear property rights within Kibera, Nubian destitution will continue long after the papers granting them citizenship have been signed. The state must take deliberate steps to redress years of Nubian exclusion in addition to ensuring that their right to citizenship is fully recognized.

The inability of the Nubians to contribute to the common good (which in their view entails serving in the security forces, an area of their specialization since colonial times) keeps them from expressing the true nature of their citizenship. This confirms Anver Salojee's assertion that 'The link between social exclusion and citizenship hinges on the manner in which individuals from racialized groups encounter structural and systemic barriers and are denied or restricted from participating in society.'[78] In fact, while increasing recognition has generated beneficial outcomes to individual members of the community, structural barriers still consign the Nubians to the same state of poverty and destitution that they were seeking to escape through their struggle for citizenship. In this case, citizenship has not brought relief.[79]

NOTES

1. While KLC pre-existed the Elders' Council, its singular focus has been on the Kibera land question rather than the broader citizenship issue.
2. Republic of Kenya, *Constitution of Kenya* (2008), Chapter VI.
3. Lonsdale and Odhiambo (2003), P. 2.
4. Section 82, Kenya Constitution. The discrimination of non-nationals is a specific exception to the non-discrimination rule in the constitution: section 82 (4) (A).
5. Section 87 (1) Kenya Constitution; initially section 2 (5) of Kenya Independence Act, 1963.
6. Generally, it has been said that from 1948, Africans in British colonies including Kenya had shared nationality status with Britons, though obviously not the same rights. See Hansen (2000), pp. 153–78.
7. Plender (1988), p. 23 (citing the British Protectorates, Protected States and Protected Persons Order, 1949 and British Nationality Act, 1948, section 30).
8. See, for example, Hansen (2000). He asserts that Asians in Kenya had two years after 1963 to apply for Kenya citizenship, failure of which their disloyalty to Kenyan

Gemeinschaft would be sufficiently proven. (p. 159). Asians in East Africa faced serious challenges to naturalization and the 'Africanization' of the economy, culminating in their expulsion from East Africa in the 1970s.

9. The assumption of the *British Nationality Act* 1948 was that all CUKC's would move smoothly from being dependent colonial subjects to citizens of an independent commonwealth country (ibid., p. 169). This did not work for neither the Asians nor the Nubians.

10. See Nairobi High Court Civil Application No. 256/2003, *Yunus Ali and Others (On behalf of the Nubian Community) v. Attorney General of the Republic of Kenya and Other*, Affidavit of the Principal Registrar of Persons, Joyce Wanjiru Mugo, in support of government's refusal to grant registration documents to members of the Nubian community, paragraphs 12, 13 and 17.

11. See, for example, *Report of the Special Rapporteur on the Situation of Human Rights and Fundamental Freedoms of Indigenous People, Rodolfo Stavenhagen-Mission to Kenya*, A/HRC/4/32/Add.3, p. 6 available at http://www.daccessdds.un.org/doc/UNDOC/GEN/G7/110/43/PRF.

12. See generally Kenya Anti-Corruption Commission (2006). See also *East African Standard*, 'Kenya's Citizenship on Sale', available at http://www.standardmedia.co.ke/mag/InsidePage.php?id=1144025169&cid=459&; Kenya Human Rights Commission (2009).

13. See Mayoyo and Otieno (2009).

14. Section 94 (1), Kenya constitution. The grounds for revocation of citizenship include disloyalty to Kenya, imprisonment for more that 12 months, support for an enemy country during a state of war and long-term residency outside Kenya. Revocation of citizenship on penal or other grounds banishes an individual to the domain of being stateless contrary to international law.

15. *Kenya Citizenship Act* (Chapter 170 Laws of Kenya, enacted in 1967), available at http://www.kenyalaw.org/kenyalaw/klr_app/frames.php. Section 9 of the Act provides that 'The Minister shall not be required to assign any reason for the grant or refusal of any application under this Act and the decision of the Minister on such application shall not be subject to appeal or review in any court.' The ousting of legal review of ministerial decision to revoke citizenship is perhaps one of the most serious blights in the Kenyan law on citizenship, and one of the most clear pathways to creating stateless persons and communities.

16. Section 88 (2) Kenya constitution.

17. R. Plender, *International Migration Law*, 379 (The Hague: Martinus Nijhoff, 1988). A/6316 (1966), 999 U.N.T.S. 171, entered into force 23 March 1976.

18. Section 89, Kenya constitution.

19. Ibid., section 90.

20. *Registration of Persons Act* (Chapter 107 Laws of Kenya), Article 1, available at http://www.kenyalaw.org/kenyalaw/klr_app/frames.php. The registration process under the Act does not confer citizenship but merely confirms that a registration officer has been persuaded that an applicant has provided documentary and oral evidence required for the issuance of an identity card.

21. Under the *Immigration Act* (Chapter 147 of 1967 as amended in 1972), non-citizens in Kenya require work permits, for example, Class A–F permits.

22. Section 81 (1) Kenya constitution. See also Kenya's *Immigration Act*, which provides that in Article 4 (1) only Kenyan citizens and such persons as may have a valid permit have the right to enter the country.

23. National Assembly and Presidential Elections (Chapter 7 Laws of Kenya, 1969) section 4A (2).

24. A non-citizen is unlikely to own land under the *Trust Lands Act* or the *Group Representatives Act*. Under the Draft National Land Policy (2005), the government seeks to regulate further the land rights of non-citizens. The problem of the proposed policy, however, is that the citizenship status of some groups in Kenya is

questionable, hence the likelihood that the policy may have negative repercussions upon their land rights. See Draft National Land Policy at http://www.ilegkenya.org/pubs/docs/DraftNationalLandPolicy.pdf.

25. The *Immigration Act* requires permits for non nationals to carry on business in the country, for example, Classes G–K.
26. See *Second Schedule Police Act* (Chapter 84 Laws of Kenya, 1961).
27. The Draft Constitution of Kenya, 2004 (Bomas Draft) (adopted by the National Constitutional Conference 15 March 2004). While this Draft was eventually amended in parliament before the final Draft was submitted to the failed referendum in December 2005, it is noteworthy that the provisions on citizenship remained largely unaltered – except for two provisions, whose impacts may be adverse to minorities. While section 21 of Bomas had explicitly narrowed the conditions for deprivation of citizenship to only those circumstances, in which acquisition was by 'means of fraud, false representation or concealment of any material fact', the Referendum Draft in section 22 seems to leave open the door for new grounds for deprivation. Similarly, section 17 (2) (b) creates uncertainty in relation to citizenship by birth in a manner similar to the current constitution. The final draft was defeated at the referendum meaning that the independence constitution is still the substantive law in terms of citizenship regulation in Kenya.
28. Ibid., section 16.
29. Ibid., section 17 (2).
30. Ibid., section 20.
31. Ibid., section 14 provides that: 'Every person who was a citizen immediately before the effective date retains the same citizenship status as from that date.' This is an important provision to ensure smooth transition, but then it fails to recognize residual effects of the current ambivalent citizenship regime.
32. Ibid., section 24.
33. bid., section 13 (b).
34. The Somali, Turkana, Borana and Galjeel minority communities in Kenya are, like the Nubians, equally discriminated against with regard to access to citizenship. See, for example, Kenya Human Rights Commission (2000).
35. *Second Schedule Police Act*, section 19 (2).
36. See generally *Convention relating to the Status of Stateless Persons,* 360 U.N.T.S. 117, entered into force 6 June 1960. See also *Convention on the Rights of the Child* and the *African Charter on the Rights and welfare of the child.*
37. The Harmonized Draft Constitution is the latest in Kenya's attempt to craft a new governance compact. It has been produced by the Committee of Experts established pursuant to the *Constitution of Kenya Review Act* 2008. The Harmonized Draft of the Constitution of Kenya, 2009 is available at http://www.coekenya.go.ke/index.php?option=com_content&view=article&id=113&Itemid=109. This Draft is intended to be debated on for one month and a further draft produced which will be ratified by parliament and submitted to a referendum for adoption or rejection.
38. See Mutua (1995).
39. Compare with section 1 Article 2, Constitution of the United States of America which requires that presidents (and vice presidents) of the United States be natural born citizens of the United States.
40. Nairobi High Court Civil Application No. 256/2003, *Yunus Ali and Others (On behalf of the Nubian Community) v. Attorney General of the Republic of Kenya and Others.*
41. Makoloo (2005), p. 17.
42. National Archives of Kenya (1933). Of the Sudanese (Nubians), the report observes that 'Their past service to Government entitles them to sympathetic consideration . . . .We shall set out the grounds for thinking that it would be of advantage both of themselves and Government that they should be allowed to do so (i.e. continue living in Kibera).'
43. The Nubians believe that strangers should be accorded respect and welcomed into their territory. Interview with the Council of Elders (see note 66 *infra*).

44. See generally National Assembly of Kenya Report of the Parliamentary Commission on Ethnic Clashes (Chaired by Kenneth Kiliku, 1993–1997).
45. UNICEF, 'Kenya's Abolition of School Fees Offers Lessons for Rest of Africa', available at http://www.unicef.org/infobycountry/kenya_33391.html.
46. See, for example, Centre for Housing Rights and Evictions (2006).
47. See M. Ufanisi, 'Kibera Integrated Water, Sanitation & Waste Management Project (K-WATSAN)', available at http://www.majinaufanisi.org/projects/k-watsan.htm.
48. For a comprehensive appraisal of Nubian land struggles in Kibera, see Sing'Oei and Hussein (2002).
49. Makoloo (2005), p. 17.
50. See section 42 (3) (f) and 42 (5) of the Kenya constitution.
51. See, for example, *Statistics Act*, Chapter 4 of 2006, Schedule I, available at http://www.kenyalaw.org/kenyalaw/klr_app/frames.php. This law mandates the state to collect information on, among others, 'communities', but the four national censuses conducted since independence have always identified Nubians as 'others'. The 2009 Population and Housing Census conducted on 24–25 August departs from previous practice and specifically desegregates the Nubians and other minorities. The Nubians were, for instance, given code 220 during the 2009 census. More information on Kenyan Census 2009 is available at http://www.planning.go.ke/index.php?option=com_content&view =article&id=219:preliminary-key-findings-20082009-kenya-demographic-and-health -survey-&catid=109:preliminary-key-findings-20082009-kenya-demograph.   Further, Nubian youth participated in the 2009 census exercise as enumerators hired by the Ministry of Planning. Interview with Rashid Ibrahim, Nubian youth on 19 October 2009 in Kibera.
52. UN Committee on Economic Social and Cultural Rights (2008).
53. See African Commission on Human and Peoples' Rights (2006).
54. Recalling this incident, Abdul Faraj, the Kenya Nubian Council Chairman says: 'I was at state house [president's official mansion]. . . . After recognizing the community, the president assured us that whatever our requests contained in the memorandum of issues submitted to him would be implemented in three days. We felt that this was a credible time-bound promise.' Interview with author, 12 August 2008.
55. The Kenyan constitution requires that a presidential candidate must also be an elected member of parliament. See section 5 (3) (f) Kenya constitution.
56. See Associated Press (2007).
57. Interview with Isa Abdul Faraj, 12 August 2008.
58. UN Human Rights Council (2008).
59. Interview with author, 13 August 2008.
60. Interview with author, 13 August 2008.
61. Interview with Adam Hussein, 15 August 2008.
62. See Hussein (2009).
63. Based on author's interview with Medina Ousman, 9 August 2008.
64. Interviewed in Amos Kareithi (2006).
65. Interview with author, 12 July 2008.
66. Refugees International (2008b).
67. This too could be changing. The author was informed that the last recruitment by the Kenya Army in Kibera sought to establish the number of applicants who were from the Nubian community. Whether this specific targeting resulted in recruitment of Nubian youth could not be ascertained. Interview with Sheikh Ahmed Ramadan, the founder of Nubian Rights Forum, a youth organization, on 19 October 2009 in Makina Primary School, Kibera.
68. Aljazeera Television (2007).
69. Makoloo (2005), p. 17.
70. As Moslims, the poverty of Nubians in Kenya has often been interpreted within the broader context of discrimination targeted at Moslims generally. In the post-9/11 period, this distinction is becoming the more salient. See, for example, Daily Nation

(2006). In response, a tacit admission of state culpability, President Kibaki appointed a Special Action Committee on 16 October 2007 to review individual complaints of alleged harassment and/or discrimination in the treatment of persons who profess the Islamic faith with regard to security operations and take immediate action to solve problems encountered by Muslims. See, Presidential Press Services (2007).

71. See Amis (1984). In Amis's sample of 95 large, informal landlords in Kibera, 71 (66 per cent) were Kikuyu and 24 (22 per cent) were Nubian. Further, 10 of the 29 (35 per cent) large landlords that they could identify were from the local administration.

72. Kibera land technically falls under the *Government Land Act*, which vests all waste and unoccupied land on the president of the republic of Kenya. It is not therefore lightly to be assumed that the president's directive is a mere political statement, since it is not unusual for the president to use this power to transfer public land into private hands. See, for example, Ogola (1996).

73. Minutes of focus group meeting held between author and Nubian Council of Elders, 12 August 2008.

74. Interview with Jamaldin Yahyah, 3 November 2009.

75. Councillor Babu represents Lindi Ward while Councillor Gore represents Makina Ward, both in Kibera Constituency. Interview with Siamah Twahib, a community elder, 19 October 2009 in Makina, Kibera.

76. Increased agency of Nubian youth is evidenced from the fact that they have formed two organizations: Nubian Rights Forum and Nubian Youth Network. The youth blame the elders for lethargy in addressing community issues and are seeking greater space for engagement with the state and other communities. Youth-led advocacy, however, sometimes run into excesses, as witnessed in the destruction of the Seventh Day Adventist Church for encroaching on Nubian land on 31 October 2009. This led to violent confrontation with youth gangs from other communities and left more than three Nubian youth dead. Interview with Jamaldin Yahya, 3 November 2009.

77. Adejumobi (2001).

78. Salojee (2005).

79. Hussein (2009).

4.   From erased and excluded to active participants in Slovenia

Jelka Zorn

In 1991, Slovenia seceded from the Socialist Federal Republic of Yugoslavia (SFRY). From the outset, the Slovene independence process seemed democratic, transparent and respectful of human rights and minorities. However, ethno-nationalist sentiments would eventually find their way into policies regarding citizenship and the treatment of foreigners (aliens); the result was that thousands of long-term immigrants[1] from other republics of the former Yugoslavia as well as some Slovenes were not only left without citizenship in the new Slovene state but were also deprived of all status and rights, including even the most basic human rights that they had previously enjoyed.

The economically motivated migration to Slovenia had begun as early as the 1960s, but it was not until the 1970s, and especially the 1980s, that these immigrants who represented territorially dispersed communities without political demands settled with their families and became visible in Slovenia[2]. When Slovenia declared its independence in 1991, these communities became the implicit target of the nationalist sentiment embedded in the citizenship and aliens' legislation of the new state. While secession legislation made it possible for the majority of these immigrants to become Slovene citizens,[3] many were less fortunate. Most troubling was that after secession a host of administrative procedures were used to strip those who did not apply for citizenship of their social, economic and political rights, giving rise to a new social category of 'erased' persons.

The term 'erasure' was coined by the journalist Igor Mekina in 1994[4] to describe a measure whereby, following the country's independence, some 25 671 persons who did not opt to become Slovene citizens or had been refused citizenship were secretly erased from the Register of Permanent Residents of the Republic of Slovenia by the Ministry of the Interior and, subsequently, were deprived of their acquired rights.[5] The term erasure was then used extensively by the Helsinki Monitor in their human rights advocacy work over the second half of the 1990s.[6] In 1999, it appeared formally in the Slovene Constitutional Court decision.[7] From 2002 onwards, ten years after the state action took place, the term was popularized by the erased themselves when they began an energetic campaign of political action.[8] Notably, following the erasure, victims did not have to cross state borders to find themselves in a new and unpredictable legal situation. On the contrary, one could say that the borders 'crossed them.'

In a symbolic sense the erasure can be viewed as an administrative act of punishment for an alleged failure to assimilate and demonstrate loyalty towards the new state.[9] Before Slovenia's secession, immigrants from other republics of the SFRY were often identified as 'others' on the basis of their ethnicity; however, in the new sovereign state of Slovenia, both their ethnicity and new status as non-citizens were treated in a highly negative way.

The oppression that the erased faced was not limited to the political sphere but encompassed a wide range of existential rights including employment, access to health care (including reproductive rights), education, social assistance, mobility, legal security, personal safety (freedom from deportation and detention), family matters and housing. The production of *de facto*, and sometimes *de jure*, statelessness was not only a temporary side effect of secession. This lack of legal status was in fact reproduced and excused for over a decade while Slovenia was, and still is, internationally praised as the only 'success story' in the territory of the former Yugoslavia.[10] Even today, certain political parties in Slovenia persistently use hate speech when referring to those whose legal status was revoked by the state, namely the erased.[11]

This chapter presents a detailed analysis of the erasure and its effects as well as a critical evaluation of attempts to resolve this problem. The harsh exclusion faced by those who remained without citizenship and residency status in the new Slovene state will serve as a backdrop for an examination of the meaning and benefits of restoring citizenship (and residency rights) to the affected population. The empirical section is based on the author's involvement in research of the phenomenon known as the erasure and the campaign of the erased[12] and draws from interviews conducted between October 2007 and July 2008.

SLOVENE SECESSION AND INITIAL CITIZENSHIP POLICY

In the Slovene example, the problem of *de facto* statelessness is associated with long-term immigrants who did not become Slovene citizens during the Slovene secession from Yugoslavia and were consequently erased from the Register of Permanent Residents of the Republic of Slovenia in

1992. To understand the erasure, composition of citizenship laws from before and after the secession must be examined. This concrete policy in the case of newly designated non-citizens was not based on the law and the Constitution but, in fact, on a lack of legislation – specifically, on the legal void created by the new *Aliens Act*. Historically formed notions of nationhood, based on ethnic belonging, that were widespread during the secession also played a role. Ethno-nationalist sentiment grew alongside the founding documents of the state, written in the spirit of political correctness, and emphasizing egalitarianism and a civic form of nationalism.[13]

According to the 1991 census, 88.3 per cent of residents identified themselves as ethnic Slovenes, suggesting that approximately 10 per cent of the population had emigrated from other areas of the SFRY (Croats, Serbs, Bosnians, Albanians, Macedonians and Montenegrins).[14]

With the disintegration of the SFRY in 1991, Slovenia became the first republic to establish itself as an independent state.[15] In 1991, the initial designation of Slovene citizenry was defined by Articles 39 and 40 of the *Citizenship of the Republic of Slovenia Act*.[16] The provisions of this Act derived from the 1974 SFRY Constitution and subsequent citizenship laws that stipulated two layers of citizenship.[17] According to the 1974 Constitution, every Yugoslav citizen was also a citizen of a republic.[18] On the basis of this Constitution, new federal and republican citizenship Acts were introduced in 1976.[19] Republican citizenship was an administrative, obligatorily ascribed status, a primer to and condition for obtaining federal citizenship. Often the citizens of Yugoslavia had little knowledge about their republican citizenship. It seems that for Yugoslav citizens, however, republican citizenship had no legal consequences.[20] It was to become relevant only after the SFRY had begun to come apart when in the successor states of Slovenia it was applied as an initial criterion for the overall determination of citizenship. Article 39 of the *Citizenship of the Republic of Slovenia Act* states:

> Any person who held citizenship of the Republic of Slovenia and of the Socialist Federal Republic of Yugoslavia in accordance with the existing regulations shall be considered a citizen of the Republic of Slovenia.

For long-term residents of Slovenia who were not considered citizens of the Republic of Slovenia (immigrants from other republics of the SFRY and their offspring), Article 40 defined the conditions for obtaining Slovene citizenship:

> A citizen of another republic that had registered permanent residence in the Republic of Slovenia on the day of the plebiscite of the independence and sovereignty of the Republic of Slovenia on 23 December 1990, and has actually

been living here, shall acquire citizenship of the Republic of Slovenia if, within six months of the entry into force of this Act, he/she files an application with the administrative authority competent for internal affairs of the community where he/she has his/her permanent residence . . .

The above Article was to prove central to the problems that resulted from the erasure. By the time the six-month window for submitting citizenship applications expired, on 25 December 1991, more than 174000 people of whom approximately 30 per cent were born in Slovenia applied for citizenship on the basis of Article 40.[21] It should be noted that this number of applicants comprised a significant percentage (8.7) of the total population. Not all non-Slovene long-term residents were granted Slovene citizenship – some applications were rejected, and some people did not apply. Many had intended to apply for citizenship but were deterred by inaccurate information provided by employees at municipality centres.[22] They were told, for example, that it was not possible to apply without a birth certificate – information which is contrary to the stipulations of the procedural law since everyone has the opportunity to apply for and, if necessary, supplement their application with the required documents in due time. Other reasons given by the erased for not applying for Slovene citizenship on the basis of Article 40 include concerns about real-estate inheritance issues and planned retirement in their countries of origin. It should also be emphasized that in the period of the six-month window for applying (from 25 June to 25 December 1991), Slovenia had not yet been internationally recognized as a sovereign state,[23] and it might be argued that its prospects were not clear at that time.[24]

In either case, those who chose not to apply for Slovene citizenship under the lenient conditions stipulated in Article 40 believed that they would be entitled to social rights as legal aliens on the basis of their permanent residence addresses, family ties and employment in Slovenia. The subsequent erasure from the Register of Permanent Residents of all those who did not become Slovene citizens, a total of 25671 persons, was impossible to predict despite growing anti-Yugoslav and anti-immigrant sentiments.[25]

LEGAL VOID OF THE *ALIENS ACT*

In addition to the *Citizenship of the Republic of Slovenia Act*, one of the fundamental laws of the new sovereign state was the *Aliens Act*.[26] Drafts of both laws were discussed at the National Assembly in May 1991 and adopted on 5 June 1991 – that is, 20 days before the independence ceremony. During the discussions on the content of the new legislation, Metka Mencin, a centre-left-wing deputy of the Assembly, proposed an amendment to Article 81 of the *Aliens Act*. This amendment stated that immigrants from other republics who did not apply for Slovene citizenship would be issued permanent residence permits based on a registered permanent residence address or employment in Slovenia. Although the Executive Council approved of this proposal, a majority of deputies in the Assembly voted it down.[27] It was said that the matter 'does not need to be regulated by the Aliens Act, but by agreements between countries' of the former Yugoslavia. However, such agreements never materialized.[28]

Ultimately, Article 81 of the *Aliens Act* did not outline provisions for persons who became aliens due to the secession.[29] This lack of regulation, which the Constitutional Court of the Republic of Slovenia *post festum* defined as a legal void,[30] was abused in order to invent and implement a measure that resulted in the total exclusion of those residents who did not become citizens of the new state. On the other hand, residence permits for foreigners with non-SFRY citizenship issued while Slovenia was a constituent republic of the SFRY continued to be legal in the independent Republic of Slovenia.[31] The Constitutional Court defined this fact as an illegal discrimination since the principle of equality before the law was violated.[32] The Court also ruled that the principles of trust in the law and security of law had been broken since the erased were not notified about the change of their permanent resident status. They found out that they had been erased solely by chance.

It was not clear how to express grievances or to whom and on what legal grounds complaints should be filed. Interviews with victims of the erasure are most revealing in this regard.[33] One participant provided the following illustration of the confusion he encountered on a regular basis when dealing with authorities following the erasure:

> In February 1992, I went to the administrative centre in order to renew my driving license. The employee said: 'Sir, you are a foreign citizen. You'll have to get an international driving license.' I replied: 'What do you mean? I passed my driving license exam here, in Slovenia. All the documentation about my exam is here and I have no intention of going and seeking a driving license anywhere else but here.' I found out that I had been erased from all sorts of registers – I don't know why and how – and without even being informed. So I didn't have a chance to complain. (Josip, 27 November 2007)

The secret manner in which the erasure was conducted gave further weight to claims that the action was, in itself, arbitrary.

REDUCING STATELESSNESS: WAYS OUT OF THE ERASURE

In the years following the erasure, approximately half of the erased acquired some form of status. Permanent resident status could be acquired under several different laws (*Aliens Act,*[34] *Temporary Asylum Act,*[35] *Act Regulating the Legal Status of Citizens of Former Yugoslavia Living in the Republic of Slovenia*[36]). The road to justice was marked by three milestones. First, in 1999 the Constitutional Court ruled that the erasure was unconstitutional as was the subsequent *Act Regulating the Legal Status of Citizens of Former Yugoslavia Living in the Republic of Slovenia.* This decision made it possible for a number of erased persons to reacquire permanent residence permits.[37] Further, on the basis of the Court's decision, the *Citizenship Act* was amended in 2002, with Article 19 now making it possible for erased persons to acquire Slovene citizenship under more lenient criteria than regular naturalization rules. Second, in 2002, the erased organized themselves into a political action group and initiated a coordinated campaign to recover their rights and receive compensation and recognition. Third, in 2003, the Constitutional Court ruled on a complaint submitted by the Organization of the Erased Residents and recognized that the *Act Regulating the Legal Status of Citizens of Former Yugoslavia Living in the Republic of Slovenia* was also not in compliance with the Constitution. Specifically, the Court stated that the Act failed to recognize revoked statuses retroactively from the date of the erasure; that it excluded those erased persons who had been removed from Slovenia; and that the three-month window it provided for filing an application was insufficient.

In spite of the Constitutional Court's actions, the decision of 2003 has yet to be fully implemented, and the legal barriers preventing many of the erased from legalizing their status in Slovenia remain. Moreover, the erased have yet to receive an apology from the state (based on an unambiguous acknowledgement of the erasure as an unconstitutional act) and compensation for damages. Attempts at reform should, however, be noted. There was a marked turning point on 3 February 2004 when the Ministry of the Interior began issuing retroactive decisions to fill the void between the erasure and reacquired residence permits.[38] Protests, however, from opposition parties and a filed interpellation against the Minister put an end to these efforts, and, as a result, only 4093 persons received such supplementary decisions.[39] When a new right-wing government took over in 2004, any progress towards the just regulation of the erasure was completely obstructed until the change of government in 2008. The current government, which was elected in 2008, decided to continue where the 2004 government had left off.

CURRENT SITUATION

The change of government in 2008 brought new reformers into the open, and, in February 2009, the new Minister of the Interior declared that she was determined to fulfil the Constitutional Court decisions by issuing supplementary decisions retroactively to those who had already acquired permanent resident status or citizenship.[40] Yet, only those erased persons who had already acquired permanent residence or citizenship are eligible at the moment. For the rest of the erased, the Ministry has promised to propose a new law that will have the potential to fully resolve the situation of all the erased persons.

While the fate of the erased remains uncertain, the Ministry of the Interior has provided the following data that helps to clarify the current scope of the problem. The number of erased people (that is, those removed from the Register of Permanent Residents on 26 February 1992) was 25 671 persons, including 5360 minors at the time of the erasure.[41] It is clear that as of 24 January 2009, some 7313 persons[42] had received Slovene citizenship.[43] Hence, less than half of the entire erased population have become Slovene citizens or foreigners with reinstated permanent residence status. It is highly likely that the majority of those who have yet to receive any status in Slovenia now live abroad; regulations that would give such persons back their revoked status have yet to materialize.

METHODS AND FINDINGS

The following section draws upon the findings from interviews conducted before April 2009 and draws upon earlier related research. Most of the persons interviewed had already regained permanent resident status or Slovene citizenship. Interviewees were found through personal contacts and using the snowball method. Out of this group, four of the interviewees were contacted again in April 2009 to further clarify some of their comments regarding the benefits they now enjoy as citizens. Two local activists were also interviewed for this chapter: Sara Pistotnik,[44] a researcher at the Peace Institute, and Katarina Vučko[45] who serves as a legal advocate at the Legal and Information Centre of Non-governmental Organizations. In addition, the author has also studied approximately 50 interviews conducted by the Peace Institute for research purposes.[46]

CASE STUDIES

Vladimir is an ethnic Serb from Bosnia who arrived in Slovenia in 1976 and acquired citizenship in 1992 through Article 40. A year after receiving his citizenship it was withdrawn and his documents were destroyed with a hole-punch. In spite of several High Court rulings that the withdrawal of his citizenship was unlawful, his citizenship was not restored. During the time when he was undocumented, he experienced torture at the hands of the police who beat him, and on two occasions attempted to deport him. He described the second attempt, which took place during the war:

> Once they failed to expel me over the Slovene-Hungarian border they took me to the Croatian border – for the second time. They should never have done that because, by nationality, I'm a Serb. They violated every convention. At the Slovene border they moved me to another car. They took me out of the police car and put me in a plain white van. The border police at the Croatian side wouldn't take me. They had to drive me back. At the Gruškovje border crossing, there's a strip of land a couple of kilometers wide that isn't in either country. There, in the middle of the two border crossings, we stopped. They pulled me out of the car. The police officer stuck an automatic rifle in my mouth and threatened that next time, he would pull the trigger – if I came back. Then he proceeded to kick me. They left me there, in that strip of land, as if to say that I should try to get into Croatia myself. I didn't know what to do. (26 June 2002)[47]

Vladimir later explained in an interview that his appearance on the radio helped him to tell his story and in the end to recover his citizenship. He described the turn of events:

> My appearance on a show on Radio Slovenia, where I had a chance to present my story, helped me get back my citizenship. At the show, there was also a lawyer from the Ministry of the Interior. In 2001 they reinstated my citizenship. Now I'm a completely different person. The police don't harass me anymore. When they stop me, I give them my documents; they take a look at them, say thanks and let me go. Before, they would call me a *četnik*, and they could beat me, but now they don't say anything. Before, they knew that I was without papers and a Serb by nationality, and it was very easy for them to manipulate and abuse me. (November 2007)

While several of the interviewees spoke of problems with the police, for many of the erased, the greatest challenge was receiving health care and accessing employment. The case of Esad below illustrates some of the benefits that the restoration of status brought this individual:

> When I got citizenship in 2003, I began to work, but I lost my employment due to my illness. I was later assessed by the disability commission. I got a disability

categorization of three, so I receive an allowance of 260 Euros per month. This is a big difference compared to the long period without documents and without any support whatsoever. I've applied for a higher category of disability, but the assessment procedure has yet to be completed. As a citizen, I am eligible to apply for a municipality apartment, and I did. I won't necessarily get one, because more people apply than there are apartments available. Citizenship means that you're not harassed, you're not vulnerable and exposed to detention or even deportation, and that you have rights. However, these rights might sometimes only be on paper, so it doesn't always mean that you can realize them. Nevertheless, citizenship has changed my life for the better, I feel safe when I go out, I travel a lot, and I receive a disability allowance. Before, I hadn't travelled for 12 years. Most importantly, I can go out in public and join various campaigns for human rights: for asylum seekers, migrant workers, the erased, against detention centers and so on. As a citizen, I have the courage to appear in the front lines of these campaigns, and I have never felt discouraged from talking to the media. This activism has also changed my life for the better. (24 April 2009)

Several participants noted similarly how the restoration of citizenship or in some cases residency status affected their sense of personal safety to the point where they felt able to engage in political action for social justice.

Several interviewees who became citizens following years of statelessness along with the activists interviewed agreed that the quality of life of those who received a permanent residence permit and especially Slovene citizenship improved greatly. Even though some of the participants in the study still cannot access certain rights (the right to employment or public housing), they at least have a feeling of basic security, that they 'belong', and like Vladimir above, that they will no longer be threatened by the police and exposed to detention and deportation. Participants generally claimed that they felt their lives would take a turn for the better. The following excerpts illustrate this conclusion in detail:

Getting citizenship is like getting back your identity. Even the dead have identities; on tombstones are the names of the people buried below. When we were erased, we didn't exist as persons, but only as bodies – we were neither dead nor alive. Now I feel that I'm acknowledged as a person again. I can identify myself by presenting a personal document. And the police leave me alone and I'm no longer oppressed by administrative employees since I no longer have to go to the aliens and naturalization offices. (Safet, 24 April 2009)

Another commented:

I believe that being a citizen means a hundred percent change – in every aspect of my life. I feel safe now; I can go wherever I wish knowing that I can always return home. If you have citizenship, you can walk the streets relaxed and calm – the police cannot harm you. Before I felt like a criminal, because I didn't have documents. It was illegal to live like that, I was aware of that, and I needed to be careful all the time. The change from before to now, when I have citizenship, is total, I think, hundred percent. Now it feels different when I talk to people, their relationship towards me has changed. Before, they would blame me for not being capable of sorting out my situation with regard to citizenship status. Now I feel safe, and I can easily talk to anybody, I'm taken seriously. It is a huge change. (Vanja, 20 April 2009)

ANALYSIS

In the case of Slovenia, there are two statuses or 'layers' of inclusion and accessibility to social and other rights: citizenship and permanent residency (for non-citizens).[48] The erased were excluded from both. As the data from the Ministry of the Interior record, the ways in which people were able to rely on particular legislation to receive status affected the degree to which they could formally reintegrate in Slovenian society. As the above official data reveals, many erased persons who have reacquired permanent residence status have also managed to naturalize. Those, however, who cannot naturalize report two key obstacles, insufficient income (they or their spouses lack proof of the permanent means to support themselves) and failure to pass the Slovene language exam.[49]

Others, however, face even greater obstacles and are effectively barred from resolving their situation. While campaigning and conducting research on the issue of the erasure, the author and her colleagues interviewed persons who had been erased and were living in Bosnia and Herzegovina, Serbia, Germany and Italy; these individuals cannot reacquire their status as permanent residents in Slovenia, and as a result of the erasure, many have not been able to return to Slovenia (since they crossed the border in 1991 or in 1992) because the border police will not let them re-enter the country.

Another group without any kind of status is found in the small minority of individuals who have remained in Slovenia since the day of the erasure and are undocumented. In principle, these individuals have the right to acquire legal status under the *Act Regulating the Legal Status of Citizens of Former Yugoslavia Living in the Republic of Slovenia*.[50] However, due to practical reasons, which the legislature failed to take into consideration (such as lack of foreign citizenship and a passport), they cannot register their alien status in Slovenia.

The situation of statelessness has persisted in situations where an erased person lacks travel documents and therefore cannot legally travel abroad (to his/her country of origin) in order to obtain foreign citizenship and documents. In a number of cases, these persons have lost all ties to their countries of origin (that is, former Yugoslav republics), and do not even have an address that could serve as a basis for requesting citizenship in these countries. Nor can they obtain the required foreign documents at the embassies of their countries of origin in Slovenia, because embassies provide services of this kind only for citizens legally residing in a country.[51]

Benefits Based on the Status of Permanent Residency

Those who have regained the status of permanent residents can claim the following social rights stipulated in various sector-specific laws:

- the right to permanent residence in the country: once a permanent residence permit has been acquired, the person in question no longer needs to spend money and time gathering documents; they no longer need to pay fees and provide costly notarized translations of personal documents in order to prolong temporary residence permits;
- access to health care on the basis of health insurance;[52]
- access to the educational system;[53]
- access to employment, irrespective of the situation and conditions in the labour market;[54]
- the right to a state pension – Persons who have no other source of income, are 65 years of age or older, and have had a permanent address in Slovenia for at least 30 years (between their 15th and 65th year of age) are entitled to state pensions;[55]
- the right to family integrity – however, aliens who possess a residence permit and would like to bring their family (spouse and/or children, parents only if the alien in question is a minor) must submit evidence of sufficient funds to support those immediate family members who intend to reside in the country;[56]
- the right to receive social assistance on equal terms with citizens;[57]
- the right to free legal aid;[58]
- safety from detention in the Detention Centre and expulsion from the state;
- the right to return to their homes in Slovenia if they cross state borders (for example, they can travel to their country of origin and return to their home in Slovenia).

Benefits Based on Citizenship Status

A wider spectrum of rights is available to those who have acquired Slovene citizenship. Besides the social rights listed above, citizenship confers the following additional rights:

- the right to the reimbursement of basic health insurance, if a citizen is unemployed and cannot afford to pay for it himself/herself (health insurance is reimbursed by their municipality);[59]
- the right to low cost housing and municipality-owned housing facilities;[60]
- political rights (the right to vote and to be elected in general elections);[61]
- the right to carry a Slovene passport.[62]

During the period of transition from state socialism to the current socio-political system and sovereign nation-state, all citizens including children had two additional rights pertaining to the distribution of collective property that was nationalized (that is, transferred to the ownership of the state) and then transformed into private property. First, every citizen received a certificate in order to become a shareholder. Second, in the case of apartments under non-private ownership, users had the right to buy the apartment at a non-commercial price, thereby converting it into private property. It should be noted that for the distribution of collective property nationality was key (beneficiaries were citizens), regardless of participation in the production of this property. This means that children with citizenship were also beneficiaries – they received certificates, although they did not necessarily play a part in the production of this property. On the other hand, the erased were completely excluded from sharing the collective property although they participated in its production.

Evaluating the Benefits of Acquiring Status

In the years following the erasure from the Register of Permanent Residents, many of the affected persons filed complaints and sought justice at various state institutions such as the Ministry of the Interior, the Slovene Ombudsman, the President of the State and the courts. These were individual actions since the manner in which the erasure was implemented kept its victims isolated from one another. Legal labyrinths were dealt with on the individual level and the term 'erasure' did not exist to inform the victims of what had actually happened. Since they were not allied, they were not able to recognize the systematic nature of the cancellation of their individual statuses.[63]

One interviewee, for example, recalled that learning about the erasure on television and contacting other erased persons was a turning point in her 'post-erasure' life:

I felt as if I had wings. I felt like the pain was going to literally fall from my body, I felt alive again and that the future exists, that there is a light at the end

of the tunnel. Finally this injustice had come out, it had been revealed! I was
not alone, I wasn't the one who screwed up; I thanked God many times for this.
(Andreja, 2 February 2008)[64]

Externalizing responsibility and learning about the magnitude of the
problem did not only bring about the psychological potential for change in
individuals (feelings of relief and empowerment), a number of cases reveal
how this change found its expression in political activism:

> There are many problems in our country. One cannot remain passive. From
> nothing comes nothing. So it happened that now, when I'm older, I take to the
> streets [attend protests]. It might sound strange or even ridiculous that now, as
> seniors, we attend street protests and rallies, but I feel it makes me stronger, it
> give us new heart. It's a small contribution that I have to offer – my participa-
> tion; but I hope this has at least a small effect in changing things for the better.
> (Vera, 5 December 2007)

In December 2008, at the first national conference on the erasure,[65]
there was a panel made up of four speakers (two men and two women)[66]
who experienced the erasure from the Register of Permanent Residents
in 1992 and were actively involved in the campaign. Instead of reiterating
the ways in which they had been excluded, they were asked to discuss the
benefits of being politically active: why they became active and how they
were introduced to the campaign; what being active means to them and
how they feel now; and the results of their campaign. Their replies and
interviews with other erased persons and two local activists make it possible to divide the results of the campaign into two categories: collective
or societal gains and personal benefits. The former include the visibility of
the erased; the inclusion of the issue of the erasure in the public agenda;
illuminating systemic failures such as the impotence of the authority of the
Constitutional Court and the misuse of a referendum[67] campaign for the
promotion of political parties; the weakness of the rule of law; the strictly
bureaucratic functioning of public institutions (that is, their total ethical
blindness); and other similar gains. Public discussions on remedying the
erasure can be thus considered a 'test' of the principle of justice and the
rule of law and a struggle for the revision of the purported 'success story'
of Slovene independence.

The personal benefits of being politically active can be summarized
as follows: empowerment of individuals (as individuals and as erased);
the ability to participate in new domestic and international networks;
the enjoyment of positive social roles; a restored sense of belonging;
and the opportunity to gain new experiences, for example, through the
possibility of travelling abroad. It comes as no surprise that those who felt

empowered by their involvement in political work also lent their support to the political campaigns of asylum seekers and migrant workers.[68] However, it should be recorded that the campaign of the erased has also met with negative responses including: the polarization of society around the issue and the breakdown of the discussion into facile 'for and against' arguments; the misuse of the issue of the erasure during the general election campaign (especially in 2004, significantly less in 2008); the stigmatization of the erased; and the harassment of individual activists and their family members.

CONCLUSION

Benefits to those who regained permanent resident status or citizenship include:

1. Possession of personal documents allows for self-identification, residence in the country, work, border crossing and accession to rights stipulated in sector-specific laws on education, health care, social assistance, employment, housing and family integrity.
2. A decreased feeling of vulnerability as a result of the fact that they have regained documents and thus basic security. They regained a feeling of belonging since they no longer live in fear of harassment by police or neighbours, deportation or detention. People feel that their lives have taken a turn for the better.
3. Reacquired legal status has enabled some to become politically active and brought the issue of the erasure, and with it the questionable functioning of state institutions, into the public agenda. They reported that becoming political and active led to feelings of connectedness and empowerment.

Although the majority of persons who remained in Slovenia for the duration of their erasure managed to naturalize or reobtain the status of permanent residents, this does not mean that their everyday situation automatically reverted to what it would have been had they never experienced the erasure. Moreover, the current legislation fails to provide compensation for the 'stolen years', as some erased individuals refer to the period when they were without documents and thus without rights. While the actions of the new Minister of the Interior are welcome, and, indeed, supplementary decisions are an important step towards eliminating this unconstitutional situation, nearly all other problems generated by the erasure currently still remain open questions.

NOTES

1. Of the 25 671 persons who were left without Slovene citizenship and the right to reside in Slovenia not all were immigrants. Owing to the non-transparent legacy on which the initial designation of citizenry was built, Slovenes were also among those excluded (Dedić et al., 2003) The number of persons was reported at the Ministry of the Interior's Press Conference 27 January 2009, available at http://www.mnz.gov.si/nc/si/splosno/cns/novica/article/12027/6214/.
2. Mežnarić, (1986).
3. 171 125 long-term and second-generation immigrants became Slovene residents in the initial designation of citizenry (Medved, 2007, p. 218).
4. The term erased appeared in Igor Mekina's article 'Izgnani, deložirani, izbrisani' (Expelled, Evicted, Erased) in a leftist weekly *Mladina*, 22 November 1994, and in Mekina (2008).
5. The administrative transformation of permanent resident status was implemented in the case of non-Yugoslav citizens. For example, an Italian citizen who had held a permanent residence address in Slovenia within the framework of the SFRY kept his/her status of permanent resident in the new sovereign state of Slovenia (Article 82 of the *Aliens Act*, Official Gazette 1/1991-I, no longer valid as of 14 August 1999). Republic of Slovenia (1999).
6. Mekina, (2008).
7. Anonymous, 'Decision No. U-I-284/94', Constitutional Court of Slovenia, 1999, available at http://ius.info/Baze/Usta/B/USTA66656335.htm.
8. Beznec (2008); Pistonik (2008).
9. Ibid.; Zorn (2009a). The assertion of European Member of Parliament Lojze Peterle (who was Slovene Prime Minister in 1992, when the erasure from the Register of Permanent Residents took place) is a telling example. In a TV show broadcast on 26 February 2009, when he was asked to explain why only former Yugoslav citizens legally residing in Slovenia were erased from the Register of Permanent Residents, whereas other foreigners kept their resident status intact, he replied: 'We were not at war with those foreigners from the UK, USA or China. It is well known who we were waging war against.' By this he meant immigrants from other Yugoslav republics, whose 'natural' position in his opinion was among the 'aggressors' threatening Slovenia. He viewed their ethnic identity as their political opinion or even action, even though 5360 children were also among these alleged 'aggressors'.
10. Dedić et al. (2003).
11. For a good analysis of hate-speech, see B. Vezjak, 'Argumentation and Rhetoric in the Case of the Erased', in Zorn and Lipovec Čebron (2008) and former Human Rights Ombudsman Matjaz Hanzek's, 'When will Words Become Actions? Reflections on Hate Speech in Slovenia' (2007).
12. Dedić et al. (2003); Zorn (2005, 2006, 2007, 2008, 2009b).
13. Bajt (2003).
14. 7.3 per cent of residents identified themselves as Croats, Serbs, Muslims, Bosnians, Albanians, Montenegrins or Macedonians; 0.6 per cent identified themselves as Yugoslavs (which was perceived as a transnational category); 0.5 per cent of the population did not wish to declare their ethnic belonging, and for 2.2 per cent there is no data (Statistical Office of the Republic of Slovenia, 2003). Hungarian and Italian national minorities and the Roma ethnic community also reside in Slovenia.
15. The sovereignty of the Republic of Slovenia was declared on 25 June 1991 on the basis of the *Basic Constitutional Charter on the Independence and Sovereignty of the Republic of Slovenia*, Official Gazette of the Republic of Slovenia No. 1/1991-1. The first legal foundation for Slovene statehood, however, was the *Constitution of the People's Republic of Slovenia*, which dates back to 1947 (Kristan, 1976, p. 50). Also, the right to secede was defined in the 1974 Constitution of the SFRY. The right to self-determination was stipulated in Part I of the *Basic Principles of the*

Constitution. The Constitution of the SFRY is available at http://sl.wikisource.org/wiki/Ustava_Socialisti%C4%8Dne_federativne_republike_Jugoslavije_%281974%29/Temeljna_na%C4%8Dela.

16. Official Gazette of the Republic of Slovenia (1991).
17. Article 249 (Chapter Relations in the Federation) of the *Constitution of the SFRY* (1974); 'Citizenship of the SFRY Act', *Official Gazette of the Republic of Slovenia*, No. 58/76; 'Citizenship of the Socialist Republic of Slovenia Act', *Official Gazette of the Republic of Slovenia*, No. 23/76.
18. Article 249, Chapter Relations in the Federation of the Constitution of the SFRY (1974).
19. 'Citizenship of the SFRY Act', *Official Gazette of the Republic of Slovenia*, No. 58/76 and 'Citizenship of the Socialist Republic of Slovenia Act', *Official Gazette of the Republic of Slovenia*, No. 23/76.
20. Some of the deputies of the Assembly of the Republic of Slovenia, when discussing new citizenship law for the independent Republic of Slovenia, emphasized that the institution of republican citizenship was generally unknown to residents of Slovenia and that records were not really kept in order. National Assembly of Slovenia (1991). See also Beznec (2008); Zorn (2008).
21. Medved (2007), p. 218.
22. Kogovšek (2008).
23. The Republic of Slovenia regards the day of its international recognition as 15 January 1992. The legal and political basis for recognition by the European Community was opinions of the special commission headed by Robert Badinter; the opinions were issued on 11 January 1992. see http://www.mzz.gov.si/index.php?id=13&tx_ttnews[tt_news]=22815&tx_ttnews[backPid].
24. Beznec (2008).
25. Ibid; Blitz (2006); Dedić et al. (2003); Lipovec Čebron (2008).
26. 'Aliens Act', *Official Gazette of the Republic of Slovenia*, No. 1/1991-I (not valid from 14 August 1999).
27. Transcripts of the National Assembly Sitting No. 19 held on 9, 15, 21, 22 and 30 May and 3 and 5 June 1991.
28. Beznec (2008); Dedić et al. (2008); Mekina (2008); Zorn (2008).
29. In 2009, the Ministry of the Interior reported that, in 1992, 5360 children had been erased from the Register of Permanent Residents. Available at http://www.mnz.gov.si/fileadmin/mnz.gov.si/pageuploads/2009/izbrisani-koncni_podatki.pdf.
30. Anonymous, 'Decision No. U-I-284/94'.
31. Third paragraph of Article 82, 'Aliens Act', *Official Gazette of the Republic of Slovenia*, No. 1/1991-I (no longer valid as of 14 August 1999).
32. Decision No. U-I-284/94 on 4 February 1999 was followed by several decisions in which the Constitutional Court reasserted its opinion: decision No. Up-60/97 on 15 July 15 1999, decision No. U-I-89/99 on 6 October 1999, decision No. U-I-295/99 on 18 May 2000, decision No. U-I-246/02 on 3 April 2003 and decision No. Up-211/04-21 on 2 March 2006.
33. Blitz (2006); Dedić et al. (2008); Lipovec Čebron (2008); Zorn (2005, 2006, 2007, 2008, 2009a, 2009b).
34. 'Aliens Act', *Official Gazette of the Republic of Slovenia*, No. 1/1991-I (no longer valid as of 14 August 1999) and 'Aliens Act', *Official Gazette of the Republic of Slovenia*, No. 61/1999 and subsequent amendments. See Republic of Slovenia (1999).
35. 'Temporary Asylum Act', *Official Gazette of the Republic of Slovenia*, No. 20/1997 (no longer valid as of 23 July 2005).
36. 'Act Regulating the Legal Status of Citizens of Former Yugoslavia Living in the Republic of Slovenia', *Official Gazette of the Republic of Slovenia*, No. 61/1999.
37. Ibid. Approximately 7000 persons received status of permanent resident under the above-mentioned law.
38. Pistotnik (2008).

39. Minister of the Interior Katarina Kresal's speech defending her work against the interpellation by the opposition parties, 1 April 2009. Available at http://www.google.si/search?hl=sl&q=dopolnilne+odlo%C4%8Dbe+rado+bohinc&meta=&aq=f&oq=.
40. Ibid.
41. As of 24 January 2009, 1302 persons had passed away.
42. 3816 of them first acquired a permit for permanent residence and then citizenship; the rest of them applied for Slovene citizenship directly.
43. It should be noted, however, that while the vast majority of those who received residency were able to rely on the Citizenship Law or *Aliens Act* (87 per cent), others had to rely on the *Temporary Asylum Act* (0.5 per cent) or could only acquire temporary residency (7 per cent).
44. Interview with Sara Pistotnik was conducted in Ljubljana on 18 March 2009.
45. Interview with Katarina Vučko was conducted in Ljubljana on 26 February 2009.
46. Peace Institute (2007).
47. Excerpts of this interview were originally published in Dedić et al. (2003). This individual was interviewed again in November 2007. Despite this, the author decided to draw on the first interview, which was conducted in 2002.
48. As the third status of inclusion and accessibility of social rights, refugee status based on the *International Protection Act* (*Official Gazette of the Republic of Slovenia*, No. 111/2007) should be mentioned.
49. Lipovec Čebron (2008).
50. See Official Gazette of the Republic of Slovenia (1999, 2003).
51. Reported by Katarina Vučko, 26 February 2009, and Sara Pistotnik, 18 March 2009.
52. Article 15, 'Health Care and Health Insurance Act of the Republic of Slovenia', *Official Gazette of the Republic of Slovenia*, No. 72/2006).
53. *Constitution of the Republic of Slovenia* (Article 57) 'Elementary School Act', *Official Gazette of the Republic of Slovenia*, No. 81/2006. 'Gimnazije Act' *Official Gazette of the Republic of Slovenia*, No. 115/2006; 'Higher Education Act', *Official Gazette of the Republic of Slovenia*, No. 119/2006).
54. Article 10 'Employment and Work of Aliens Act', *Official Gazette of the Republic of Slovenia*, No. 4/2006'.
55. Pension and Disability Insurance Institute of the Republic of Slovenia, 'Kako do državne Pokojnine? (How to Obtain a State Pension)'. Currently the state pension amounts 178 euros per month.
56. Article 36 of the Aliens Act (2006).
57. Article 5 (Beneficiaries), 'Social Assistance Act', *Official Gazette of the Republic of Slovenia*, No. 36/2004.
58. Article 10, 'Free Legal Aid Act', *Official Gazette of the Republic of Slovenia*, No. 96/2004.
59. Point 21 of Article 15, 'Health Care and Health Insurance Act of the Republic of Slovenia', *Official Gazette of the Republic of Slovenia*, No. 72/2006.
60. Paragraph 5, Article 87, 'Housing Act', *Official Gazette of the Republic of Slovenia*, No. 69/2003.
61. Article 7, 'National Assembly Elections Act', *Official Gazette of the Republic of Slovenia*, No. 109/2006.
62. Article 1, 'Passports of the Citizens of the Republic of Slovenia Act', *Official Gazette of the Republic of Slovenia*, No. 65/2000.
63. Blitz (2006); Dedić et al. (2008); Zorn (2005).
64. This quotation is taken from an interview conducted by colleagues from the Peace Institute for the research project entitled 'The Erased Residents of Slovenia: A Challenge for a Young Democratic State'. The head of the project is Neža Kogovšek. Slovene summary available at http://www.mirovni-institut.si/Projekt/Detail/si/projekt/Izbrisani-prebivalci-Slovenije-Izziv-za-mlado-drzavo/.
65. The conference '*16 Years Later: Political and Legal Aspects of the Erasure in Slovenia*' was held on 3 and 4 December 2008 in Ljubljana. It was organized by the Peace

Institute. see http://www.mirovni-institut.si/Dogodek/Detail/si/dogodek/ 16-let-poznej e-Politicni-in-pravni-vidiki-izbrisa-v-Sloveniji/.

66. Irfan Beširović, Nisveta Lovec, Aleksandar Todorović and Mirjana Učakar were speakers at the panel entitled 'European Tour of the Erased: From Copenhagen to Belgrade'.

67. A referendum to decide on a law that would fill the void in the legal status of the erased, called the *Technical Act*, was initiated by opposition parties as their unofficial pre-election campaign. The campaign pitted 'loyal citizens', who would have to pay compensation to the 'traitors' of the Slovene nation, the erased and thus against the law. The referendum was held on 4 April 2004; 31.1 per cent of the electorate cast their vote; 94.7 per cent voted against the law. At the national elections, held on 3 October 2004, the former opposition won (Pistotnik, 2008).

68. Unfortunately, the struggles of asylum seekers and migrant workers against exclusion and exploitation provoked extremely negative responses from the Ministry of the Interior (in the case of asylum seekers) and individual employers (in the case of migrant workers). For the activists involved, these negative responses included negative decisions on their asylum applications or dismissals in the case of migrant workers.

5. From statelessness to citizenship: Up-country Tamils in Sri Lanka

P.P. Sivapragasam

Source: © Greg Constantine 2010.

Figure 5.1   *Hill Tamils working on tea plantations in Sri Lanka have historically been discriminated against and were denied Sri Lankan citizenship for decades. While many have obtained Sri Lankan citizenship in recent years, thousands are still stateless.*

The history of plantation people in Sri Lanka goes back at least two hundred years. Because there is limited information available from that time period, there is much room for interpretation, and it is important to note that contemporary accounts may be coloured by an individual's academic tradition, ethnic, religious and ideological perspective; or their relationship with the contemporary trade union movement.

The origin of plantations themselves can be traced back to the Portuguese Canary Islands in the fifteenth century. In the sixteenth and seventeenth centuries, they were established in the New World where they mainly produced sugar and cotton for the European market – subsidized by African slave labour.[1] Subsequently, and despite the abolition of slavery in the nineteenth century, plantations spread under the aegis of an expanding Western imperialism into parts of Africa and Asia. A wider range of food, beverages and raw materials for industrial use were cultivated for the consumer markets and factories of the West. To this day, plantations remain an important form of agricultural production in many countries of the world.

An important and recurring issue in plantation studies is the problem of definition. The issue is not trivial. Acceptable definitions and conventions are a prerequisite for meaningful comparison and generalization, and in the field of policy, it is important to set universal, or at least widely applicable, standards. A plantation is usually a large farm or estate, especially in a tropical or semi-tropical country, on which cotton, tobacco, coffee, tea, sugar cane or trees are cultivated, usually by resident labourers. A plantation is an intentional planting of a crop, on a larger scale, usually for uses other than cereal production or pasture. The term is currently most often used for plantings of trees and shrubs. The term also tends to be used for plantings maintained for economic purposes other than that of subsistence farming.

Most of these involve a large landowner, raising crops with economic value rather than for subsistence, with a number of employees carrying out the field labour. Often it refers to crops newly introduced to a region. In the past, it had been associated with slavery, indentured labour and other economic models of high inequity. Arable and dairy farming are usually (but not always) excluded from such definitions.

The term plantation is defined in the International Labour Organization's (ILO) Plantations Convention 110 of 1958 as:

> any agricultural undertaking regularly employing hired workers which is situated in the tropical or subtropical regions and which is mainly concerned with the cultivation or production for commercial purposes of coffee, tea, sugarcane, rubber, bananas, cocoa, coconuts, groundnuts, cotton, tobacco, fibers (sisal, jute and hemp), citrus, palm oil, cinchona or pineapple; it does not include family or small-scale holdings producing for local consumption and not regularly employing hired workers. (Article 1(1) of the ILO Convention 110, as amended by the Protocol)[2]

Another widely accepted definition provided by Kirk is:

> A plantation is an economic unit producing agricultural commodities for sale and employing a relatively large number of unskilled laborers whose

activities are closely supervised. Plantations usually employ a year round labor crew of some size, and they usually specialize in the production of one or two marketable products. They differ from other kinds of farms in the way in which the factors of production, primarily management and labor are combined.[3]

PLANTATION WORKERS IN SRI LANKA

Historically, plantation workers in Sri Lanka shared a fate similar to that of millions of workers in many neo-colonial Third World countries. They were products of the nineteenth century phase of Western capitalist expansion under colonialism, which was characterized by the establishment of plantation economies. From 1830 onwards, coffee plantations were developed in Sri Lanka. By 1880, tea had replaced coffee.[4] Immigrant Indian workers became the cheap and easiest source of labour for the plantations of Ceylon (Sri Lanka).

The systematic recruitment of Indian labour began in 1839, and, in that year alone, 2432 male labourers arrived in Ceylon.[5] There are, however; no details of the number of women who arrived with them. Planters soon recognized the advantages of employing women workers. Women provided a reserve army that the planters could draw upon when needed, thus enabling the establishment of an elastic and cheap supply of labour. Through the development of household structures, women gave birth to children, enabling the plantation owners to reproduce their own supply of labour and, thus, to subsidize the plantation. The fact that several members of the same family were employed lent justification in the eyes of the planters to the lowering of the individual wage. Both men and women were subjected to exploitation on the plantations. However, it should be noted that suffering was inflicted on the women workers jointly by both the capitalist class and by male workers. If domestic work is defined as labour, then women laboured free of charge and alone. Cooking, sweeping, washing the dirty linen of the infants, cleaning, removing garbage and washing pots and pans were some of the burdens imposed by capitalists on women under the cover of family responsibility – and this with the connivance of male workers (themselves cruelly exploited by the capitalists) who accepted this exploitation as their culture.

One of the most striking developments of the 1920s was the militant action of the urban workers to improve their living and working conditions. A.E. Goonasinghe played an important role in developing a workers movement in the urban sector.[6] The estate workers, however, were faced with great barriers at every stage of their struggle to organize themselves.

K. Natesa Aiyer, an Indian Brahmin, joined with A.E. Goonasinghe in trade union action, but the association between the two men did not last long. Natesa Aiyar eventually founded the first trade union for the plantation workers – the All Ceylon Estate Labor Federation – in 1931 with its headquarters in Hatton. In May 1931, a meeting of 5000 workers was held in Hatton, and resolutions were adopted protesting against wage cuts.[7] The later years saw a multiplicity of trade unions, and the major trade unions in the plantation sector became politically motivated.

Today's Up-country or Plantation Tamils derive their origins from a British colonial era project. According to Professor Bastianpillai, workers around India – the Tamil Nadu cities of Thirunelveli, Tiruchi, Madurai and Tanjore – were recruited from 1827 by Governor Sir Edward Barnes on the request of George Bird, a pioneering planter. The nature of their labour also defined Tamils of Indian origin who lived on the plantations under a regimented system of labour management where they were denied any right to mobility and were restricted to a narrow area in the plantation. It is important to note that the Plantation Tamil communities are not directly related to the Tamils in other parts of Sri Lanka who have been involved in a civil conflict with the government. Unlike other Tamil communities, the Plantation Tamil labour force speaks Tamil, is Hindu by religion, and the majority of them are Dalits[8] who traditionally have resided in the central part of Sri Lanka among the local Sinhala Buddhist population of the surrounding areas. Restricted to tea and rubber estates, and a smaller number to coconut estates, the Tamil population did not have much opportunity to interact or integrate with other communities. For over 150 years, the management of the plantations has been responsible for the welfare of workers, including their health and education.

The contribution of the Plantation Tamils cannot be understated. Sri Lanka has one of the finest social welfare records among developing countries, and it is important to note that the island's welfare policies are funded through revenue derived from the agricultural sector, which is still dominated by tea plantations; hence the important contribution of the Plantation Tamils who make up just 5.4 per cent (2001) of the total population of Sri Lanka. According to the Ministry of Estate Infrastructure, the total number of families living on plantation is around 230000, and the best estimate of the population of Plantation Tamils is 900034 (2006). The population of women living on the tea plantations, unlike those of the other ethnic groups of Sri Lanka and areas other than plantations in the world, is especially significant: of the total labour force, about 46.7 per cent is made up of women.

In spite of their role in the Sri Lankan economy, the people living on the plantations, particularly women, have been continuously subjected to various forms of oppression and have been denied civil, political, economic, social and cultural rights, and the right to development. Nadesan, a trade unionist describes the historical restrictions on the Plantation Tamils:

> The estate workers, however, were faced with great barriers in every stage of their struggle to organize themselves; no other section of the working class of Ceylon was confronted with comparable obstacles. The estates were sacred territories not to be blemished by any intruder agitator. There was the 'Protection of Produce Ordinance No. 38 of 1917' hanging like the sword of Damocles over any outsider entering the estates. According to Section 3 of this Ordinance, any person found loitering or lurking about in a plantation was liable to imprisonment for a period of six weeks and a fine of Rs. 25.[9]

Today, the Plantation Tamils remain isolated from the rest of the population and are subject to discrimination in many areas, including the denial of political rights such as voting as well as the right to freedom of movement; they are also prevented from opening bank accounts. They encounter a host of practical problems in their daily lives. One retired worker on the Greatwelly Estate, Deltota, described the situation he experienced before he received citizenship.

> I retired after working for 40 years on this estate as a laborer. For the last many years, many including me have been without citizenship – as second-class citizens. Many of us did not get the opportunity of voting. Therefore neither a politician nor a government officer cares for us. We have been living sidelined for the last many years. (N., 10 May 2009)

The description of plantation workers as 'second-class' citizens, however, does not take into consideration the magnitude of the problem as the estate system comprised an entire world for the Plantation Tamil workers who were bound by both formal and informal contracts to the estate. The room that housed workers and their families symbolized their captivity, as they had no right to leave the estate or own land or a house elsewhere.[10]

Trade unions played a crucial role among the Indian Plantation workers in the 1990s; however, the system has undergone significant changes in ownership with the nationalization of plantations and subsequent privatization. One result of these changes is the growing poverty among the plantation people. In 2002, the level of poverty in the plantation sector was well above the national average, and international aid agencies have noted that their welfare has been neglected for a long period of time.[11]

CIVIL AND POLITICAL RIGHTS OF THE PLANTATION PEOPLE

After Sri Lanka became independent in 1948, the new parliament soon enacted the *Citizenship Act* of 1948. This law conferred citizenship by descent on all persons who were born in Sri Lanka and whose father was born in Sri Lanka (*Citizenship Act* No. 18 1948). The *Indian and Pakistan (residents) Citizenship Act No.* 3 1949 provided for citizenship by registration. Application for citizenship by registration was in the first instance only open to persons who were, and could be proven to be, of Indian origin. The citizenship law of 1948 discriminates against people who have come to Sri Lanka 'recently', namely after the law entered into force, and has placed the community of the Plantation Tamils in a vulnerable position that has been further aggravated by the discriminatory implementation of the law. This situation gave birth to statelessness.

The problem of the stateless Tamils was taken up in negotiation with India in 1964 when the two parties reached an agreement called the Sirimavo-Shastri Pact. The pact extended until 1974 when the number of stateless Plantation Tamils was estimated at around 975000. An agreement was reached whereby 600000 Plantation Tamils would be repatriated to India and 375000 registered for Sri Lankan citizenship.[12] A subsequent agreement in 1974 agreed to split the remaining population between India and Sri Lanka.

In the aftermath of the July 1983 violence, when a large number of Sri Lankans ended up in India as refugees, India linked the problem of refugees arriving on its shore to the repatriation process for the Plantation Tamils. It should be noted that as a result of the violence in Sri Lanka, some of those who had previously opted for Sri Lankan citizenship now preferred the possibility of relocating to India. In 1986, it was estimated that there were still 94000 Estate Tamils without status but, given the inter-state tensions and complex ethnic political situation, Sri Lanka decided to grant Sri Lankan citizenship to this population and passed legislation for this purpose in January 1986.

CITIZENSHIP REFORM AND EVIDENCE OF GOOD PRACTICE

Over the past 50 years, all of Sri Lanka's post-independence governments have attempted to resolve the problem of the stateless Plantation Tamils. To this end, the Indian government has also played an important role. Both governments, however, have considered the issue more as a political, rather than humanitarian or human rights issue. Nonetheless, the Sri Lankan government's efforts to resolve the problem in 2003 were commendable both in terms of outcome and the way in which the issue galvanized political constituencies in both Sri Lanka and India. Remarkably, all parties in the Sri Lankan parliament unanimously supported the government's motion to address the situation. Although the people of Indian origin had previously been critical of the earlier approaches of the Sri Lankan and Indian governments over the last 50 years to resolve the issue, both states proved willing and able to cooperate on this issue.

The introduction of the *Grant of Citizenship to Persons of Indian Origin Act No. 35*[13] by the Sri Lankan parliament in October 2003 gave immediate citizenship to people of Indian origin who had lived in Sri Lanka since October 1964 and to their descendants. The innovation of this legislation lies in its simplified procedure whereby, rather than applying to state authorities for citizenship, individuals could obtain a 'general declaration' that was to be countersigned by a justice of peace and serve as proof of citizenship. The UNHCR's, which led an active media campaign to inform

Source: © Greg Constantine 2010.

Figure 5.2   *Once children finish primary school, they can go to secondary school but Hill Tamils have an incredibly high drop out rate. Low wages and poverty force many to follow in their parents' footsteps as workers on the plantations instead of going to school.*

people about the new citizenship procedures, has subsequently described Sri Lanka as a success story. Amin Awad, UNHCR's Representative in Colombo, went on record declaring 'almost overnight, the stateless population in Sri Lanka was more than halved . . . . It was a huge success story in the global effort to reduce statelessness' (p. 21).[14]

Yet the issue has not been resolved for thousands of individuals and continued discrimination against the Plantation Tamils is suggested by the regular involvement of civil society and international organizations, trade unions and UNHCR which have engaged in awareness-raising programmes, lobbying efforts and advocacy. Out of 300 000 identified stateless persons in 2003, only 190 000 individuals were eventually registered as citizens.[15] Numbers registered also varied widely from one region to another; in the northeast of the country, 679 persons registered for citizenship through mobile services in Vavuniya, and 320 persons registered in Trincomalee.

There were many reasons why the registration campaigns in the above regions were less successful, including ignorance among the plantation community about the significance of registration. It should be noted that ignorance is interrelated with the poor standard of education of the marginalized plantation community. Other reasons include bureaucratic processes[16] and a lack of clarity among the government officers regarding the issue and content of the new citizenship law. It was expected that most stateless persons of Indian origin who wished to register as citizens would have done so by the end of December 2004. The state was required to maintain continued registration facilities in government offices for those people who, for some reason, did not or were unable to register during the respective campaigns. But this did not happen and especially in the North and Eastern districts many individuals were unable to obtain information or participate in the registration process because of civil conflict taking place in these areas. Moreover, thousands of stateless persons who would have qualified for citizenship under the latest Act fled the country. Many of these are currently residing in refugee camps in South India.[17]

While the citizenship issue has been largely resolved in law, several problems have not been addressed. These include the following challenges:

- The state administration bodies have not been made fully aware of the legal arrangements that followed the 2003 law.
- In practice, the government insists on citizenship certificates from people of Indian origin who approach them; yet many are still unable to obtain these documents.
- There is widespread ignorance about the value of citizenship certificates.[18]

- Individuals who cannot provide citizenship certificates are often denied the right to be included on the list of voters.
- There is a need to conduct a campaign to re-register or clarify the situation of individuals in Tamil Nadu, India, where many stateless people have sought refuge.

To make the resolution of statelessness meaningful for the Plantation Tamils, the aforementioned issues must not only be identified but also implemented, principally through the education of administrative officers at all levels in order to ensure affected individuals equal rights and opportunities.

RESEARCH AND FINDINGS

For the present project, the researcher interviewed individuals on plantations in Kandy and Nuwaraeliya, Sri Lanka, in February and March 2009. Interviewees identified a number of positive effects of obtaining citizenship. One individual stated in summary, 'As far as I am concerned, I feel that those who have been granted citizenship are treated as human beings.'

A change repeatedly noted by interviewees is the newly granted freedom to participate in the country's political system. Specifically, the right to vote and to stand as a candidate for local elections was recorded. Individuals highlighted the fact that their nationality and national identification was ensured. It was also mentioned that children of the new citizens have the right to basic documents. Others claimed that since their political rights had been realized, they could engage in political processes in a meaningful way. Moreover, the degree to which they could demonstrate their community's political importance and enter into bargains and alliances gave them greater access to development activities.

The interviews also highlighted the fact that younger workers were more likely to benefit from the citizenship campaigns. There is evidence of migration from the estates to the large cities of Colombo and Kandy. This trend supports some of the recent findings obtained by UNHCR. For example, Perera records the testimony of an individual named Kalyani who was able to move out of the plantations and establish a career outside the tea industry in the nursing sector in Colombo:

> I was really thankful when my national identity card arrived because it allowed me to travel to Colombo and find work here, said the 23-year-old. 'I am earning much more than I would have if I stayed on at the estate.' Her husband is also applying for his national identity card and will then join her in Colombo. He is with my two-year-old son in Hatton. My mother takes care of the child

while he goes to work, but very soon all of them can join me here for a much better life.[19]

It should be noted here that, in addition to age, obtaining a National Identity Card (NIC) was considered essential to being able to leave the plantation as recorded by one young shop worker from Hatton:

> Many Plantation Youth migrate to Colombo or Kandy for job, as they do not wish to work on the estate like slaves. Getting NIC [is] easier for me as I had the citizenship certificate but quite a good number of my fellow workers are being arrested by police in the absence of NIC.

In spite of the granting of citizenship, formal documentation appears to be a major factor in personal and social development. Other participants, especially older individuals, offered a more nuanced view and felt that the impact of citizenship has been mixed or that there has been no real change. One person said:

> Many of those who obtained citizenship have been registered as voters; they have been politically strengthened and their political rights have been guaranteed. Though this is a progressive step, their economic conditions cannot be said to have improved.

Another stated, '[I]t is not possible to state that any significant change has occurred for better in the lives of beneficiaries.' Several participants reported that it was only by applying through dedicated NGOs that they were able to receive citizenship certificates. Others who applied through trade unions were less successful. Given the influence that the tea and rubber estates have in the region, it is possible that the authorities are more sensitive to trade unions and less inclined to support applications for citizenship sent to them by NGOs, although given the small number of interviews, it is not possible to reach this conclusion on the basis of this research alone.

Interviewees also mentioned problems that remain for the community. There are individuals who still face difficulties getting their names on the list of voters. One interviewee stated:

> They say that we are all citizens of Sri Lanka. I cannot say that our lives have become better because we are citizens. Our wages have not been increased. And indebtedness grows. Our day to day life becomes hard as we depend on the estate work alone without other options, and we do not have our own land to cultivate.

Some participants noted that administrators are not informed of legal developments and this has negatively affected their rights to participate in

*Figure 5.3   A group of women take a break from picking tea. Some Hill
              Tamils who have received Sri Lankan citizenship say their lives
              have changed very little.*

political and other activities. For example, it was noted that *grama niladari*
(local government official) officers are not clear about the *Citizenship Act
of 2003* and its procedures, a fact previously recorded by other commenta-
tors.[20] This lack of awareness has resulted in people approaching certain
officers, in the hope of registering on the list of voters, only to encounter
problems. Several interviewees mentioned that the right to citizenship has
not yet addressed the high degree of poverty.

   Generally poor living conditions have not changed for the Plantation
Tamils. The lack of documentation means that person without proof of
citizenship cannot apply for a plot of land, request credit from banks or
financial institutions to purchase a plot of land, construct a house or set up
a business and so on. One retired worker from Golinda Estate, Hettimulla,
offered this account of the economic and personal challenges he faced
without documentary proof of his citizenship:

   I was born and bred on this estate and, was working here. To date I have not
   cast vote. According to the estate management my birth has not been registered. Therefore I have not been able to obtain a National Identity Card. As a

result, I do not know whether I can receive even my Employee Provident Fund benefits. All have sent application for citizenship through a trade union. But up to date nobody has received [a] citizenship certificate . . .

There also appears to be little improvement with regard to educational development of the population as a result of their recently regularized status, though citizenship does allow formerly affected persons to now hold employment, such as a teacher, in the government sector.

CONCLUSION

Sri Lanka is one of the few countries in the world that uphold two different types of citizenship: citizenship by descent and citizenship by registration. While most residents of Sri Lanka obtained citizenship by descent, the Plantation Tamils are required to use the registration process. However, expedient – and it must be repeated again that the simplified registration procedure introduced following the 2003 *Grant of Citizenship to Persons of Indian Origin Act. No. 35* more than halved the number of stateless people in Sri Lanka – the dual procedures still leave Plantation Tamils at a disadvantage relative to other Sri Lankans.

Nevertheless, the law has not been implemented sufficiently, and there is widespread ignorance among public officials about which procedures to apply. Many stateless people remain ignorant about the benefits of applying for a certificate of citizenship.

Plantation workers of Indian origin were brought to Sri Lanka to help maintain a sector of the country's economy, which later became Sri Lanka's backbone. Such plantation labour constituted the first modern working class of the country. However, the opportunity to overcome poverty and powerlessness has yet to be seized[21]. Further reforms are essential, including the introduction of sustainable programmes that meet the strategic challenge to end elite dominance so long associated with control over the plantations and the workers on these estates.

NOTES

1. Kemp and Little (1987).
2. International Labour Organization (1958).
3. Kirk (1987).
4. Nadesan (1993).
5. Ibid.
6. Ibid.

7. Ibid.
8. Dalits are identified as so-called oppressed caste people particularly in India.
9. Nadesan (1993), p. 83.
10. Shanmugaratnam (1997).
11. World Bank (2007).
12. UNHCR Citizenship for All, Focus on Protection' (2004b).
13. Government of Sri Lanka (2003).
14. Perera (2007).
15. Ibid.
16. Ibid.
17. Ibid.
18. Sulakshani Perera explains some parents refuse to regularize the status of their children. She quotes the principal of a small school saying, 'We try and educate students about the need for national identity cards and proper documentation . . . . But when they tell their parents, the children's comments are simply brushed aside. Some parents also question why national identity cards and birth certificates are important, because they themselves have managed perfectly fine without them. So these children grow up with absolutely no evidence of their parentage, except a piece of paper issued by the estate management' (Perera, 2007, p. 23).
19. Ibid.
20. Ibid.
21. World Bank (2007).

6. Citizenship reform and challenges for the Crimean Tatars in Ukraine

Rustem Ablyatifov

Source: © UNHCR/Greg Constantine 2010.

Figure 6.1 While many Crimean Tatars have returned to the Crimea, they face challenges obtaining documentation as well as owning land. Crimean Tatars have created unauthorized settlements on self-captured land like this area outside the city of Simferopol.

The Crimea is a unique region of Ukraine with respect to geography, climate, geology and history. It is inhabited by people of various ethnic origins with distinctive languages, cultures, traditions and history. However, the region's history has left many knotty questions and problems unresolved. One such matter, inherited from the recent past, was the issue of forced deportations that affected among others the Crimean

Tatar people. This situation was not created by the Ukrainian people or the Ukrainian government but rather was a legacy from Stalinist times and the repressive policies of the Union of Soviet Socialist Republics (USSR). Today more than 250 000 Crimean Tatars and other formerly deported persons (FDP) have returned to the Crimea. However, the measures adopted by the Ukrainian government to accommodate the repatriates are insufficient, and many citizenship issues have not been resolved. This chapter evaluates efforts by the Ukrainian government to reintegrate repatriated Crimean Tatars and, in particular, the citizenship campaigns instituted for their benefit. The aim of this chapter is to assess whether or how the governmental reforms improved the situation of formerly stateless Crimean Tatars.

HISTORICAL CONTEXT

The Crimean Tatars are indigenous to the Crimea. Their place in the ethnic matrix of former Soviet peoples is, however, extremely complicated. Their language belongs to the group of Turkic languages, and most Crimean Tatars are Muslim. In the fifteenth and eighteenth centuries the Crimean Tatars had their own state – the Crimean Khanate part of present day Ukraine. The Crimea was later annexed by the Russian empire in 1793. The native Crimean Tatars were decimated by the colonial policies of Russia and the Soviet Union that brought war to the Crimea, deprived people of their land and prompted forced emigrations. The repressive policies associated with the period of Soviet collectivization of agriculture dealt a further blow to the Crimean Tatar people, which decreased from 98 per cent to 20 per cent by 1939.

Soviet rule was established in the Crimea in 1921 with the creation of the Crimean Autonomous Soviet Socialist Republic, then part of Soviet Russia. Although autonomy was limited, there was a particular ethnic and territorial character to the reorganization of Crimea in the USSR. In 1921, the conception of *Korenizatsiya* (strengthening of roots) was introduced in the USSR as an attempt to address the multinational challenges of managing the vast Soviet state, which was organized into ethnic and public entities and territorial units of different levels (including autonomous republics, autonomous sub-regions and the like). The *Korenizatsiya* provided some minority rights including opportunities for the development of native languages and cultures and also ensured that ethnic groups were formally represented in these ethnically defined sub-national entities. Such policies were also carried out in the Crimea.

During this period, both the Crimean Tatar and Russian languages were recognized as official. Crimean Tatar national symbols were also visible and featured on flags and other political markers. The Soviet principle of ethnic representation was reflected in the administrative division of autonomy in the Crimea. In 1921, the Crimea was divided into 15 *raions* (territorial units), and in 1930 a further 145 rural districts were designated for Crimean Tatars, in addition to five raions. The rest of the Crimea was divided up for the other nationalities present and included 102 districts for Russians, 29 for Germans, 7 for Bulgarians, 5 for Greeks, 1 for Armenians and Estonians, respectively; the remaining 54 rural districts were for mixed populations and functioned in parallel to the ethnically designated territories.

In 1944, the Crimean Tatars were falsely accused of having collaborated with Nazi Germany and were then forcibly deported to Central Asia and Siberia by an extra-judicial procedure. Two years of illnesses, starvation and slave labour took a toll on more than 46 per cent of deported Crimean Tatars. The Crimean Tatar people were targeted and victimized to the point of destruction on account of their ethnic origin. With the Crimean Tatars either dead or deported, new settlers moved into the Crimean peninsula, most of whom were ethnically Russian. Soon after the Crimean Tatars were deported, the necessity for autonomy had fallen away, and in 1946 the Crimea became an ordinary *oblast* (region) of the USSR.

In 1954, the Crimean *oblast* was officially transferred from Russia to the Ukrainian Soviet Republic. This event was particularly significant and later paved the way for the mass return of the Crimean Tatar people to their homeland during the period of 'perestroika' in the late 1980s. However, until that time, the Crimea was off limits to Crimean Tatars. In 1956, military regulations and laws regulated the living conditions of Crimean Tatars who were housed in special settlements which bore many similarities to the ghettos Nazis had established for Jews just a decade earlier. Every Crimean Tatar was obliged to undergo a monthly personal check, which took place in the commandant's office. Those who wanted to visit other settlements for personal or family reasons, such as attending a funeral, required special permission, which could only be granted by the military authorities. Individuals who broke these rules were punished severely and were sentenced to 25 years in a prison camp.

The Crimean Tatars began their struggle to return to their Motherland on their first days in exile. The Crimean Tatar national movement for right to return to the Crimea was a unique phenomenon in the former USSR: it was a single mass movement uniting a whole people and was guided by principles of non-violence. The collapse of the USSR in 1991 and the establishment of the Ukrainian independent state had a huge impact on the process of return and resettlement of the Crimean Tatars. It was of principal importance that independent Ukraine, both the state and Ukrainian democratic political forces, unambiguously supported the return of the deported Crimean Tatars and other ethnic groups to their historic homeland. The openness shown by the government of Ukraine to the return of the Crimean Tatars not only ruled out the possibility of any conflict between the indigenous minority and the state but also fostered a sense of loyalty among the Crimean Tatars who supported the idea of the independent Ukrainian state.

The Autonomous Republic of the Crimea (ARC) was created in its present form as an integral part of Ukraine in 1991. It was founded in response to the demands of the Crimean Tatar people who were returning from places of deportation, but, in practice, the granting of autonomous status benefited the Russian speakers. The interests of the Crimean Tatars were ignored.

The problems facing the 250000-member Crimean Tatar community are multi-faceted and include social, economic, cultural, political and legal issues. The economic challenges are particularly worrisome, and there is a high degree of destitution among the Crimean Tatar whose situation is by all accounts appalling. In addition, there are a number of political and legal problems associated with the return of the Crimean Tatars to Ukraine. Problems with the protection and enforcement of minority rights are among the issues most often stressed by Crimean Tatar leaders. These include: the need for effective legal mechanisms that guarantee Crimean Tatars representation in Crimean and Ukrainian bodies of power; official recognition of the Crimean Tatar People Majlis (a legislative body elected by the Crimean Tatar people) and the Qurultay (National Congress) as representative bodies of the Crimean Tatar people; official recognition of the Crimean Tatars as an indigenous people in Crimea and Ukraine rather than a national minority; and the recognition of the Crimean Tatar language as one of the official languages of the ARC.[1]

CITIZENSHIP STATUS OF THE FORMERLY DEPORTED ETHNIC GROUPS IN UKRAINE

For over 45 years, the Crimean Tatar people struggled under the Soviet totalitarian regime, which prevented them from returning to their native land. Thousands suffered in labour camps and prisons. It was only in late 1989 that their commitment and dedication bore fruit; assisted by Soviet and foreign human rights activists, the Crimean Tatars were finally able to overcome the resistance of the state authorities and were allowed to repatriate en masse. Their return took place against the backdrop of the dissolution of the former Soviet Union and the establishment of 15 newly independent states on its territory.

The peak of the repatriation of Crimean Tatars coincided with the formation of the Commonwealth of Independent States (CIS) and created many additional problems. In particular, individuals returning to the peninsula after August 1991 faced problems in renouncing the citizenship of their countries of previous abode or affiliation (Uzbekistan, Tajikistan, Kazakhstan, Kyrgyzstan, Turkmenistan, Russian Federation and Georgia) and acquiring citizenship in their new home country, Ukraine.

Between 35000 and 40000 people repatriated every year from 1990 to 1995. This trend decreased slightly in the following years. By December 2001, the All-Ukrainian Population Census counted 248000 Crimean Tatars.[2]

Though Ukraine was one of the first CIS countries to adopt its own citizenship law (8 October 1991) and recognized the citizenship of all 'citizens of the former USSR who at the moment of declaration of independence (24 August 1991) were permanently residing in the territory of Ukraine', the same law completely disregarded the growing mass return of Crimean Tatars.

The lack of Ukrainian citizenship was one of the most serious problems of formerly deported Crimean Tatar people as well as for Armenians, Greeks, Bulgarians and Germans. Of the approximately 250000 Crimean Tatars, 108000 returned after 13 November 1991 when the *Law of Ukraine Of Citizenship of Ukraine* entered into force. This law did not provide for automatic Ukrainian citizenship but required applicants to go through a process of naturalization. Of this group, approximately 25000 were stateless persons who were able to benefit from a simplified naturalization procedure that was introduced in the 1997 law on citizenship.[3]

From 1991 to 1996, non-citizens of Ukraine lived in an indeterminate situation because neither the authorities nor civil society were aware of their legal situation. The remaining 83000 repatriates were not able to obtain Ukrainian citizenship because of financial and legal barriers. Several administrative obstacles were put in their way as a means of refusing citizenship to those who held citizenship in another CIS state. For example, the majority of repatriates (62000) were considered nationals of Uzbekistan, and one important hurdle facing Crimean Tatars who wanted to renounce their Uzbek citizenship was the high consular fee (US $100) established by Uzbekistan. It should be noted that the average monthly wage of a Ukrainian citizen amounted to less than that amount. For the average Crimean Tatar repatriate who was usually unemployed and without adequate housing, spending this sum was inconceivable. In addition, individuals were required to apply in person at the Embassy of Uzbekistan in Kyiv and then wait one year.

Ukrainian authorities unjustly accused the Crimean Tatar repatriates of being unwilling to naturalize in Ukraine. In response to this, in 1997–98 the Majlis of Crimean Tatar people organized a collection of Crimean Tatars' applications that required the state to grant them Ukrainian citizenship. As a result of this campaign more than 80 000 applications of formerly deported Crimean Tatars were collected and presented to the Presidential secretariat. In addition, the repatriates organized mass protests where they converged at the call of the Majlis in front of the Office of the Permanent Representative of the President of Ukraine in the Crimea every day over a four-month period during 1997–98.[4]

In 1997, the government introduced the first of three citizenship campaigns, which was arguably propagandistic in nature. During 1997–98, the militia passport service and one NGO Foundation on Human Rights and Naturalization 'Assistance' dealt with citizenship issues on behalf of Crimean Tatars from Uzbekistan, Tajikistan and Kyrgyzstan and encouraged them to naturalize in Ukraine. However, the challenge of granting Ukrainian citizenship to large numbers of returnees was soon frustrated by the legal arrangements and incompatible systems in their former places of residence and only a fraction of people were able to benefit from this particular campaign.

Real assistance could only be given to stateless persons who had returned to Ukraine during the window in 1991, after Ukraine had declared its independence and before they could obtain foreign citizenship in the successor states to the USSR in the CIS where they had been resident. Those who benefited were a large number of Crimean Tatars – refugees from Tajikistan who had escaped the civil war. The number of stateless people who fell in the above category, and were able to take advantage of Ukrainian citizenship at this time, was approximately 20 000. About 5000 Crimean Tatar refugees who escaped the civil war in Abkhazia, Georgia faced difficulties because many had to leave behind not only their property but also their documents. The few who had passports still held those of the former USSR because the separatist administration in Abkhazia refused to recognize Georgian sovereignty and hence the Georgian authorities were unable to issue passports to people in the breakaway region of Abkhazia. This problem was finally settled within the framework of the Ukrainian citizenship campaigns in 1998–2000 thanks to cooperation from the Georgian diplomatic missions in Ukraine and support from the 'Assistance' foundation and the UNHCR. As a result all Crimean Tatar refugees from Abkhazia acquired Ukrainian citizenship due to the joint work of state bodies and the Crimean Tatar public.[5]

The second 12-month citizenship campaign was launched in 1998, and while it was similar to the previous campaign, a larger group of people were able to benefit, thanks to an inter-state agreement between Ukraine and Uzbekistan, which addressed the problems that had so frustrated the campaign of 1997–98. A major problem for Crimean Tatar repatriates from Uzbekistan was removed in August 1998 when under international pressure, particularly from the Organization for Security and Cooperation in Europe (OSCE), Ukraine and Uzbekistan signed an agreement that provided formerly deported persons with a simplified procedure for renouncing Uzbek citizenship and obtaining Ukrainian citizenship. On the whole, more than 65 000 repatriates took advantage of the opportunity to acquire Ukranian citizenship under a simplified procedure at that time. This procedure, though originally time limited, was later extended to 31 December 2001. Moreover, about 10 000 Crimean Tatars in Uzbekistan were also granted citizenship through this procedure.

A third campaign from 1999–2001 built on the Ukraine-Uzbek accord of 1998. During this campaign the Crimean Tatars formerly based in Uzbekistan were provided with ample opportunity to renounce former citizenship and to acquire Ukrainian citizenship. It should be noted that the UNHCR took an active part in these campaigns and exerted its influence on the Ukrainian government to settle the problem of citizenship of the Crimean Tatars.

In practical terms, UNHCR supported two Crimean NGOs that offered legal aid to repatriates as well as training to lawyers working in NGOs, officials of the Ministry of the Interior, staff in the passport service, local government bodies and the militia (police). Thanks to the financial and technical assistance provided by the UNHCR, it was possible to establish a network of NGO field offices across the Crimea and, thus, reach returnees who needed assistance.

INTERNATIONAL COOPERATION AND THE GRANTING OF CITIZENSHIP

The problem of lack of citizenship was resolved through a complex set of measures that received wide support from international institutions, above all the UNHCR. Local representative bodies, in addition to the Crimean Tatars self-governing institutions, also helped to advance a solution to the problem, and on 1 January 2002, an estimated 235 043 formerly deported Crimean Tatars became citizens of Ukraine – approximately 90 per cent of the total number of the Crimean Tatars based in the ARC.

There were, however, some lingering issues and there are individuals who have still not managed to obtain citizenship, including, 4100 Crimean

Source: © UNHCR/Greg Constantine 2010.

*Figure 6.2   A Crimean Tatar, 36, and his wife lived in Uzbekistan and
              moved back to Crimea in 1996. While she has obtained
              Ukrainian citizenship, he remains stateless.*

Tatars who returned to the Crimea from Uzbekistan. Also, the simplified
procedure for obtaining citizenship in Ukraine (which was established by
the law on citizenship and the 1998 Ukrainian-Uzbek Agreement) concerned only formerly deported persons and their descendents. It did not
cover spouses in case of mixed marriage – an estimated 26 100 people (10
per cent of repatriates) who lived permanently in the ARC and remained
as foreigners or stateless persons. The numbers of people affected are
recorded in Table 6.1.

In this regard, the Ukrainian government appealed unsuccessfully to
the governments of Kazakhstan, Tajikistan, Turkmenistan, Kyrgyzstan
and Russia to sign similar agreements for a simplified procedure for the
obtaining of Ukrainian citizenship for Crimean Tatars.

An estimated 150 000 to 200 000 Crimean Tatars remain in Uzbekistan,
and while the overwhelming majority of them might want to return to
the Crimea, because of complications with the process for return, many
cannot meet the time requirements. The Representation Office of Majlis of
the Crimean Tatar people in Central Asia (Tashkent) repeatedly applied
to the Uzbek President (and Ukraine's Embassy in Uzbekistan) to extend

*Table 6.1 Stateless people not covered by the 1998 Ukrainian-Uzbek
Agreement*

Country of citizenship	Approximate number
Russia	11 200
Kazakhstan	3100
Tajikistan	2900
Kyrgyzstan	1600
Georgia	1000
Azerbaijan and Armenia	657
Moldova	51

a campaign to provide a simplified procedure for the renunciation of
Uzbek citizenship in order to obtain Ukrainian citizenship.

Over the past decade, the domestic situation has changed considerably.
As recorded above, Crimean Tatars who registered their Ukrainian citizenship in Uzbekistan before 31 December 2001 experienced significantly
fewer problems than those current waves of Crimean Tatars who are
returning to Crimea as citizens of Uzbekistan. Conditions for the returning of Crimean Tatars who hold Uzbek citizenship have become increasingly complicated.[6]

Unfortunately, there is no legislation on repatriation or legal status of
formerly deported persons of ethnic origin. One explanation for the lack
of legislation may be due to continued prejudice against the Crimean
Tatars as an ethnic group.

CITIZENSHIP AND COLLECTIVE RIGHTS: AN EVALUATION

Initially, the right to Ukrainian citizenship for all returnees resettling in
their homeland was one of the main political demands of the Crimean
Tatars. Citizenship was considered by the Crimean Tatar political forces
as one of the instruments to protect their rights as a people. The Crimean
Tatars consider themselves as indigenous people of the Crimea and thus
strive to participate in decision-making processes that take place at the
regional Crimean and local levels. They want to influence decisions that
directly affect them. In order to accomplish this, they believe Crimean
Tatar representatives should be elected to representative bodies and
appointed to governmental bodies.

Until the reforms discussed above took hold, the right to vote and to be elected to Ukrainian institutions could only be granted to citizens of Ukraine. Crimean Tatar political forces viewed their struggle for acquisition of nationality in terms of fighting for their collective rights. As a representative body, the Majlis of the Crimean Tatar people constantly raised this problem to the Ukrainian authorities. On the eve of elections in February–March 1998, Crimean Tatars conducted mass protests about their ambiguous position regarding citizenship. The protests by the repatriates developed into clashes with the Interior Ministry's troops on several occasions.[7]

Even though the Crimean Tatar people had 14 deputies united in the 'Qurultay' faction in the Crimean representative body of convocation of 1994–98 and, in spite of the fact that they had been elected within the united Crimean Tatar electoral district, the majority of Crimean Tatars were deprived of their opportunity to vote during the 1998 election by the Ukrainian state. The Crimean Tatars were deprived this right in spite of OSCE pointing out that their right of suffrage, which had been granted earlier could not be deprived. During the parliamentary elections in 1998, approximately 85 000 Crimean Tatars (that is, more than half of the population of voting age) had no opportunity to vote because of their lack of citizenship. The denial of the right to vote by such a large section of the population had a great influence in the outcome of the 1998 election results: none of the Crimean Tatar candidates were elected to the ARC's representative body, the Verkhovna Rada, and only a few Crimean Tatars were elected to local councils. For example, two Crimean Tatar deputies out of 80 were elected to the Simferopol City Council where the share of the Crimean Tatar dwellers accounted for about 12 per cent of the total population.[8]

However, after the 1998–2001 citizenship campaign, the situation regarding the political representation of the Crimean Tatars improved dramatically, and seven Crimean Tatar representatives successfully won seats in the Crimea's Verkhovna Rada in the elections of 31 March 2002. In all, 6614 persons were elected as deputies of local councils in the ARC, including 922 Crimean Tatars (or 13.9 per cent); in towns where there was a tendency to vote for Republican candidates, 63 (or 4.9 per cent); in rural areas, 839 (or 16 per cent) of the number of elected deputies. Thirteen Crimean Tatars were elected as village mayors, including in Bilohirsk *raion*, six; in Kirovske, two; in Dzhankoi, Lenino, Pervomaiske, Krasnohvardiiske and Chornomorske, one.

As noted above, the Crimean Tatars' success in the 2002 local government elections was possible because they were seen as a large and important constituency. In contrast to 1998, there were approximately an additional 85 000 people who were eligible to vote, thanks to the adoption of the new citizenship law and the successful implementation of the bilateral Ukrainian-Uzbek Agreement on citizenship for formerly deported

Source: © UNHCR/Greg Constantine 2010.

Figure 6.3   *This 70-year-old Crimean Tatar woman returned to the Crimea in 1997. It took her family seven years to obtain Ukrainian citizenship. While they were stateless, they missed out on the opportunity to get land. Now they live in a dilapidated home on somebody else's property.*

persons and their descendants. As a consequence of their electoral success, the number of Crimean Tatars elected and appointed to public and local bodies increased considerably and in each *raion* in Crimea, the deputy head of state administration was a Crimean Tatar. In addition, the Crimean Tatars also entered the Council of Ministries of the ARC.[9]

The situation was different for the Crimean Tatars in rural areas. Among other things, they were denied the right to participate in the process of the privatization of rural Crimean agricultural lands because, at the time, most rural Crimean Tatars were stateless. This policy of deprivation resulted in a now serious imbalance between Russian-speaking landowners (the vast majority) and the few Crimean Tatar landowners. Further, despite numerous appeals of the Crimean Tatar politicians and the general public, the introduction of the Land Code of Ukraine in 2001 consolidated this inequality. Both political experts and the Crimean Tatars consider this land allocation process a telling illustration of ongoing discrimination against the Crimean Tatars and a violation of their rights.[10]

CURRENT SITUATION

The citizenship law of 2001, most recently amended in 2007, liberalized the procedure of naturalization and introduced sweeping reforms. Most importantly, this law now provides a range of options for acquiring citizenship. Article 6 stipulates the following means for acquiring citizenship:

1. by acquisition of nationality by birth;
2. by territorial origin;
3. by common procedure of acquiring citizenship;
4. by procedure of restoration of citizenship;
5. by adoption;
6. as a consequence of establishing care or trusteeship of a child by an individual or the state;
7. as a consequence of establishing care for a person who is recognized as an incapable person by the court;
8. for the reason that one or both parents of a child are citizens of Ukraine;
9. as a consequence of acknowledging paternity or maternity;
10. by other reasons that are provided for by the international treaty of Ukraine.

Most Crimean Tatar repatriates have received Ukrainian citizenship on the basis of territorial origin. Article 8 of the law reads:

A person who him/herself or at least one of whose parents, grandfather or grandmother, brother or sister were born or permanently resided within the territory, which became the territory of Ukraine in accordance with the Article 5 of the Law of Ukraine 'On Legal Succession of Ukraine' and within other territories, which consisted a part of the Ukrainian People's Republic, the Western Ukrainian People's Republic, the Ukrainian State, the Ukrainian Socialistic Soviet Republic, Trans-Carpathian Ukraine, Ukrainian Soviet Socialistic Republic (URSR) and who is a person without citizenship or a foreigner, and who has obliged him/herself to terminate foreign citizenship and who submitted an application to acquire the citizenship of Ukraine and his/her children are registered as citizens of Ukraine.[11]

Under the rules of the Interior Ministry of Ukraine, based on the above-mentioned law, an individual who can prove his Ukrainian origin and has filed all necessary papers can become a Ukrainian citizen after one month of submitting their application. In 2008, some 45873 persons received Ukrainian citizenship by means of a presidential decision.[12] It should be noted, however, that others have been less fortunate, and Crimean Tatar repatriates who have come back, mainly from Central Asia, still encounter difficulty largely because of legal inconsistencies between the systems in other post-Soviet states and Ukraine.

It is important to highlight some key reforms. In December 2003, Ukraine cancelled a 1996 bilateral agreement with the Republic of Uzbekistan on the prevention of cases of dual citizenship and allowed tens of thousands of deported persons and their children and grandchildren who had already returned to Ukraine (particularly the Crimea) to finally receive citizenship. Since 7 October 2004, when the cancellation law came into force, citizens of the Republic of Uzbekistan residing in Ukraine have been able to acquire Ukrainian citizenship without having to pay the fee of more than US $100 to renounce their Uzbek citizenship.

METHODS AND FINDINGS

Interviews were conducted in April and May 2009. Participants were selected because they were among the former Uzbekistan-based applicants who had applied to the researcher's NGO for legal assistance in their bid for Ukrainian nationality.

Overall, the participants noted that the citizenship campaigns sponsored by the Ukrainian government, with the assistance of the UNHCR, were generally positive but two participants also noted that there had been a period of inactivity on the part of the government and that it was later forced to react to this issue. They claimed that the government was pressed to introduce the citizenship campaigns because of many protests by Crimean Tatars who demanded a resolution to the problem.

Two female participants, a middle-aged woman and a young woman in her 20s who returned in 1993, went on record to say that they returned because they identified with the Crimea, and described the problems that they had encountered when they did not have citizenship and how these had been rectified.

Zarema Zinabadinova, who arrived in Ukraine as a minor, noted that when she applied for a job and a place at a public university without a Ukrainian passport, her applications were unsuccessful. However, once she received citizenship and Ukrainian documents, new opportunities presented themselves and the above barriers were removed. To her, the key benefits of citizenship included the opportunity to work with public services and to receive a public university education.[13] For the older Adile Niiazova, citizenship also meant that it was now possible to secure a plot of land or social housing.[14]

For Anatolii Basalayev, a young man who arrived from Uzbekistan in 1992, the granting of citizenship made his life much simpler. Whereas previously he could not work legally and was 'holed up', in fear of being found by the militia without papers, he no longer felt threatened. He described the immediate benefits of citizenship. First, the district militia officer stopped 'watching him' when he saw that he now held a Ukrainian passport. Second, he was able to find a regular job. Third, he noted that as a result of his change of status he was no longer so vulnerable to exploitation by employers and that he had a choice over the types of jobs he could do. Fourth, he states that he was now invited to participate in elections. Just as with Zarema and Adile, Anatolii claimed that receiving citizenship opened up new possibilities. In addition to feelings of assertiveness and the possibility of holding down a good job with decent pay, he felt that the possibility of acquiring a plot of land on which he could build was especially significant. The ability to acquire land enabled him to start a family and have a base of security.[15]

For Server Izzetov, a thirty-something man born in the Fergana region of Uzbekistan, the return to the Crimea was marked with obstacles and opportunities. Having an uncle in the Crimea gave him a base of support as he raced to meet the filing deadline for citizenship in 2002. However, he had problems with local civil servants and could not register for housing as a formerly deported person; as a result his application for a plot of land was not processed. He claimed that his life changed after naturalization in Ukraine but not dramatically. He had found a job while still a foreigner, however, when the chief of personnel saw his foreign passport, service record and diploma he was told he could only be employed once he had acquired the citizenship of Ukraine. He was officially hired once he obtained his Ukrainian passport. His personal story is fairly positive in that Izzetov is still working in the same organization as an information system administrator and his family eventually received a plot of land. They intend to complete the building of their house. He identified the benefits of citizenship as including the opportunity to become a 'free man' with all rights to participate in the country's life, to receive state assistance that is provided for its citizens, namely, the ownership of land and participation in elections.[16]

Ali Hamzin, living in Bakhchisarai town, is a member of the Majlis of Crimean people, where he is Chief of the Foreign Affairs Division. He was born in Uzbekistan and obtained Ukrainian citizenship in the Ukrainian Embassy in Uzbekistan, thanks to the simplified procedure administered by the UNHCR. Being the official Majlis representative, he and his family members were among the first to acquire Ukrainian citizenship. Ali Hamzin states that neither his family nor his compatriots had special difficulties when they formalized their abandonment of the Uzbek citizenship.

According to him, it was accomplished quickly and was free of charge. Taking into account the fact that Ali Hamzin and his family acquired Ukrainian citizenship in Uzbekistan, they did not encounter any problems associated with the lack of citizenship once they reached Ukraine. When they arrived in the Crimea their family promptly received Ukrainian internal passports. They then received governmental compensation for travel and luggage costs.

According to Hamzin, his family adapted to life in Ukraine rather smoothly. While he acknowledged that some areas of his personal life were problematic (because of his higher education, he expected a better job), he felt that he had a responsibility to represent Crimean Tatars through the regional and communal political structures. He believed it necessary to represent the Crimean Tatars, ensuring that their rights to land, representation and continued repatriation are respected, especially in the face of alarmist and populist stereotypes, including suggestions by some parties that the Crimean Tatars seek a 'Kosovo solution' in the Crimea. He also cited the following benefits of citizenship: the right to education, social and economic rights and the right to vote.[17]

Some of the most notable benefits of the campaign by the Crimean Tatar representatives included a greater degree of confidence and assertiveness among the Tatar community. This was partially due to the adoption of a new law regarding proportional representation, which guaranteed the representation of Crimean Tatars in local self-government and the Verkhovna Rada of the ARC.

For individuals, there were some personal benefits; for example, the possibility of finding employment in public service, a sector that is traditionally secure. Individuals were also now in a position to participate in the privatization schemes of public property and, in theory, have a greater possibility of becoming landowners.

For younger people, the granting of nationality status enabled them to receive valid travel documents, which permitted them to travel not just in the former Soviet Union but also to other parts of Europe and Turkey. More important was the possibility of entering public institutions and receiving free tuition. The only perceived negative effect for young people was the fact that military service was compulsory and took them out of the labour market.

On balance, however, while the right to citizenship was one of the central political and legal demands of the formerly deported Crimean Tatars, the citizenship campaign could not solve the issue of legislative rehabilitation nor address some of the systemic problems of unemployment, the lack of decent housing and public infrastructure, high levels of morbidity, the lack of access to sufficient medical care, limited social integration, the restoration of property rights and the multiple challenges involved in the allocation of land. Formerly stateless people could not escape from the slow and complex legal and bureaucratic machinery that was necessary to guarantee access to rights. Moreover, for many, their exclusion from the state educational system had long-term effects on their potential earning capacity and some of the less educated Crimean Tatar returnees were resigned to low-pay work.

Further, it should be noted that the reforms of the last decade have not been able to address the situation of close on 2000 stateless Crimean Tartars, mostly settled in urban areas in Central Crimea, who are still without valid documents and have yet to receive Ukrainian nationality.

CONCLUSION

The Ukrainian Citizenship Law defines the Ukraine's citizenship as a 'permanent legal bond between individuals and the Ukrainian State that reveals itself in mutual rights and obligations'. Belonging to the Ukrainian citizenry provides for a wide range of rights and freedoms in various spheres of life. Thus, citizens of Ukraine have a right to participate in public administration through their participation in elections and national and local referenda under the current legislation of Ukraine. Ukrainian citizens have the right to demand protection of their rights from the state. Ukraine's diplomatic missions and consular offices must take measures to provide for the citizens of Ukraine to enjoy the rights granted by the legislation of their country of residence and also to abide by the international agreements in which Ukraine and the country of residence are parties in full; they must protect their interests, which are guaranteed by law in accordance with the established procedure; and if necessary, the state must take steps to restore infringed rights of Ukrainian citizens.

Belonging to the Ukrainian citizenry is the most important precondition of the state's obligation to protect, in full, the rights and freedoms of its citizens that are guaranteed by the constitution and laws of Ukraine not only on the territory of the state but also abroad. Equally important are provisions of the Constitution and laws of citizenship that prevent Ukrainian citizens from being deported or extradited to a foreign state.[18]

The mass statelessness of the Crimean Tatars was, first of all, a violation of their legitimate right to have and realize their human rights on the same basis as other citizens of Ukraine. For the vast majority of repatriates, the deprivation of Ukrainian citizenship significantly complicated their resettlement and reintegration in the Crimea. The deprivation of citizenship was also accompanied by violations of other fundamental rights, above all their economical, social, cultural and other rights, which contributed to the societal and political tension on the Crimean peninsula. The lack of citizenship and persistence of statelessness among so many Crimean Tatars and their exclusion from the electoral franchise were the causes of the numerous public meetings, protests and other demonstrations that brought them into conflict with the militia on the eve of the parliamentary elections in March 1998. The mass statelessness of the Crimean Tatars also impeded a realization of their rights in the areas of investment, business development and other entrepreneurial activities. Their lack of citizenship status violated their rights to labour, social security, housing, education, equal participation in public life and freedom of movement. It should be noted that the endeavour of the Crimean Tatar people itself was marked by the international community: the legendary leader of the Crimean Tatar people, Mustafa Dzhemilev, received in 1998 the Nansen Medal Award for his outstanding efforts towards the resolution of statelessness and citizenship issues of the Crimean Tatar people.[19]

While both repatriates and their leaders, the Majlis of the Crimean Tatar people, regularly urged the government of Ukraine to improve this unjust legal situation, it was only after the international community became engaged, represented by the OSCE and UNHCR, that the situation improved. Between 1999 and 2001, the joint efforts of the government of Ukraine, the UNHCR and the Crimean Tatar public then brought about fundamental changes that had been long awaited by tens of thousands of repatriates after long years of forced exile. As a result tens of thousands of repatriates carved out a new life, however imperfect, in Crimea.[20]

NOTES

1. Shevel (2002).
2. Personal archive of author.
3. Prybytkova (1999).
4. Ahtem Zeytullayev, manager of the NGO 'Assistance' Foundation, Simferopil City, interviews with author May–July 2009.
5. Personal archive of author.
6. Ibid.
7. Kotyhorenko (2004).
8. Tyshchenko et al. (2004).
9. Chubarov (2002).
10. Tyshchenko (2004).
11. Law of the Ukraine, 'Of citizenship of the Ukraine', available at http://zakon.rada.gov.ua/cgi-bin/laws/main.cgi?nreg=2235-14.
12. See http://president.gov.ua.
13. Zarema Zinabadinova, Oktiabrske urban village, Krasnohvardiikyi *raion*, ARC, interview with author, 5 June 2009.

14. Adile Niyazova, Krasnohvardiiske urban village, ARC, interview with author, 12 June 2009.
15. Anatolii Basalayev, Trudove village, Saky raion, ARC, interview with author 24 June 2009.
16. Server Izzetov, Simferopil city, interview with author, 17 July 2009.
17. Ali Hamzin, Bakhchisarai town, interview with author, 27 July 2009.
18. Pohorilko and Fedorenko (2006).
19. Information bulletins of 'Assistance' foundation and the UNHCR (1998–2000) Grazhdanin (citizen), entire publications consulted.
20. 'Crimean Tatar Activist Receives Nansen Medal', available at http://www.unhcr.org/cgi-bin/texis/vtx/search?page=search&docid=3ae6b81840&query=mustafa%20dzhemilev.

7. The Urdu-speakers of Bangladesh: an unfinished story of enforcing citizenship rights

Katherine Southwick

Source: © Greg Constantine 2010.

Figure 7.1 *Overcrowding plagues every camp. Living conditions are cramped and pose safety and health problems as families, some as large as 15, live in 8 x 10 feet living spaces. In a room decorated with old newspapers glued to the walls, a family of seven lives and works in Kurmi Tola Camp in Dhaka.*

Members of the Urdu-speaking minority in Bangladesh have always had a right to citizenship under national law, but the challenge has come from enforcing that right and the benefits that attach to it. Bangladeshi courts have recognized Urdu-speakers as citizens in successive cases over the years. However, since the country gained independence from Pakistan in 1971, the state has failed to acknowledge them as citizens on a broad political and administrative level. This protracted disconnect between law and policy has made the group's status uncertain, effectively stateless.

For nearly four decades, the unwillingness of either government, Bangladeshi or Pakistani, to formally recognize this community as citizens has rendered an estimated 160000–500000 people vulnerable to extreme poverty and without equal access to education, health services and livelihoods.

Time, however, as well as the accretion of case law, has confirmed this group's citizenship. Since the most recent 2008 High Court decision ordering government agencies to register individuals to vote and to issue national identification cards, perceptions have shifted to the point where few can credibly deny that most of the Urdu-speakers (also known as Biharis and stranded Pakistanis) are Bangladeshi citizens. Time has healed some scars from the violent war for independence, during which both Bengalis and Urdu-speakers committed atrocities against each other. Time has also allowed a new generation of Urdu-speakers to grow up with limited ties to Pakistan and a natural affinity for Bangladesh. A whole generation of young people in Bangladesh has no personal memory of the liberation war. Yet progress for this community may ultimately arise not by ignoring the role of Pakistan nor by repressing memories but by collectively acknowledging the victims on all sides.

Some Urdu-speakers appear to have taken advantage of such progress by pursuing higher education and obtaining jobs. Others report that discrimination continues, particularly regarding access to public schools, government jobs and passports. Individuals are most affected who report addresses in slum-like settlements in urban areas where around half of the community has lived since the early 1970s. Poverty, resulting in part from years of effective statelessness, has also created barriers to opportunities and upward mobility.

Community leaders acknowledge the progress that has been made yet vacillate between accepting that change will not occur overnight and feeling frustrated that vindication of their clearly established rights continues to take so long. Based on the momentum for citizenship rights generated by recent court decisions, more can be done to integrate this minority into the country's social fabric and economic development. Bangladesh is a poor country with massive challenges, but the Urdu-speaking minority has seen progress. There is the potential for genuine success in ending statelessness and ensuring the right to a nationality.

ORIGINS OF THE URDU-SPEAKING MINORITY

Most Urdu-speakers of Bangladesh are descendants of Muslim minority groups originating in the Indian state of Bihar, close to Bangladesh. Accordingly, the Urdu-speakers are sometimes referred to as 'Biharis', a term which is problematic in part because not all Urdu-speakers can trace their background to Bihar. Some of their forbearers also came from other states, such as Uttar Pradesh, West Bengal and what is now Jharkhand.[1] As the term 'Urdu-speaking minority' suggests, this group is primarily united by language rather than by ethnicity or geographic origin.[2]

Some members of this community were civil servants in the British colonial administration, through which they were posted to East Bengal (now Bangladesh) to serve in the railways, police and other civil services.[3] Thousands of railway workers brought their families to live near stations such as Syedpur, Parbatipur, Rangpur, Shantahar, Khulna, Jessore and Chittagong.[4]

In the years leading up to the Partition of India and Pakistan in 1947, the region was plagued by communal riots between Hindus and Muslims in several states, including Bihar. Communal tensions resulted in part from decades of debate over whether Hindus and Muslims could or should coexist in one united state of India or whether the country should be split apart along religious lines. Ahmed Ilias, former journalist and Executive Director of Al Falah,[5] a non-governmental organization working in the Urdu-speakers' settlements in Dhaka, writes:

> [t]he Bihar riots generated immense feelings of Islamic brotherhood among the Muslims of other provinces . . . . Bengali Muslims contributed generously in cash and kind to help the affected Bihari Muslims. Sheikh Mujibur Rahman, then a student leader [who would later lead the call for Bangladesh's independence from Pakistan in 1971], toured the affected villages in Bihar with his relief team. He was so moved and excited by the scene of the refugee camps that he urged the Bihari refugees to come to East Bengal for their shelter and settlement.[6]

At the time of India's independence and Partition of the country in 1947, communal violence between Hindus and Muslims intensified. Tensions in Kashmir prompted revenge attacks against both Hindus and Muslims in several parts of India. Until the 1960s, millions of Muslims poured into East Pakistan (previously East Bengal, and by this time part of post-Partition Pakistan) as refugees, and Muslims in that state in turn committed violence against Hindus, forcing as many as four million across the border into India. Ilias notes that '[t]he local Bengali community was also very sympathetic towards [the Muslim] refugees [from India], whom they absorbed as workers and executives in their business and commercial set-ups'.[7]

Many also came in search of economic opportunities and because of cultural ties.[8] Some invested in industries such as jute, sugar and paper, owning their own factories and businesses. The Adamjee Jute Mill, built 20 kilometres south of Dhaka in Narayanganj in 1951 by the Adamjee Group of West Pakistan, was at one point the largest in Asia. Before closing in 2002, it reportedly employed thousands of Urdu-speakers.[9] In addition to finding jobs in the railway department or police forces, Ilias recounts:

> Unlike the other refugee groups, Biharis were small businessmen, petty traders, and shopkeepers. Most of them . . . belonged to the working class and only a handful emerged as factory owners . . . . [T]hey penetrated into mills and factories as laborers, supervisors, and administrators of commercial firms and factories.[10]

Culturally and linguistically distinct from the majority Bengali Muslim population, the Urdu-speaking minority did not systematically learn Bangla (or Bengali), the predominant language favoured by political elites from East Pakistan. They settled in their own urban enclaves, such as in Mohammedpur and Mirpur in the Dhaka area. Ilias chided his own group during this period, stating that 'they only thought about their economical interests disregarding the social and economic aspirations and hopes of the forty-two million Bengali Muslims and sufferings and agony of the Bengali Hindus'.[11]

THE WAR OF INDEPENDENCE

Beyond political and economic favouritism West Pakistani elites shared with the Urdu-speaking minority in East Pakistan, Bengalis were also stung by Pakistani Governor-General Muhammad Ali Jinnah's declaration in 1948 that the national language of Pakistan, East and West, would be Urdu. Pakistan's obstinacy on this issue stoked protests within the Bengali-speaking majority of East Pakistan, leading to the creation of the Language Movement, which advocated that Bengali be taught in schools and used in government relations. Following a series of mass protests in which several people were killed or beaten by police, the Bengali language was granted official status along with Urdu in 1956.

The Language Movement helped form the basis for the Bengali nationalist Awami League's call for greater autonomy. Other factors contributed to Bengali frustration with being part of Pakistan. Although East Pakistan contained a slight majority of the population, government spending dis-proportionately favoured West Pakistan. The limited response of West Pakistan to a cyclone that hit East Pakistan in November 1970, killing 300 000 to 500 000 people, was widely criticized. Bengalis were underrep-resented in the military, and political power was concentrated in the presi-dent and the military. Any elected prime minister from East Pakistan was promptly deposed by the predominantly West Pakistani political-military establishment.

In 1970, the Awami League, East Pakistan's largest political party and led by Sheikh Mujibur Rahman, won a majority of seats in the National Assembly. Zulfikar Ali Bhutto, leader of the Pakistan Peoples' Party, refused to allow Rahman to become prime minister of Pakistan and proposed having two prime ministers, one from the West and one from the East. Talks failed in March 1971, prompting Rahman to call for a nationwide strike and to declare independence.

The Pakistan Army's plan to quell Bengali nationalism, Operation Searchlight, was promptly put into action. Some members of the Urdu-speaking minority, along with Islamist groups and Bengalis opposed to independence, formed paramilitary forces to support West Pakistan. Targeting students, the intelligentsia, Hindus and anyone thought to be supportive of the Awami League, the operation led to large-scale destruc-tion of property, rape and murder. Death toll estimates range from 300 000 to 3 000 000. Over one third of the population was displaced, with eight to ten million refugees fleeing across the border to India. In the course of conflict, the Urdu-speaking minority also experienced brutal revenge attacks 'as they were seen as symbols of Pakistani domination'.[12] Anthony Mascarenhas, a South Asian journalist, then writing in the *Sunday Times*, recounted:

Thousands of families of unfortunate Muslims, many of them refugees from Bihar who chose Pakistan at the time of the partition riots in 1947, were mercilessly wiped out. Women were raped, or had their breasts torn out with specially fashioned knives. Children did not escape the horror: the lucky ones were killed with their parents; but many thousands of others must go through what life remains for them with eyes gouged out and limbs amputated. More than 20,000 bodies of non-Bengalis have been found in the main towns, such as Chittagong, Khulna, and Jessore. The real toll, I was told everywhere in East Bengal, may have been as high as 100,000, for thousands of non-Bengalis have vanished without a trace.[13]

Responding to Indian support of Bengali resistance fighters, the Pakistan Air Force launched a pre-emptive strike against India, prompting India to invade East Pakistan. Out of concern that growing Indian influence in the region would upset Cold War power balances, the Nixon Administration in the USA provided military supplies to Pakistan. A few months later, in December, Pakistan surrendered, and conflict with India formally ended under the July 1972 Simla Agreement.

POST-INDEPENDENCE: DISPLACEMENT AND REPATRIATION

The Liberation War, as it is known in Bangladesh, gave birth to an independent country,[14] which swiftly established a parliamentary democracy. Amidst these developments, the situation of the Urdu-speaking minority took a dramatic turn for the worse.

As the Pakistani military and civilians evacuated from Bangladesh, the Urdu-speaking minority found themselves unwanted by both countries. Pakistan was reportedly concerned that a mass influx of people would create tensions within culturally mixed populations, particularly in the Sindh region.[15] Bangladesh, on the other hand, rejected the community for having supported the enemy. Revenge attacks continued. As Ninette Kelley explains, 'Witnesses reported summary executions by firing squads, mass decapitations, rape and mutilation. Although the government estimated that 15,000 were killed, most estimates place the number of deaths of Urdu-speakers at between 70,000–100,000 people in a matter of months'.[16]

Hundreds of thousands of internally displaced members of the Urdu-speaking minority sought refuge in some 166 camps quickly constructed by the International Committee of the Red Cross (ICRC). These camps were situated mostly on public land in or near urban areas such as Dhaka, Rajshahi, Khulna and Chittagong divisions.[17] Some of the camps in Dhaka were established in areas in which Urdu-speakers had long been settled, such as Mohammedpur and Mirpur. As the population crowded into the ICRC camps, many members of the group were purged from government posts and their property confiscated under presidential orders.[18] Property was seized on grounds that it was deemed abandoned or that it belonged to enemy aliens.[19]

On 15 December 1972, a presidential order on citizenship, the *Bangladesh Citizenship (Temporary Provisions) Order*, 1972,[20] was promulgated. In this same period, Pakistan, India and Bangladesh sought to address the status of displaced persons. Under the *New Delhi Agreement* of August 1973, Pakistan and India, with the concurrence of Bangladesh (which Pakistan had not yet recognized), set out to solve 'the humanitarian problems resulting from the conflict of 1971'.[21] Pressure on the Pakistan government mounted from the Urdu-speaking population in the Sindh province of Pakistan who insisted that members of the group be admitted from Bangladesh, and from the Bangladeshi government who conditioned the establishment of diplomatic relations on resolution of the humanitarian situation.[22] The parties agreed to the simultaneous repatriation of all Bengalis in Pakistan and all Pakistanis in Bangladesh.[23] In particular:

> the Government of Pakistan, guided by considerations of humanity, agrees, initially, to receive a substantial number of such non-Bengalis from Bangladesh. It is further agreed that the Prime Minister of Bangladesh and Pakistan or their designated representatives will thereafter meet to decide what additional number of persons who may wish to migrate to Pakistan may be permitted to do so.[24]

The *New Delhi Agreement* provided that India would work out a time schedule for the completion of repatriation in consultation with Pakistan and Bangladesh. Pakistan, India and Bangladesh further stated that in carrying out logistical arrangements for repatriation of individuals from and to their respective countries, they 'may seek the assistance of international humanitarian organizations and others'.[25] They were 'confident that the completion of repatriation . . . would make a signal contribution to the promotion of reconciliation in the sub-continent'.[26]

On 19 September 1973, three weeks after the *New Delhi Agreement* was signed, repatriation processes commenced.[27] In February 1974, Pakistan recognized Bangladesh as a sovereign state. In the April 1974 *Tripartite Agreement* between Bangladesh, Pakistan and India, the three governments reviewed progress and made new commitments regarding repatriation. Regarding 'non-Bengalis in Bangladesh':

> the Pakistan side stated that the Government of Pakistan had already issued clearances for movement of Pakistanis in favor of those non-Bengalis who were either domiciled in former West Pakistan, were employees of the Central Government and their families or were members of the divided families, irrespective of their original domicile. The issuance of clearances to 25,000 persons who constitute hardship cases were also in progress.

The Pakistan side reiterated that all those who fall under the first three categories would be received by Pakistan without any limit to numbers. With respect to persons whose applications had been rejected, the government of Pakistan would, upon request, provide reasons why any particular case was rejected. Any aggrieved applicant could at any time seek a review of his application provided he was able to supply new facts or further information. The claims of such persons would not be time-barred. In the event of the decision of review of a case being adverse, the governments of Pakistan and Bangladesh might seek to resolve it by mutual consultation.[28]

Under the *New Delhi* and *Tripartite Agreements*, about 500 000 'stranded Pakistanis' registered with the ICRC for repatriation to Pakistan, but only about 108 000 people were repatriated.[29] The majority of the population was refused citizenship, and thousands of families still suffer from decades of separation. Despite Bangladesh's calls for continuing repatriation processes, Pakistan resisted.

In the years that followed, several thousand more Urdu-speakers reportedly moved to Pakistan illegally.[30] Thousands remaining in Bangladesh continued to subsist in the government-managed camps (the ICRC departed in 1973)[31] which evolved into squalid, overcrowded slum-like settlements where entire families live in rooms no larger than eight feet by ten feet. Most are denied access to social services, including public education and health care, and as a result of poverty and discrimination, find their livelihoods in the informal sector as barbers, mechanics or rickshaw drivers. Some, including children, engage in traditional weaving and the embroidery of saris, techniques known as *Benarasi* and *Karchupi*. Although these products are prized for their luxurious quality, the artisans are paid less than one tenth of the retail price.[32] While most settlements have electricity, sanitary conditions are grave. The few toilets and washing facilities, combined with poor drainage and nearly non-existent garbage disposal, have resulted in high levels of dysentery, particularly among children, and the risk of water-borne diseases such as cholera is high.

During the 1970s, as living conditions deteriorated and as Pakistan faced political pressure to honour its agreements regarding repatriation, the Stranded Pakistanis General Repartriation Committee (SPGRC) was formed. It vigorously continued advocacy for repatriation. In 1985, Pakistan President Zia-ul Haq offered to accept the remaining Urdu-speakers in Bangladesh on humanitarian grounds, offering international assistance. Millions of dollars were raised, and the Saudi charity, Rabita al-Alam al-Islami (World Muslim League) created the Rabita Trust for Repatriation of Stranded Pakistanis from Bangladesh in 1988 to facilitate the repatriations. The World Muslim League and the Pakistan High Commission in Bangladesh reportedly carried out a population survey of the camps in Bangladesh.[33]

Some small progress was made in 1993, when under a Joint Declaration between Bangladesh and Pakistan, 50–60 families out of an anticipated 3000 were repatriated from the Adamjee camp in Narayanganj.[34] By 1994, the Rabita Trust reportedly had constructed 1000 housing units (out of an anticipated 41 500 throughout Punjab) in the Mian Channu district.[35] Repatriation was controversial within Pakistan, as non-Urdu-speakers in the Sindh region raised concerns that they would become a minority in their ancestral land and that the Urdu-speakers would join paramilitary groups.[36]

Figure 7.2 *Most Bihari camps in Bangladesh are comprised of people born after 1971. Young Bihari consider Bangladesh their home and feel it is essential to their cultural identity that they are provided with the rights granted to all Bangladeshi citizens. Bihari youth gather at a rally in Dhaka in 2006.*

With a change in government in Pakistan, the issue became a low priority. In early 2006, a Pakistan government representative told Refugees International (RI), a humanitarian advocacy organization that has published several reports on the Urdu-speakers, that 'we see this as a humanitarian issue'.[37] When asked about movement toward resolution, the representative responded, 'we are not aware of any steps at this time'.[38] On an August 2008 visit to Bangladesh, RI could not reach the Pakistan High Commission in Dhaka for comments.

Left with few belongings, limited opportunities and perhaps permanent separation from their families, some Urdu-speakers, particularly those who consider themselves 'stranded Pakistanis', vacillate between despair and a dogged resolution to continue advocacy for repatriation. The SPGRC continued its call for repatriation and reunification of 3000 families during the organization's November 2009 summit.[39] Despite feelings of resentment, some, particularly the elderly, continue their desire to go to Pakistan.

THE NEXT GENERATION

Since the 1970s, another generation of Urdu-speakers, fluent also in Bengali, has grown up in Bangladesh. With no first-hand memory of the Liberation War and with a limited affinity for the idea of 'Pakistan', many members of this generation identify with Bangladesh and have developed a desire to be recognized as Bangladeshi citizens. Some members of the older generation, either pragmatically acknowledging that repatriation was unlikely or feeling more at home in Bangladesh having spent their lives there, also shared this inclination.

These perceptions coincided with worsening conditions in the camps, which became more overcrowded and uninhabitable. Today, about 160 000 of around 300 000 Urdu-speakers in Bangladesh live in 116 camps and settlements.[40]

In Geneva camp, one of the largest (named for the city of the ICRC headquarters), only 250 public latrines are available for 25 000 people.[41] Young couples limit the number of children they have simply because there is no space in which to raise them.[42] A settlement address is often construed as barring access to public education, jobs and passports[43] because such a residence denotes that the individual is a 'Bihari' or 'stranded Pakistani' and therefore not entitled to the full benefits of citizenship.[44] To avoid such outcomes, Urdu-speakers 'often give non-settlement addresses in order to obtain the required services'.[45] Because few Urdu-speakers can afford to send their children to private school, 'only 10 per cent of primary school aged children and 2 per cent of secondary school aged children attend school'.[46] Paulsen notes that 'their freedom of movement is not restricted, and they are free to live in or outside the settlements, and travel anywhere in the country'.[47] While this statement may be true in principle, poverty, due in part to discrimination, prevents many in the camps from exercising this freedom.

Some Urdu-speakers living outside the camps have managed to obtain a relatively middle-class or higher economic status and have integrated into society. Some groups have raised funds to support education, microfinance projects or sanitation services.[48] Others, as will be discussed later, have assisted with litigation on behalf of the minority group's rights. Overall, however, the relationship between those living outside the camps and the camp-dwellers, is unclear. Paulsen claims that for those living outside the camps, 'their origin is neither a bar nor an issue' and that this particular 'class has evolved away from those living in the settlements'.[49]

Over time, some individuals, especially those living in the camps, perceived that their separation from mainstream society had led to uncertain citizenship status, which in turn led to discrimination, poverty and lack of opportunities. They determined that the first step toward genuine progress would require clarification of their right to citizenship under national law.

REALIZING THE RIGHT TO CITIZENSHIP

The laws of Bangladesh establish that most Urdu-speakers in Bangladesh qualify as citizens, yet a number of factors – social, political and even legal – have confused the group's status over the decades.

The *Constitution of the People's Republic of Bangladesh*, adopted in 1972, provides that 'the citizenship of Bangladesh shall be determined and regulated by law'.[50] The *Adaptation of Existing Bangladesh Laws Order* of 1972 kept in force all laws from before independence, subject to any necessary changes.[51] Accordingly, the primary laws governing citizenship include the *Pakistan Citizenship Act* of 1951 and the *Bangladesh Citizenship (Temporary Provisions) Order (Citizenship Order)* of 1972. As the Appellate Division stated in *Bangladesh v. Professor Golam Azam*, 'the provisions of the Act and the Order are to be read together to get a complete picture of the law of citizenship in Bangladesh'.[52]

Under the *Citizenship Act*, every person born in the territory after 1951 is a citizen by birth.[53] An individual can claim citizenship by descent if she is born after 1951 and her father is a citizen at the time of the individual's birth.[54] Citizenship may be revoked if the individual obtained certificates of domicile or naturalization through concealment of material facts, expressed disloyalty to the Constitution through actions or speech, or engaged with or illegally traded with an enemy during a war.[55]

Under Article 2 of the *Citizenship Order* of 1972, every person shall be deemed to be a citizen of Bangladesh:

1. who or whose father or grandfather was born in the territories now comprised in Bangladesh and who was a permanent resident of such territories on the 25th day of March, 1971, and continues to be so resident; or
2. who was a permanent resident of the territories now comprised in Bangladesh on the 25th day of March, 1971, and continues to be so resident and is not otherwise disqualified for being a citizen by any other law. . .[56]

Under Article 2 (b), a person cannot qualify for citizenship if he 'owes, affirms or acknowledges, expressly or by conduct, allegiance to a foreign state'.[57] According to Article 3 of the Order, 'in case of doubt as to whether a person is qualified to be deemed to be a citizen of Bangladesh under

Article 2 . . . the question shall be decided by the government, which decision shall be final'.[58]

The repatriation policies articulated in the 1973 *New Delhi Agreement* and the 1974 *Tripartite Agreement*, the displacement of so many Urdu-speakers to ICRC-administered camps, the conflation of support for Pakistan during the war of independence with the concept of 'enemy alien' under the abandoned property laws, and the explicit desire on the part of some Urdu-speakers to go to Pakistan helped confuse the status of the community within Bangladesh, at least in a practical sense if not a legal one.

The *New Delhi Agreement* spoke of repatriation of 'all Pakistanis in Bangladesh', the Pakistan government's willingness to 'receive a substantial number of such non-Bengalis from Bangladesh', and referred to 'non-Bengalis who are stated to have 'opted for repatriation to Pakistan'' as 'Pakistanis'.[59] In the 1974 *Tripartite Agreement*, Pakistan is said to have 'issued clearances for movement of Pakistanis in favor of those non-Bengalis' who fell into the three categories described earlier.[60] Such interchangeable usage of 'Pakistani' and 'non-Bengali' reflects a perception that non-Bengalis in Bangladesh, particularly those wishing to repatriate, are actually Pakistani citizens. Urdu-speakers displaced to ICRC camps were all presumed to have filed applications for repatriation to Pakistan. The expropriation of Urdu-speakers' property under the abandoned property orders suggests that many were deemed to have been enemy aliens, as opposed to citizens who opposed the creation of Bangladesh.[61] Neither Pakistan nor Bangladesh clearly articulated terms for citizenship for those who did not wish to repatriate to Pakistan or for those who did not qualify for repatriation. The absence of clear citizenship policies, particularly for minorities with ties to more than one country, is a pitfall in the course of state succession.[62]

CASE LAW

Some cases clarified whether support for Pakistan during the Liberation War, or if expressing or acting on a desire to live in Pakistan after independence, constituted expressions of disloyalty or allegiance to another state or created any other grounds for losing Bangladeshi citizenship. For example, in *Mukhtar Ahmed v. Government*, the court found that 'the mere fact that the petitioner filed an application for going over to Pakistan cannot take away his citizenship . . . . He could voluntarily renounce it or he could be deprived of it if he . . . incurred any disqualification . . . . He filed an affidavit affirming his allegiance to Bangladesh in 1972. The petitioner having not acquired the citizenship of any other country, his citizenship of Bangladesh, which he acquired long before, cannot evaporate and he continues to be a citizen of this country.'[63]

The case of *Bangladesh v. Professor Golam Azam* was especially important in clarifying the limits of the exceptions to citizenship. Golam Azam was president of the Jamaat-e-Islami Party of the former East Pakistan and was known to have supported Pakistan before and during the Liberation War. In August 1971, the party's paper quoted him as saying, 'but God forbid, if Pakistan does not exist, then Bengali Muslims will have to face the death of dishonor'.[64] He claimed that pro-liberation forces were enemies of Pakistan and addressed paramilitary groups responsible for atrocities against Bengalis. He went to Pakistan in 1971 and returned to Bangladesh in 1978, after years of trying to obtain an exit visa from Pakistan. He no longer carried a Pakistani passport and had applied for restoration of Bangladeshi citizenship. In seeking to deport him back to Pakistan, the government contended that Azam could not be deemed a citizen of Bangladesh under Article 3 of the *Citizenship Order*.

The Appellate Division determined that Article 3 could be invoked 'only when a "doubt" arises as to whether a person fulfills all or any of the conditions "deeming citizenship" under Article 2'.[65] Since Azam was a permanent resident on 26 March 1971, he was a citizen on grounds of permanent residence under the *Citizenship Order*. He was not a Pakistani citizen because 'one cannot continue to be a citizen of Pakistan merely by his choice to stay in Pakistan unless the State of Pakistan accepted him as such'.[66] Moreover, 'law cannot be interpreted according to the respondent's alleged contemplation or notion about Pakistan's sway over his mind. Even a diehard pro-Pakistani, born in this country, is entitled to be a citizen of Bangladesh if he fulfills the requirements under Article 2 and is not disqualified under clause 1 of Article 2(b)'.[67] The court went on to underscore that deprivation of nationality could not be used as punishment for holding certain political opinions. It stated that:

Even if the [criminal] allegations are correct, our citizenship law does not deny citizenship to those who opposed the creation of Bangladesh and even killed freedom fighters and were engaged in murder, rape, and so on . . . . There were many Muslims (and Hindus as well) who opposed the creation of Pakistan . . . . Yet, the Pakistan Citizenship Law did not deny them citizenship. They were deemed to be citizens of Pakistan if they had permanent residence in the territory of Pakistan and did not leave the same. Bangladesh also followed the same principle . . . . In Bangladesh, collaborators and Razakars (paramilitaries) were prosecuted under the Collaboration Order, President's Order No. 8 of 1972, but they were not denied the citizenship of Bangladesh.[68]

Further regarding permanent residence, 'the domicile of origin is
not lost by abandonment nor is it extinguished by mere removal . . . .
Overwhelming evidence is required to rebut the presumption in favor of its
continuance.'[69] More generally, the court articulated the resilient quality
of citizenship rights, stating that 'Citizenship, though not mentioned as a
fundamental right in our Constitution, is to be considered as the right of all
rights as on it depends one's right to fundamental rights expressly provided
for a citizen in Part III of the Constitution and his right to seek a Court's
protection of those rights.'[70] In addition, 'it can be safely said that citizenship involves a determination of a very vital issue concerning an individual
by which his fundamental, political and civil rights are affected'.[71]

Perhaps because the Urdu-speakers' identity still seemed so bound up
in the idea of Pakistan, at least on a social and political level, the implications of the Mukhtar Ahmed and Azam decisions had limited effect on
altering perceptions of the citizenship status of the Urdu-speaking community as a whole. The 2003 High Court decision in *Abid Khan and others
v. Government of Bangladesh* managed to touch more broadly on Urdu-
speaking persons' right to citizenship. In that case, ten Urdu-speakers
filed a petition requesting the court to direct the Election Commission
to register them as voters. The Commission had asserted that because
the petitioners lived in Geneva camp in Mohammedpur, they were not
entitled to voter registration. The court found that those petitioners born
before independence were citizens by permanent residence under the
1972 *Citizenship Order*. Being only two and four years old at the time of
independence, and with no claims to the contrary by the respondent, the
petitioners did not fall into the exception of having expressed allegiance to
a foreign state.[72]

Regarding whether residence in Geneva camp raised any special concerns, the court took judicial notice of 'the fact of liberation struggle of
Bangladesh and subsequent connection of the Urdu-speaking persons in
this camp . . . after the liberation of Bangladesh for security reasons'.[73]
The court did not find that 'only because of the concentration of Urdu-
speaking people, who were citizens of erstwhile East Pakistan, the so-
called Geneva Camp has attained any special status so as to be excluded
from the operation of the laws of the land . . . . So mere residence of the
first group of petitioners at the Geneva Camp cannot be termed as allegiance to another state by conduct.'[74] Referring to *Mukhtar Ahmed v.
Government of Bangladesh* and *Abdul Khaleque v. The Court of Settlement*,
the court noted that petitioners at issue were 'in a much better footing
[because] they did not even apply for citizenship of another country nor
did they apply for repatriation to Pakistan'.[75] The court determined that
the petitioners born after independence were citizens under the 1951

Citizenship Act. No exceptions applied. Accordingly, the court directed the Election Commission to register the petitioners to vote. The government did not appeal the decision.

Nonetheless, Paulsen observes that the citizenship status of Urdu-speakers remained unclear despite the Abid Khan decision, primarily because the government had not clarified its policies or acted unequivocally following the order.[76] The UNHCR has also noted that 'the effect of the 2003 decision was limited to the ten petitioners'.[77] Whether that effect was limited in a legal or policy sense is unclear. However, as with any other precedent, the same reasoning presumably applies to all others so as to prevent requiring each individual to seek a court's confirmation of his or her citizenship.

Sadakat Khan and Others v. The Chief Election Commissioner, May 2008

The landmark 2008 decision, *Sadakat Khan and Others v. The Chief Election Commissioner*, as well as certain government actions that followed, addressed the citizenship rights of Urdu-speakers as a group more explicitly than in previous cases. A political crisis created an opportunity. In 2006, the Bangladesh National Party (BNP) gave power temporarily to a non-elected caretaker government, provided for in the Constitution to ensure that new elections take place freely and fairly. The opposition Awami League led nationwide protests demanding electoral reforms, prompting the caretaker government to declare a state of emergency and to extend its term to make the reforms.

The Election Commission was tasked with preparing new voter registration lists, which would be used for issuing national identity cards to all citizens for the first time. The Chief Election Commissioner wrote to the Chief Advisor (head of the caretaker government) on 7.June 2007, requesting clarification as to whether the Urdu-speakers living in the ICRC-created camps were citizens and should therefore be registered to vote. The Election Commission did not question whether Urdu-speakers living outside the camps were citizens, and those individuals were enlisted in the electoral rolls.[78] As the High Court stated, 'till [May 2008] the Chief Advisor could not find time to give any policy guidance'.[79] Irrespective of whether the Chief Advisor responded or not, this kind of constitutional question, in part because it affected a whole community, could only be decided through a writ petition.[80]

Sadakat Khan, leader of the Urdu-Speaking Peoples' Youth Rehabilitation Movement (USPYRM), and ten others filed a petition, requesting that they be enrolled as voters. Most of the petitioners resided in camps in Mirpur, north Dhaka. The Election Commission did not appear in the case. The Chief Election Commissioner, as conveyed in his letter to the Chief Advisor, only sought clarification of the law and had no reason to oppose the petitioners. The Commissioner 'solicited an urgent decision on the matter of citizenship of the people'. He reasoned that after introduction of a national identity card as a condition for delivery of a number of services, 'these people may lose access to many services they currently enjoy. Even renewal of a rickshaw license would require presentation of an ID card and no ID card will be issued to a person who is not a citizen of Bangladesh'.[81] Moreover, the Commissioner reportedly stated that the Commission 'was of the view that the time has come to look at the issue objectively and with compassion. The case of the Urdu-speaking people needs to be separated from 'stranded Pakistanis' and a decision on their citizenship may be taken expeditiously. It also desired the Chief Advisor may consider holding an inter-ministerial meeting with all relevant government agencies'.[82]

Having reviewed the law, including the Abid Khan and Mukhtar Ahmed decisions, the court concluded that 'members of the Urdu-speaking people, wherever they live in Bangladesh . . . have already acquired the citizenship of Bangladesh by operation of law' if they meet the requirements under the 1951 *Citizenship Act* or the 1972 *Citizenship Order*.[83] '[N]o intervention of the government is necessary . . . and the Election Commission is under constitutional obligation to enroll [those who wish to enroll] in the electoral roll as voters. No functionary of the Republic can deny such rights of the Urdu-speaking people who want to be enrolled as voters'.[84] The court found the petitioners to be citizens of Bangladesh and entitled to voter registration. The court also directed the Election Commission to 'enroll the petitioners and other Urdu-speaking people who want to be enrolled in the electoral rolls accordingly', and to 'give them National Identity Card[s] without any further delay'.[85]

Underscoring the importance of the constitutional right to citizenship, the court also stated:

> Miseries and sufferings of such people due to statelessness were time to time reported in the national media, electronic and print . . . . [T]hey are constantly denied the constitutional rights to job, education, accommodation, health, and a decent life like other citizens . . . . By keeping the question of citizenship unresolved on wrong assumptions over the decades, this nation has not gained anything rather was deprived of the contribution they could have made in nation building. The sooner the Urdu-speaking people are brought to the mainstream of the nation the better.[86]

Under the Sadakat Khan decision, the Urdu-speakers' right to citizenship was unequivocal. A number of factors were at play in the result, such as the earlier decisions that set important precedent in interpreting Bangladesh's citizenship laws,[87] the pressure felt by the Election Commission to carry out sweeping electoral reform, the Chief Election Commissioner's integrity in seeking 'to look at the issue objectively and with compassion,' and the willingness of petitioners and their attorneys to pursue the case, no matter the risks. Rafiqul Islam Miah, the attorney in the Sadakat Khan case, is Bengali and essentially took the case pro bono. Having seen the 'inhumane conditions' in the camps, he felt that the camp-dwellers, especially those born after the Liberation War, were 'still suffering' due to no fault of their own. 'These Biharis are very hard-working; they are not thieves or terrorists,' he stated. The denial of rights was clear to him. M.I. Farooqui, an Urdu-speaking attorney who had brought earlier cases, including the Abid Khan case, acknowledged that 'we took some risk in bringing these cases'.[88] In deciding whether to litigate, 'we not only read the law; we read the judges'.

Other factors that contributed to this success included 'advocacy on the part of local organizations, such as the USPYRM, Al-Falah, and RMMRU (Dhaka University's Refugee and Migratory Movements Research Unit), as well as international advocates who encouraged interest in the issue; UNHCR's studies of the situation and discrete advocacy with the government; and the government's restraint in declining to appeal the decision, either because of benign neglect or 'in tacit recognition that a solution had been delayed for far too long'.[89]

Three months later, the Election Commission began its drive to register eligible voters throughout the camps. As recounted by Refugees International, 'Over several long days and through weekend hours, Election Commission "enumerators" took forms door to door, registering hundreds of people each day . . . . After a person was registered for voting, he or she was instructed on where and when to report for national ID registration'.[90] During this author's August 2008 visits to some of the camps during voter registration, the atmosphere was enthusiastic and hopeful. One enumerator, a high school teacher, found the work 'very satisfying because everyone is so cooperative'.[91] Family members gathered around individuals in their homes as they worked with the enumerators to fill out the forms. Reams of completed forms were proudly bound and stacked for delivery to the Election Commission.

Around 80 per cent of eligible Urdu-speakers, men and women of all ages, registered to vote and obtained identity cards.[92] The cards enable an individual to access numerous rights and services, such as 'getting a passport, opening a bank account or securing a loan, getting utility connections, registration for public examinations, applying for public services, marriage registration, applying for government subsidies, selling and

*Figure 7.3   While stateless, most Bihari could not work in the private
            sector and were not given government jobs. Most work petty
            jobs that cater to others living in the Bihari camps. A man runs
            a small printing press out of the one room his family occupies.*

buying land and vehicles, admissions to schools and lodging petitions and
appeals in court'.[93] Reactions to the process were positive to uncertain.
Several parents believed the ID cards would enable their children to go
to schools, find jobs and avoid harassment when travelling in rural areas.
Others had heard rumours that obtaining a national ID card could lead
to eviction from the camps.[94] One pragmatic woman stated, 'We will just
have to wait and see if [the ID card] brings us any benefit.'[95]

CURRENT SITUATION AND INTERVIEWS

Fifteen months after the voter registration drive and issuance of national
IDs (November 2009), interviews of individuals living in camps in
Mohammedpur, Mirpur and Narayanganj (outside Dhaka) were carried
out. People were selected at random for interviews based on availabil-
ity and willingness to speak. Interviewees ranged in age from 18 to 70,
male and female. Assessments of the current situation were mixed. Some

individuals reported that their ID cards gave them a sense of national belonging and identity, that they had opened doors to education and jobs, while others felt that discrimination continued or that nothing had changed because their poverty was simply insurmountable.

Some individuals were positive to ambivalent about having citizenship and a national ID card. For instance, Ali[96] is 22 years old with a Master's degree in management. He voted for the first time last year. He sought an ID card to show that 'I am a national of this country,' and felt that an ID card brought tangible benefits, such as the opportunity to attend government schools and obtain jobs in public service. Still, Ali is not totally confident that having a national ID card makes him or others immune to discrimination. He stated that he provided a non-camp address when he applied to go to school because 'if they knew you were a stranded Pakistani, you didn't get access'.[97] Even now, he claims that individuals applying for government jobs or education are better off using non-camp addresses. Moreover, 'if you have money, you can get a job'.[98] According to Ali, having a national ID is less of a guarantee than the means to bribe your way to opportunities.

Some interviewees' perceptions of the ID cards were primarily optimistic. For example, Sara is 40 years old and the mother of four small children. She said she felt she had no opportunities until she obtained a national ID card. It enables her to say that 'I am a national of this country, I have rights, and I expect that when I want to open a bank account, obtain a passport, or buy land, I will be able to do so.'[99] She is 'happy to have become a voter. With the national ID card, my kids are able to say that they are educated gentlemen, and equal with others. The ID is very useful for my kids.'

Farida, who is 21 years old, married and studying to receive a Bachelor's degree in business studies, was similarly positive. She reported that she feels 'more important' having obtained a national ID card. 'If you don't have an ID, you have lots of problems.'[100] With her card, she voted for the first time, opened three bank accounts and applied for shares in the national stock exchange. She needed an ID card to apply for her job and believes that having an ID helps keep her job secure.

For Munni, another young woman living in a camp in Mohammedpur, the ID card affirms her sense of identity and aspirations. She is 18 years old and became a voter last year. Her father is a butcher, her mother is a housewife and she has four sisters. Two of her sisters are in 'open university' and two are in government schools. As for her, 'I'm an educated girl' she said, studying commerce in her higher secondary school. When asked to speak about her identity, she responded, 'Of course I am Bangladeshi.' An ID card 'is necessary to prove I am Bangladeshi, that my motherland is Bangladesh. It is necessary to go into the outside world, to apply for a government job.' She would like to join the army because it is 'honorable, established, and comes with benefits and facilities'.[101] She claims that one potential barrier to her success is that 'some men think women should not study', but this has nothing to do with having an ID card.

Others' impressions of having an ID card were characterized by ambivalence, with some expressing uncertainty, a sense of powerlessness despite having a card, and even fear. Shahanaz has four children and all attend private school. She believes that she is in the same position since she obtained an ID card. 'I am confused. I do not know if having an ID helps or not. Twenty-six years ago, many of my relatives went to Pakistan, but I did not have enough money at the time. Now, only two relatives live in Bangladesh. I prefer to go to Pakistan.' She voted for the first time last year, but 'many people said different things, such as that if we became voters, our children would become more secure in Bangladesh. On the other hand, we also heard that the government would evict us if we became voters.'[102]

Sajia, a mother of six, was also ambivalent. All of her children study at home 'because of financial problems'. Most of her boys work in handicrafts, making two saris per week. They are paid 500 Taka for a sari that sells on the market for 4000 Taka. 'What will happen next? I don't know. It depends on the government.'[103] One of her sons, Raja, is 20 years old, registered to vote last year and spends several hours a day embroidering saris. He said, 'Without an ID card we can't do anything.' He needed an ID to enroll in university, and he would like to use his ID to obtain a passport. He wants to go overseas and become a fashion designer. 'I want something bigger', he said with a grin. Whether or not Raja can fulfil his dreams and truly enjoy the benefits of citizenship will depend on whether or not he can overcome his family's poverty.

Josim is 35 years old and was born in Bangladesh. He said that there has been 'lots of suffering, but the next generation will lead a better life'.[104] He elaborated that 'we need an ID card to have a national identity, to feel secure, to fulfill our needs, to get jobs, and attend government schools'. He nonetheless expressed fears that with an ID card, he would not be permitted to live in the camp.

In Mirpur, Sadakat Khan, who successfully brought the 2008 petition seeking voter rights, claims that little has changed for individuals who live in the camps. In principle, having an ID clears the way to applying for certain jobs, going to school and seeking rehabilitation from the government. Yet having a camp address still creates barriers to accessing basic services. Living conditions in the camps, especially poor sanitation, are unchanged. Several cases involving housing rights are still pending in the legal system; the courts are being asked to prevent government evictions from the camps. According to Sadakat Khan, '[w]e need more legal assistance to continue to litigate our rights. We still do not know how to seek compensation for property that was lost in 1971.'[105] In making these statements, Khan is not content to rest on any laurels he may have earned in successfully bringing the 2008 case. He is modest and matter-of-fact.

In Adamjee camp near Narayanganj, views on the community's current status were pessimistic. Many individuals claimed that they had applied for jobs in the 'Export Processing Zone', a complex of factories being constructed near the camps, but that they were turned away because they were 'Biharis'. They felt that the ID cards had made no difference in their lives. One group said they wanted to go to Pakistan but that they would be all right staying in Bangladesh if they had 'full rights and dignity'.[106] Worth noting is that many camp-dwellers in Adamjee had been previously employed in the now defunct nearby jute mills and that the most recent group of individuals who went to Pakistan in 1994 originated from Adamjee. The school in the camp where the emigrants reportedly gathered 15 years ago to say goodbye to the community is now derelict.[107]

ANALYSIS AND CONCLUSION

Overall, interviewees' sentiments ranged from ambivalent to positive regarding the impact of being recognized as citizens and having obtained a national ID card. Because having a national ID card permitted access to public schools, jobs, bank accounts, licences and passports, many individuals perceived that their prospects and their children's futures had substantially improved. However, poverty, corruption and ongoing confusion within certain administrative agencies over the legal effect of having a camp address continue to block access to these opportunities. Enduring perceptions by the majority of the country's population (and perpetuated by the media) that the group consists of 'stranded Pakistanis' also feed notions that the Urdu-speakers are not from Bangladesh.

These conditions in turn diminish the meaning and value of nationality in the country. More broadly, they reflect weaknesses in legal institutions. If people cannot access their legal rights because they are indigent, because bureaucrats are corrupt or unhelpful, or because average individuals just do not believe that they are entitled to these rights, what is the use of such rights? Moreover, national ID cards do not by themselves reunite individuals with family in Pakistan. Solving statelessness does not solve all problems. Yet while some expressed concerns that having a national ID card might increase the likelihood of eviction, no one reported that national ID cards had actually made their lives worse than before.

Notably, when asked about why it was important to have a national ID card, several interviewees first stated that it enabled them to say that they were citizens of Bangladesh. They understood that from this fact, many benefits flowed. As one woman said, 'I am a national of this country, I have rights.' One did not need to be an eminent jurist to grasp that nationality, for all practical purposes in Bangladesh, constituted the 'right to have rights'.[108] This relationship between citizenship and other rights has profound psychological implications. In Bangladesh and elsewhere, for persons without citizenship, life is a giant negation. Stateless persons have conveyed feelings of dislocation, stasis, powerlessness, hopelessness and depression. To say 'I am a national of this country', in the slums of Dhaka or anywhere, is an affirmative statement that 'I exist.' As Sadakat Khan stated after the May 2008 judgment, 'We hope to get our life back'.[109] Moreover, 'We can live in Bangladesh with dignity'.[110]

Although interviewees' assessments of their situation since obtaining national ID cards are not resoundingly enthusiastic, the success of the Urdu-speakers in confirming their citizenship rights through the courts is unquestionably significant. On a basic level, statelessness is a legal problem.[111] Through successive court judgments and with the help of sympathetic attorneys, community members confronted the root of their predicament and obtained legal remedies. It was a triumph not only for the Urdu-speakers, but also for rule of law more broadly, for '[t]he petitioners succeeded in a judiciary vulnerable to political influence and lengthy delays'[112] and elicited powerful language from the courts regarding citizenship rights and the group's need for integration into society. Thanks to these efforts, most Urdu-speakers living in Bangladesh can claim Bangladeshi nationality. The community is definitively not stateless, and no one can legitimately assert that Urdu-speakers, living inside or outside the camps, are legally barred from enjoying the benefits of citizenship.

However, as some of the interviewees suggest, legal victories are not enough.[113] The remaining challenges for genuinely ending statelessness among the Urdu-speakers of Bangladesh are the political, social, economic and administrative obstacles that frustrate implementation of the group's rights as citizens. As the American Ambassador to Bangladesh, James Moriarty, stated to community leaders when he visited Geneva camp in November 2009, 'I came here to call attention to your community, to show that political rights exist, but that there is still much ground to cover'.[114]

Groups such as the RMMRU call for 'rehabilitation with dignity', and along with Al-Falah, advocate for government and non-governmental plans to support education, livelihoods and general integration developed in consultation with the community. While remaining persistent with its advocacy that Pakistan take more responsibility for the community, SPGRC also affirms rehabilitation as a solution, stating that 'we are ready to stay [in Bangladesh], but with all basic needs and rights'.[115] An attorney in the Sadakat Khan case further averred that '[i]f you give them some support, they will be excellent citizens'.[116]

Ahmed Ilias of Al-Falah accepts that expectations must be realistic. 'Things will not change overnight. We must have our own policy and programs to rehabilitate the community, and match it with the government's plans. I have to own Bangladesh, including its problems. I must acknowledge that the government is facing problems more challenging than the Biharis'.[117] Since the government generally aims to benefit the majority, the strategy should seek to make the government see the Urdu-speakers as part of the population, while still allowing the community to retain its linguistic traditions.[118] Community leaders also foresee the need for more litigation to protect rights. Yet the government can easily avert the need for costly litigation and facilitate the community's integration by unequivocally affirming the rights of Urdu-speakers and prohibiting discrimination and unequal treatment.[119] It should also continue to raise with Pakistan the rights of certain individuals to reunite with family members. Such gestures might form part of a concurrent process of post-liberation reconciliation.

The story of the Urdu-speaking community of Bangladesh provides important lessons regarding successful advocacy for nationality rights. It also demonstrates that ending statelessness does not always resolve all of its consequences, nor does it eliminate all of its causes. This fact in turn raises questions regarding how to define and measure statelessness, how to determine when the predicament has actually ended and when victory can truly be declared. Due largely to individual initiatives, unsung heroes and increasing international attention, the Urdu-speakers of Bangladesh stand and deserve a fair chance of carrying their success forward to full enjoyment of citizenship, to the 'life with dignity' that Sadakat Khan and others have long sought.

NOTES

1. Ilias (2003), p. ix, fn. 1 and p. xi.
2. Terminology used to define the group is somewhat contentious. Ahmed Ilias of the non-governmental organization AL-falah asserts that '[i]n Bangladesh, "Bihari" is a word usually considered offensive for a non-local, speaking Urdu.' (ibid., p. ix). Members of the young generation express that terms such as 'Bihari' or 'stranded

Pakistani' are unhelpful to their efforts to advocate for integration and rehabilitation within Bangladesh, as they imply that the group is from and therefore belongs somewhere else (Author interviews with members of Al-Falah in their early to late 20s, August 2008 and November 2009). 'Urdu-speaking minority' is the preferred term of those who wish to claim Bangladeshi citizenship, because they consider it to be more accurate and inclusive than other terms while still retaining a sense of cultural distinctiveness. Perhaps appealing to linguistic identity is also helpful for inspiring unity within the Bangladeshi context. As will be discussed below, the Language Movement played a significant role in shaping national identity before independence in 1971, partly through promoting appreciation for Bengali language and culture. Reference to an Urdu-speaking minority is arguably a call for cultural recognition and celebration to which the Bengali majority can relate.

By contrast, another group organized within the community is called the Stranded Pakistanis General Repatriation Committee (SPRGC). As the name suggests, the group has pressed for the community's repatriation to Pakistan and prefers to identify the minority as 'stranded Pakistanis.' This term references the group's historical identification with Pakistan before Bangladesh's independence and alludes to deep grievances against Pakistan's refusal to accept those individuals who wish to migrate to Pakistan.

Connotations related to the term 'stranded Pakistani' carry validity. Yet mindful of the diversity of opinion among community members in Bangladesh, I have chosen to use the term 'Urdu-speakers' and 'Urdu-speaking minority' throughout this chapter because these terms do not carry strong implications as to where the group ultimately belongs.

3.   Ibid., p. ix.
4.   Ibid., p. x.
5.   Al-Falah means 'welfare' in Urdu.
6.   Ilias (2003) p. 39.
7.   Ibid., p. 60.
8.   Ibid., p. 56.
9.   'Author interview with SPGRC at Adamjee camp, Narayanganj, November 2009; see also Khan (2004).
10.   Ilias (2003) p. 62.
11.   Ibid., p. 66.
12.   Minorities at Risk Project (2007). According to the Minority at Risk Project, 'Bengalis reportedly killed over 1,000 Biharis', though other estimates are much higher.
13.   Anthony Mascarenhas, *Sunday Times*, London (13 June 1971), quoted in Kelley (2009). Mascarenhas subsequently published two books, *The Rape of Bangladesh* (1971) and *Bangladesh: A Legacy of Blood* (1986).
14.   Bangladesh means 'Bengal nation or land'.
15.   Lynch and Calabia, (2006).
16.   Kelley (2009), pp. 349, 356 (citing Sen, 2000, p. 41).
17.   Paulsen (2006), pp. 54–5.
18.   See South Asia Forum for Human Rights (n.d.).
19.   The *Bangladesh Abandoned Property (Control, Management and Disposal) Order*, 1972 (President's Order No. 16 of 1972, 28 February 1972, Preamble and Article 2.
20.   Paulsen notes that '[t]he supposedly temporary law has yet to be consolidated or codified.' (Paulsen, 2006, p. 57).
21.   *New Delhi Agreement between India and Pakistan*, Article 3, (28 August 1973).
22.   Kelley (2009), p.357 (citing Shah (1997)).
23.   *New Delhi Agreement*, Article 3 (a) (iii).
24.   Ibid., Article 3 (a) (v).
25.   Ibid., Article 3 (a) (vii).
26.   Ibid., Article 3.
27.   *Tripartite Agreement of Bangladesh-Pakistan-India*, Article 6 (9 April 1974).

28. Ibid., Article. 12.
29. Chowdhury (1998).
30. Kelley, (2009), p. 358.
31. Refugee and Migratory Movements Research Unit (2007).
32. Calculations based on author's interviews with *Benarasi* and *Karchupi* weavers and embroiderers in camps in Narayanganj and Mohammedpur, November 2009.
33. *Survey of Stranded Pakistanis Conducted by Pakistan High Commission*, Rabita Islami, and Assisted by SPGRC, Table 4: Distribution of population by camp and location of residence (1992).
34. Daily Star (1993). Apparently, most of the 1110 families living in the Adamjee camp believed that they would also be imminently repatriated to Pakistan. In anticipation, many left their jobs and sold property. See Khan (1993).
35. Ibid.
36. See, for example, (1992).
37. Lynch and Calabia (2006).
38. Ibid.
39. The Dhaka Declaration, Summit of SPGRC 1, 5 November 2009).
40. See Hussain (2009); McKinsey(2007) author interview with Al-Falah, August 2008.
41. 'The Story of Khalid Hussain', Durban Review Conference, Geneva, 2009, available at http://www.un.org/durbanreview2009/story27.html.
42. Author interview with young Urdu-speaking mother, August 2008.
43. Author interview with Khalid Hussain, November 2009. See also Paulsen (2006), p. 56.
44. Paulsen (2006), also author interviews with Urdu-speakers, August 2008 and November 2009.
45. Paulsen (2006), p. 56.
46. Kelley (2009), p. 360.
47. Paulsen (2006), p. 56.
48. See, for example, OBAT Helpers, Inc. (n.d.), at http://www.obathelpers.org/index.html.
49. Paulsen (2006), p. 57.
50. *Constitution of the People's Republic of Bangladesh*, Article 6 (1972).
51. *Adaptation of Existing Bangladesh Laws Order*, Preamble (1972).
52. *Bangladesh v. Professor Golam Azam*, 46 DLR (AD) 192 (1994).
53. *Pakistan Citizenship Act*, Article 4 (1951).
54. Ibid., Article 5 (1951).
55. Ibid., Article 16 (1951).
56. *Bangladesh Citizenship (Temporary Provisions) Order*, Article. 2 (a) (1972).
57. Ibid., Article 2 (b) (1972). Certain persons residing in the United Kingdom may also encounter obstacles to citizenship under Article 2.
58. Ibid., Article 3 (1972).
59. *Delhi Agreement*, Article 3 (iii), 3 (v), and 3 (viii).
60. *Tripartite Agreement of Bangladesh-Pakistan-India*, Article 12 (1974).
61. See Farooqui (2000) (exploring the confusion between 'non-Bengali' and 'Pakistani citizen' within the context of abandoned property orders).
62. Certain international instruments articulate emerging international standards on statelessness and state succession. See, for example, International Law Commission Draft Articles on the Nationality of Natural Persons in relation to the Succession of States, available at http://www.unhcr.org/refworld/type,INTINSTRUMENT,,,4512b6dd4,0.html, and *Council of Europe Convention on the Avoidance of Statelessness in Relation to State Succession* (2006), available at http://conventions.coe.int/Treaty/EN/Treaties/Html/200.htm.
63. *Mukhtar Ahmed v. Government of Bangladesh*, 34 DLR (1982) 29, cited in Farooqui (2000), p. 28. See also *Abdul Khaleque v. The Court of Settlement*, 44 DLR 273 (filing an application for repatriation does not result in loss of citizenship), cited in *Abid Khan and Others v. Bangladesh*, 55 DLR 318 (2003).

64. Paulsen (2006), p. 63.
65. Ibid., 46 DLR (AD) 220-21 (1994).
66. Ibid., 46 DLR (AD) 215 (1994).
67. Ibid., 46 DLR (AD) 207 (1994).
68. Ibid., 46 DLR (AD) 222 (1994).
69. Ibid., 46 DLR (AD) 207-08 (1994).
70. Ibid., 46 DLR (AD) 197 (1994).
71. Ibid., 46 DLR (AD) 238 (1994).
72. *Abid Khan and Others v. Government of Bangladesh*, 55 DLR 318 (2003).
73. Ibid.
74. Ibid.
75. Ibid.
76. Paulsen (2006) pp. 67–8.
77. UNHCR (2009), [paragraph 5].
78. *Sadakat Khan and Others v. The Chief Election Commissioner*, Writ Petition No. 10129, 10 (2007).
79. Ibid. Writ Petition No. 10129, 16 (2007).
80. Ibid.
81. Ibid. Writ Petition No. 10129, 9-10 (2007).
82. Ibid. Writ Petition No. 10129, 10 (2007).
83. Ibid. Writ Petition No. 10129, 14 (2007).
84. Ibid. Writ Petition No. 10129, 14, 17 (2007). ('Till now option lies under the law with a citizen to enroll as a voter.')
85. Ibid. Writ Petition No. 10129, 17 (2007).
86. Ibid. Writ Petition No. 10129, 16 (2007).
87. M.I. Farooqui, the Urdu-speaking attorney who brought the Abid Khan case, among others, acknowledged that the 'government is acting because of the accumulation of earlier cases.' Author interview with M.I. Farooqui, August 2008.
88. Author interview with M.I. Farooqui, August 2008.
89. Southwick and Lynch (2009), p. 17
90. Southwick and Calabia (2008), p. 2.
91. Ibid.
92. UNHCR (2009) [paragraph 8] author's visit to Bangladesh on behalf of Refugees International, August 2008.
93. Research for Development (2008), see also UNHCR (2009) [paragraph 7.].
94. The RMMRU of Dhaka University alleged that the eviction rumours had been spread by 'a small group . . . having been frightened by the empowerment of the general members of the community as citizens of the country'. (Refugee and Migratory Movements Research Unit, 2008).
95. Southwick and Calabia (2008).
96. Interviewees' names have been changed.
97. Author interview, Mohammedpur, November 2009.
98. Ibid.
99. Ibid.
100. Ibid.
101. Ibid.
102. Ibid.; see also Parveen (2008), ('Biharis residing in camps are in fear of eviction and uncertainty after the High Court on May 18 granted them citizenship, ending a long-lasting argument over their status.')
103. Author interview, Mohammedpur, November 2009.
104. Ibid.
105. Author interview with Sadakat Khan, Mirpur, November 2009.
106. Author interviews facilitated by SPGRC, Adamjee camp, Narayanganj, November 2009.
107. Author interview with SPGRC, Adamjee camp, Narayanganj, November 2009.

108. *Trop v. Dulles*, 356 U.S. 86, 102 (1958).
109. Parveen (2008).
110. Author interview with Sadakat Khan, August 2008.
111. According to the 1954 *Convention relating to the Status of Stateless Persons*, Article 1, a stateless individual is 'a person who is not considered as a national by any state under the operation of its law'.
112. Southwick and Lynch, (2009), p. 17.
113. Ibid. 'RI's visit to Bangladesh in August 2008 revealed that a court judgment confirming citizenship rights, while significant, is itself insufficient to end nearly four decades of poverty and discrimination.'). See also author interview with SPGRC, November 2009. ('The High Court decision is not enough. It is the political hurdle we are still facing.')
114. American Ambassador. Moriarty's visit to Geneva camp, Mohammedpur, November 2009.
115. Author interview with SPGRC, November 2009.
116. Author interview with Rafiqul Islam Miah (August 2008), quoted *in* Southwick and Calabia (2008), p. 2.
117. Author interview with Ahmed Ilias, November 2009.
118. Ibid.
119. Refugee and Migratory Movements Research Unit (2007). See also Southwick and Calabia (2008).

8.   Mauritania: citizenship lost and found

Julia Harrington Reddy

In January 2008, an important exercise began: the first of tens of thousands of Mauritanian refugees, exiled since 1989 in Senegal, returned to their country under the terms of a tripartite agreement between the UNHCR and the Senegalese and Mauritanian governments.[1] The tripartite agreement specifies that Mauritanian refugees in Senegal shall have the right to return to Mauritania and be recognized as Mauritanian citizens. The logistics of the returns are to be organized by the UNCHR, with the Mauritania government doing its part by issuing the necessary citizenship documents to the returnees.[2]

Some months later, the first of these returnees did obtain their Mauritanian ID cards. The story of how they lost recognition of their Mauritanian citizenship and became refugees in the first place is an all-too-common story of ethnic discrimination transformed by state policy into the destruction or denial of legal identity. Similar attacks on the legal status and rights of minority groups happen across Africa and around the world.

The events in Mauritania are worthy of note because the actions of the state were so stark and explicit; because an international tribunal condemned the denationalizations and expulsions as a violation of international treaty law; because those affected maintained coherent and consistent demands for repatriation for nearly 20 years; and because there are now concrete steps towards a happy resolution, one that will see those arbitrarily denationalized restored to the citizenship they had lost.

MAURITANIAN CITIZENSHIP LAW

Mauritanian citizenship law is based on French citizenship law. Under colonial rule, Mauritania had no government or laws of its own, and no citizens. The status of the inhabitants of its colonies changed several times over the centuries as France oscillated between idealism, assimilationism and racism. The French Revolution developed the notion of state sovereignty flowing from an organized civil community of equals in which each citizen had a share in making the law.[3] The First Republic voted in 1791[4] to abolish slavery and, as if this were a necessary consequence, declared all men living in French colonies to be French citizens entitled to enjoy all the rights provided by the Constitution. This burst of assimilationist idealism lasted only eight years, until the Consulate restored slavery in 1802.[5] In 1848, at the beginning of the Second Republic in France, the idealism briefly returned. French citizenship rights were again extended to the population of French colonies, and four communes in what is now Senegal (St Louis, Dakar, Rufisque and Gorée) gained representation in the French National Assembly.[6] Residents of these communes retained their right to citizenship, but the populations of Mauritania and other French territories in West Africa later lost their French citizenship, notional as it may have been. Rather, they became French subjects.

Under French colonial rule, Mauritania was governed from St Louis, now in present-day Senegal. The population of Mauritania has for hundreds of years been ethnically mixed, usually divided into three main groups: the north of the country was populated chiefly by 'Moors' (Arab-Berber) pastoralists and so-called 'Haratines', descendants of black Africans taken into forced labour in the thirteenth century[7] and who became permanently attached to specific families, essentially as slaves.[8] Several sub-Saharan African groups, including Hal-peulaar (Fulas), Soninkés, Sarahulés and Wolofs, were concentrated in the south where they practised agriculture in the most fertile part of the country, the Senegal River Valley. Estimates are that the population was divided roughly in thirds among these groups.[9] The country has always been sparsely populated; at independence, a population of about one and a half million was scattered over a million square kilometres, 70 per cent of which is desert or semi-desert.[10]

Mauritania became independent in 1960. The independence constitution, adopted in November 1961, did not define whom the citizens of the state should be. This was dealt with in a separate law[11] adopted in the same year. Article 8 of the nationality law provides that anyone born to a Mauritanian father was Mauritanian as a matter of right from birth ('*citoyen d'orgine*').[12] Obviously, in a newly independent country, such a provision was not very meaningful. Article 9 (1) now resolves the problem by providing that anyone born in Mauritania or to a father or mother born in Mauritania or in the territory that became Mauritania shall be considered a citizen of origin (as of right, from birth). This provision is based directly on the French civil code of 1889, which provides a child born in France of a parent born in France became French,[13] regardless of the parents' legal citizenship.

Mauritanian nationality law discriminates on the basis of gender: whereas children born to Mauritanian fathers are automatically Mauritanian, those born to Mauritanian mothers are only Mauritanian if the father is stateless, of unknown nationality or if the child rejects his or her father's (non-Mauritanian) citizenship before the age of majority; the presumption is that the father's nationality trumps the mother's.[14] Similarly, children born in Mauritania to mothers born in Mauritania become citizens only if they do not decline Mauritanian nationality in the year before they reach the age of majority.[15]

The law also provides in Article 13 for acquisition of Mauritanian citizenship by election for children born to Mauritanian parents abroad; by children born in Mauritania of foreign parents who have lived there for at least five years and by children adopted by a Mauritanian citizen if they live in Mauritania for five years.[16] These individuals can obtain citizenship by opting for it in the year before they reach the age of majority.

Naturalization is available to others upon application after five years 'habitual residence'[17] in Mauritania. This residence requirement is waived for those born in Mauritania, for a man married to a Mauritanian woman and for those who have rendered extraordinary service to the country.[18] The only other requirement for naturalization is that the candidate must be able to speak one of the several languages spoken in the country fluently: Peul (Fula), Sarahulé, Wolof, Bambara, Hassaniya (which is the Mauritanian dialect of Arabic) or French.[19]

Although Mauritania has had several constitutions since the original one, the citizenship law has remained unchanged. The 1991 Constitution added the requirement that to be eligible for the presidency, a candidate must be Mauritanian from birth.[20] Otherwise, no aspect of the right to citizenship has been altered.

Mauritanian citizenship law is, prima facie, relatively liberal. While it discriminates against women, it does not discriminate absolutely. It is possible for women to give their nationality to their husbands and to their children; it is simply not automatic. The law does not discriminate on grounds of ethnicity. The provision granting citizenship to those born in the territory of a parent born in the territory (Article 9 (1)), modelled on the French civil code, assured that the vast majority of the population in the country obtained citizenship at the time of independence.[21] Mauritania, unlike countries who denied citizenship to certain groups at the time of independence, has no historically stateless population.[22]

The provision that allows children born in the territory to acquire Mauritanian citizenship after five years residence ensures that even children of stateless or foreign parents can become Mauritanian quite easily. Even the naturalization provisions are relatively liberal, requiring only five years' residence and barring only those with physical infirmity or mental illness. These are unfortunate but common provisions. The language requirement cannot be seen as too rigorous because it requires only spoken fluency, not literacy, and can be fulfilled by knowledge of any of the languages spoken in the country; anyone who lived in the country for five years would be almost certain to speak one of the languages listed in the citizenship law. Although language requirements can easily be manipulated to bar individuals from naturalizing, in Mauritania this has never been a problem. Rather, it is politics, not law, which has made citizenship in Mauritania so vexed.

POLITICS AND ETHNICITY IN MAURITANIA AND THE EVENTS OF 1989

Although tens of thousands of Mauritanian citizens became *de facto* stateless in 1989 and only now are having their citizenship restored, this cannot be blamed upon deficiencies in Mauritania's 1961 citizenship law. The law is innocent of any reflection of the fractured nature of Mauritanian society.

To understand how citizenship became such a bitter contest in 1989, one must look well beyond the law and into the politics of language and ethnicity in the country – specifically, to the struggle for dominance between Moors and 'black Mauritanians'.[23] After independence, the official language of the country was French, as it had been before. However, the Moors, who assumed a dominant position in national politics after independence, soon began a process of elevating al-Hassaniya Arabic, the Mauritanian dialect of Arabic that is heavily influenced by Berber, to official status. Language became a key point of contention in the competition between Moors and black Mauritanians seeking political and cultural dominance.[24]

The substantial movement of population between Mauritania and Senegal, which had been taken for granted under French rule, continued in the decades after independence. Many Mauritanian Moors were small businessmen and traders in the sub-region. Individuals who originated in what became independent Senegal continued to work in the civil service and in parastatals in Mauritania. Many black Mauritanians living in the Senegal River Valley had family on the south side of the river in Senegal, and some Senegalese farmers had plots of land on the north side of the river in Mauritania, which they continued to farm. There were few official border crossings, and most of the long frontier between the two countries was not policed: for the inhabitants of the villages along the river, crossing the border was a simple matter of a short boat ride. In some places and for much of the year, the river is narrow enough for a person to easily swim across.

However, after the 1984 *coup d'état* which brought Maouiya Ould Taya to power, the Mauritanian government's policy of 'Arabization' heightened tensions between the Moors and black Mauritanians, as well as between Mauritania and Senegal. Arabization had its origins in Baathism, which had a significant presence in Mauritania.[25] The Baathist ideology first developed in Syria and Egypt and was eventually adopted by Saddam Hussein in Iraq. Baathism emphasized the notion of an Arab nation made up of individuals who speak Arabic; the strengthening of Arab identity was 'the ultimate expression of freedom and as the realization of an Arab *baath*, or renaissance'.[26] This ideology did not sit easily with the multi-ethnic population of Mauritania, specifically with the black Mauritanians who resisted the progressive entrenchment of Arabic at the expense of French.

In early 1989, there were so-called 'border skirmishes' that were linked with the rustling of livestock over the border. There followed a general sense of unease, which provoked an exodus of both Mauritanian and Senegalese business people living in the other country. Although the true sequence of events may never be known, it appears that the 'border tensions' may have been engineered by, or were at least cover for, the Mauritanian government in order to carry out a plan for 'ethnic cleansing' that had been some time in the making.[27]

Beginning in early April 1989 and lasting through June, tens of thousands, estimated to be as few as 60 000 and as many as 100 000,[28] of black Mauritanians were expelled from the country; a majority were from the Senegal River Valley, but others came from deep in the interior. These events were often mischaracterized by the Mauritanian government at the time as a civil conflict which caused people to flee. In reality, most individuals were forcibly expelled by the army or police, some in planes,[29] some in trucks, some in boats across the river to neighbouring Senegal. As one expellee described it:

> Soldiers gathered all the men, and loaded them into trucks. When the men had been taken away, they came back for the women. They were the great big yellow open-air trucks used for carrying animals. People were packed into the trucks like animals, as many as they could fit, even people who were sick or hurt. There were 100 persons packed into the truck I was in.[30]

In some areas, Haratines were armed by the army or police and instructed to terrorize the local population.[31] Those expelled from the interior of the country, from as far north as Nouadhibou, were chiefly civil servants, including police officers and teachers rather than farmers. Most expellees arrived in the neighbouring country with little more than the clothes on their backs, having abandoned land, animals and other possessions. Perhaps 10 000 to 20 000 pastoralists in the extreme east of Mauritania fled across the border to Mali or were already in Mali as part of their regular seasonal migration pattern when the expulsions took place.

THE SYMBOLISM OF DOCUMENTATION

That the expulsions were the result of a deliberate Mauritanian government policy against its own citizens as opposed to a spontaneous flight of foreigners is clear. The army and the police, using airplanes to expel those in the interior of the country, could only have been mobilized by the government itself. A deliberate effort was made to confiscate and destroy citizenship documents as most adults had birth certificates and national identity cards; children also had birth certificates. Some people intuited in advance that they were likely to be expelled; one man gave his identity documents to his brother for safekeeping.[32]

Some survivors describe how, prior to being expelled, they were called by the local commissariat of police and ordered to hand over their identity cards. Sometimes this was justified with the explanation that their identity as Mauritanians (rather than Senegalese) had to be verified. Some saw their cards destroyed before their eyes:[33]

> They asked me for my *carte d'identité* (issued in Mbout, 1981), and ripped it up in front of me and put it in a bucket. The same thing happened to everyone who came into the Commissariat at that time.[34]

Another relates:

> There was an Arabic teacher named Oumar Galo Ba, also a Peul, who the village had brought from Aleg to teach our children. He rented a room in our house. At one of these meetings where the gendarmes asked for identification papers, Oumar Galo Ba brought out his papers. The gendarmes then made him come with them, in their vehicle. We didn't see him again until we were expelled, when we found him in Senegal.[35]

Some individuals were told to leave their identity documents, which were to be returned later; they were then expelled without the documents ever being returned. Others were taken from their homes and their identity documents were left behind:

> They were shouting at us, 'You're not from here.' Some were speaking in al-Hasaniya, others in French or Peul. All the identity documents – mine and

the children's – were in the house, and they were all taken with the rest of our things.[36]

The Mauritanian government insisted that not a single Mauritanian had been expelled; they were all Senegalese. Although there was some acknowledgement that identity cards had been confiscated, the government's justification was that all such identity cards were forged.[37] However, there was no attempt to verify the validity of the cards prior to expelling those who held them.

Survivors of the events described being told by the officials who were expelling them that they, the expellees, were not Mauritanian, a judgement apparently based on the expellees' ethnic identity rather than their legal citizenship, the documentary proof of which was being destroyed as part of the same operation. This attitude was consistent with the view that placed primacy on membership in a specific social group over legal qualifications for citizenship. As described by one expellee, 'The Commander said, "You are not Mauritanian. You must return to Senegal. This is a country for the Moors."'[38]

Despite the close ties between the two countries, many of the expellees had never set foot in Senegal and had no family there. Being told that they were Senegalese, rather than Mauritanian, especially when this characterization was offered as a justification for their expulsion, was wrenching. Losing the state's recognition of their Mauritanian identity at the hands of state agents sent a powerful, if unofficial, message of being disowned:

> We didn't get any explanations. They drove us to the river. It's only 12 kilometers. When we got to the edge of the river, they took us out of the vehicle and said, 'Go home and don't come back.' They called pirogues from the other side of the river – the river is very narrow – to come and take us. The Senegalese with boats came quickly, and said to us that they came to help us because sometimes they had seen people being beaten on the riverbank, or women being raped under the trees. We didn't really know what was going on. We were traumatized, we were crying.[39]

LEGAL IDENTITY IN EXILE

Most expellees arrived in Senegal without either possessions or identity documents. The Senegalese government offered help and soon the UNHCR mounted a substantial operation to assist the expellees. The expellees were registered, received food, shelter, and within a few weeks or months, temporary refugee documents. The populations of some villages were expelled in their entirety, but they soon re-established themselves on the south side of the river calling the new village by the old village's name. Expellees who had originally been grouped in a large camp on the outskirts of Dakar, such as those expelled by plane, were in due course relocated to smaller refugee 'sites' throughout the river valley.[40]

Despite the cultural similarities between many expellees and the Senegalese communities that they lived alongside, there was no doubt that the expellees were foreigners and refugees. Even outside Senegal, few were fooled by the Mauritanian government's rhetoric that those expelled were all Senegalese. What made their foreignness most obvious was their lack of possessions or livelihoods; the expellees subsisted on UNCHR rations for several years after the expulsions. Another clear indicator of their foreignness was, naturally, their lack of Senegalese identity documentation.

Perhaps, the clearest evidence of the expellees' Mauritanian identity was the intense loyalty they articulated towards Mauritania, their ongoing bitterness and shock at their rejection by its government, and their determination to return and regain recognition as citizens. One expellee said, 'Even when I am watching football, when the Mauritanian team is playing, I care so much more, because I want them to win.'[41]

One key to the survival of the expellees, both physically and as a political force, was their tight social organization. The leadership of the expellee communities soon formulated a list of demands for the Mauritanian government, and all along the length of the Senegal River Valley where expellee 'sites' were located, the leaders of the communities consistently framed these demands. Among the demands were repatriation to Mauritania supervised by an international body such as the UNCHR; compensation for their lost property; and the return of their identity documents.

The importance of the Mauritanian citizenship they had lost became clear to the expellees in light of the difficulties they suffered living as poorly documented foreigners in Senegal. Their state had withdrawn from them its protection and recognition; this left them eligible for international protection, in this case to be provided by the UNCHR. International protection, however, is a poor substitute for state protection under the best of circumstances, and in this specific case, UNCHR's issuing of identity documents was never well managed. Most refugee cards were valid only for a period of a few months or a year and when they expired or were lost it was extremely difficult to get them renewed or replaced. There came a time when replacement refugee cards were issued only at UNCHR's office in Dakar. Without a valid identity document, it is very difficult to travel on the national highways in Senegal: passengers on public transport are subjected to regular identity checks, and those without documents can be prevented from travelling farther. Thus, the very fact of needing a replacement refugee card made it nearly impossible to travel to get one. This problem was quite apart from the expense of travelling from far-flung expellee settlements in the river valley to Dakar. Even unexpired refugee cards were sometimes not accepted by the Senegalese police as valid identification.

Things grew more difficult for the expellees after 1994 when the Senegalese and Mauritanian governments re-established diplomatic relations. As early as 1992, Mauritanian President Ould Taya stated that Mauritanians outside the country were free to return and enjoy all their rights.[42] One casualty of improving relations was UNHCR's role as provider for the expellees. As the Mauritanian government tried to play down the scope of the continuing refugee situation and to buttress its claims that the expulsions had been of Senegalese citizens only, it pressured Senegal to withdraw UNHCR's mandate to assist expellees. UNHCR's very presence was a testament to the fact that there were non-Senegalese living in the river valley who required international protection. The idea in government circles was that the cessation of food assistance would force the expellees to either return to Mauritania or to fully integrate into the Senegalese population, and that Ould Taya's statement would provide further encouragement for voluntary repatriation. It was to be seen, however, that while the Mauritanian government wanted the expellees to vanish for political reasons, this did not mean that it was about to recognize them again as Mauritanian citizens.

A substantial number of expellees did move back to Mauritania. The UNHCR reported assisting over 37 200 people between 1995 and 1999.[43] However, these returns were termed 'spontaneous' because the UNCHR did not pay for transport nor monitor them. The returnees did not receive any assistance from the Mauritanian government nor any compensation for the property that they had been forced to leave behind years earlier. Those who had been civil servants did not get their jobs back, although they formed the Association of Formal Civil Servants to lobby for their reintegration into government service.[44] Many of these 'spontaneous' returnees had great difficulty regaining their Mauritanian documents. Some reported being able to get Mauritanian documents upon the presentation of copies of their documents that had been destroyed. Some had relatives who had kept their documents, enabling them to apply for renewal; others had former colleagues trace the 'file number' from their civil service employment.[45] Those who were educated and able to get documents could begin functioning as citizens with relative ease.[46] Due to the informality of the return process during these years, however, many individuals who were unable to exert pressure on the bureaucracy, including a high proportion of women, were never able to receive their documents and remained stateless in their own country.

As for the expellees who remained behind in Senegal, they continued to be a thorn in the side of the Mauritanian government, which had not counted on their resilience, tenacity or social cohesion. UNHCR food support ceased in 1995 but, by this time, many of the expellees had acquired small plots of land or a small number of animals that enabled them to survive in Senegal. The cessation of food support was not sufficient therefore to make them return to Mauritania without more specific promises of restoration of property and status. Ould Taya's statement was insufficient in that it did not contain any explicit acknowledgement that Mauritanians had been expelled by their own government, nor did it make any apology. He made no promises with respect to restoration of citizenship, property or compensation. For these reasons, many expellees refused to return.

In the face of UNHCR's failure to provide them with valid documents, many expellees obtained an alternate legal status: Senegalese citizenship. Senegalese law at the time of independence provided that individuals from neighbouring countries who were habitually resident in Senegal could opt for Senegalese nationality.[47] In 1979, a revised law provided for naturalization of those who had been habitually resident for ten years (shortened to five years for those married to Senegalese citizens or those employed in the civil service). Habitual residency is defined as residence with the intention of remaining.[48] Thus, the expellees, who had been in residence for only six years and intended to return to Mauritania, would not have qualified. Some indeed married Senegalese. Others, however, were able to obtain Senegalese identity documents by paying bribes for them, and, as the years passed, the expellees did fulfil the physical residence requirement, if not the requirement of intent to remain.

Few, however, would admit to the possession of Senegalese documents, so their numbers cannot be accurately estimated. One reason for denying Senegalese citizenship was a legal action challenging the expulsions and demanding recognition of their Mauritanian citizenship. This had been pending before the African Commission on Human and Peoples' Rights since 1991. Many expellees naturally felt that to take Senegalese citizenship, or publicly admit that they had done so, would be to validate the Mauritanian government's contention that they had been Senegalese all along and to undermine the basis for their case.

RECOGNITION OF CITIZENSHIP IN PRINCIPLE AND PRACTICE

The expulsions were only one part of the African Commission case, whose plaintiffs included several different Mauritanian NGOs, international

NGOs and individuals in Mauritania submitting cases under pseudonyms.[49] In the years just prior to and after the expulsions, numerous other violations of human rights had occurred, including the torture and murder of hundreds of black officers in the Mauritanian Army, another consequence of the policy of 'Arabization'. The cases, submitted over the course of several years, were joined together by the African Commission. A decision on the cases was no doubt delayed by the uneven quality of the submissions, not to mention the Mauritanian government's strenuous diplomatic efforts to woo the Commission, including hosting a session of the Commission in Mauritania in 1996.

Throughout the years that the Mauritanian cases were before the African Commission, Mauritanian civil society organizations, including associations representing the expellees in Senegal, regularly attended sessions of the Commission, continuously protesting the delays and contradicting statements of government representatives that the events complained of had never happened or had been resolved.

In 2000, the expellees' claim to Mauritanian citizenship was finally validated by the Commission, which found:

> Evicting Black Mauritanians from their houses and depriving them of their Mauritanian citizenship constitutes a violation of article 12,1 [of the African Charter on Human and Peoples' Rights]. The representative of the Mauritanian government described the efforts made to ensure the security of all those who returned to Mauritania after having been expelled. He claimed that all those who so desired could cross the border, or present themselves to the Mauritanian Embassy in Dakar and obtain authorization to return to their village of birth. He affirmed that his government had established a department responsible for their resettlement. The Commission adopts the view that while these efforts are laudable, they do not annul the violation committed by the State.[50]

Many plaintiffs were deeply satisfied by this moral victory. To have their version of events recognized by an organ of the African Union ended the debate over what had actually happened in 1989 and vindicated their claims for the restoration of Mauritanian citizenship, as well as for their lost property. The Commission's decision contained six highly specific recommendations for what the Mauritanian government should do to remedy the numerous violations found.[51] The second of these relates to the expellees; the Mauritania government is ordered:

> to take diligent measures to replace the national identity documents of those Mauritanian citizens, which were taken from them at the time of their expulsion and ensure their return without delay to Mauritania as well as the restitution of the belongings looted from them at the time of the said expulsion; and to take the necessary steps for the reparation of the deprivations of the victims of the above-cited events.[52]

It was predictable that Ould Taya's government, which was still in power, would ignore the African Commission's decision. It was to be five more years before Ould Taya was overthrown in a *coup d'état* in August 2005, and the political landscape was transformed. The transitional government, which took power after the coup against Ould Taya, seemed to view the African Commission's decision as a concise list of prescriptions which, if implemented, would re-establish Mauritania's respectability as a human rights-respecting state in the eyes of the international community. Early on, the head of the transitional government apologized for the expulsions.

The democratically elected government, which followed the transitional one, took power in April 2007 and seemed to recognize the importance of implementing the African Commission's decision. It signed the tripartite agreement with Senegal and the UNCHR for the return of the remaining expellees in November of that year.[53]

The tripartite agreement specifies that those who have returned are able to use UNHCR issued documents as identity cards until the Mauritanian government reissues them national identity cards.[54] It promises returnees restoration of their identity documents within three months. For the vast majority of returnees, this deadline has been missed, although it is still unclear whether this is due to reluctance on the part of the government to restore full citizenship to the returnees, or whether it is simply an oversight or the result of bureaucratic obstacles. The process was certainly slowed down by a *coup d'état* in August 2008, which overthrew the democratically elected government and ushered in another period of transition and political stalemate.

Mauritania again became officially a democratic government after elections were held in July 2009. Throughout the period of transition, the coup government maintained its intention to abide by the tripartite agreement and continue the repatriation of expellees. This is interesting because there are certainly significant forces within Mauritania that oppose the repatriations. They are the same forces that were behind the expulsions in the first place. Even though the returns were halted for some months in mid-2009 due to the rainy season, they resumed again towards the end of the year. As of December 2009, it has been estimated that over 15 000 expellees have returned since the repatriations began nearly two years before.[55]

Although those who have recently come back are frustrated by the slow return of their documents, the question of documentation of citizenship has been partly overshadowed by other problems, such as lack of permanent shelter, access to clean water and health care, and lack of provision of land or livelihoods.

Those in the current wave of returnees have had their rights to

Statelessness and citizenship

citizenship and documentation clearly set out by the tripartite agreement. The greater difficulties in accessing recognition of citizenship are faced by those who returned 'spontaneously' between 1995 and 1999. Because there was no formal system for providing them with identity documents at the time of their return, there is little pressure and no clear, formal procedures to resolve their problems now.

THE PRACTICAL BENEFITS OF CITIZENSHIP

The obvious difficulty faced by those returnees who have not received identity cards, whether they came 'spontaneously' or in the current wave, is continuing vulnerability to charges that they are not Mauritanian and consequent political disenfranchisement. Although the tenor of Mauritanian politics seems to have shifted, and future expulsions now seem highly unlikely, and despite the more immediately pressing problems of poor living conditions and lack of livelihoods, lack of formal recognition of citizenship presents immediate obstacles to daily life and becomes more problematic the longer it continues.

First, there is the difficulty in freedom of movement. As in Senegal, Mauritanian highways have frequent checkpoints at which passengers in public transport are asked to show their identity cards. Between Rosso, the town on the main highway at the border with Senegal, and Medina Salaam, a settlement of both first and second wave of returnees, there are 13 checkpoints within 50 kilometres. For the time being, gendarmes accept UNHCR repatriation papers, so individuals possessing these documents have freedom of movement; there is no guarantee of how long this will continue.

Lack of identity documents is a particular problem for many women who returned 'spontaneously' between 1995 and 1999. If a woman stays within her home village, she may not be affected by the lack of documentation. Travelling on highways, however, can be difficult or impossible. As recently as November 2009, a young woman returnee was trying to reach Nouakchott for medical reasons, but at a gendarmerie check point near Rosso, she was ordered to return to her village, Keur Madicke, because she was not able to show a valid card.[56] One woman had a letter of endorsement from the wilaya to the effect that she should be permitted to move freely, but the gendarme at the checkpoint did not recognize its validity and complained that it was the fourth time that he was forced to return her to her village for lack of an identity card. Now that more than ten years have passed since the first wave of repatriations, identity cards for this population are difficult to obtain.

Access to identity cards appears to be linked more to the date of repatriation and where the returnees settle within Mauritania than with any reasonable suspicions on the part of the government that the individuals are not entitled to citizenship. For the current wave of returnees, some villages have seen all their inhabitants receive cards, while in Medina Salaam, populated by many individuals who returned 'spontaneously', many have failed to receive them.

The system for obtaining identity cards has recently become more efficient: President Aziz has made the distribution of cards a priority. This policy began prior to the most recent presidential elections as part of an attempt to cement his legitimacy. Since his election, the improved policy has continued, but there is a substantial backlog of individuals waiting for their cards.

Individuals who have Senegalese cards can fairly easily exchange them for Mauritanian ones; this, too, was a provision in the tripartite agreement.[57] A birth certificate from either Mauritania or Senegal is sufficient for operations such as school registration and marriage. A national identity card is required for buying and selling land, collecting funds from Western Union and opening a bank account.

However, even national identity cards are not sufficient proof of citizenship in all cases. True proof of nationality is the '*certificate de nationalité*' (certificate of nationality). Obtaining a certificate of nationality is substantially more difficult than getting a national identity card. An official explanation for the confiscation and destruction of national identity cards in 1989 was that all these cards were forged. It would be far more difficult to forge a certificate of nationality. According to some, in the early days after independence for Mauritania, the government readily granted these certificates to skilled individuals from Senegal and others who were ready to join the Mauritanian Army.[58] To register for exams at state schools, civil service exams or university admission, a certificate of nationality is required. In the only known case thus far of a returnee who required a certificate of nationality, the individual was given an exemption, not a permanent solution.

Thus, although the process of granting national identity cards seems to be proceeding somewhat more smoothly than in the first year of repatriations, another documentation hurdle may be looming in the future as certificates of nationality become important for more people.

THE SYMBOLIC SIGNIFICANCE OF CITIZENSHIP AND ITS INSUFFICIENCIES

When returnees are asked why they have chosen to come back to Mauritania, despite knowing that the living conditions in the resettlement sites are very hard and that many of the promises in the tripartite agreement are still not being implemented, they give several answers. One is attachment to the land per se, as much as to Mauritania as a country. One returnee put it thus: 'Here where my ancestors are buried.'[59] Others state that (and this is directly linked to regaining legal recognition of citizenship itself) belonging to Mauritania should be a given. 'The real fight for our rights must be undertaken in our own country, not outside',[60] said one returnee. This conveys the idea that, while citizenship itself does not guarantee all rights, it is an essential tool in the struggle for rights, which must take place through the domestic political process. Notwithstanding how relatively effective the expellees in exile were in keeping implementation of the African Commission's Mauritania decision on the agenda year after year, this battle was waged at the international level. Vindicating their rights in the future will have to be done through the domestic Mauritania political process, and only individuals with citizenship can play a meaningful and active role in domestic politics.

Other returnees have said, 'By getting back our citizenship rights, we recover our pride and self-respect. We disprove those who lied, saying that we were not Mauritanians.'[61] This attitude emphasizes the symbolic importance of citizenship. It explains why many plaintiffs in the African Commission case were nearly satisfied with the decision itself, long before actual return of their citizenship was on the horizon. Taking back citizenship is a symbolic undoing of the wrongs that were committed in 1989.

In contrast to this is a pragmatic attitude, no doubt due in part to what many individuals have undergone, such as having their documents confiscated or destroyed before their eyes, being issued refugee documents in Senegal which were then not renewed, prompting them to take Senegalese citizenship through naturalization, or simply to obtain Senegalese identity cards through bribery, and to then return to Mauritania with new refugee documents to begin a prolonged, frustrating process to obtain new identity cards. Many returnees view citizenship as something that they need in order to obtain employment, to travel and to function on a daily level, but not of great symbolic importance.

In addition to attitudes learned through personal experience, the idea of citizenship is coloured by local culture: in Mauritania, individuals may be more loyal to a specific piece of land ('where my ancestors are buried'), their village or village leader, than to the state. The returnees recognize that legal citizenship is essential to vindicating and protecting their rights, but in addition to the long-term problem of certificates of nationality and in addition to national identity cards is the even more pressing problem of access to land, which has not been solved by the recognition of citizenship. The return of property is a key, equal part of the African Commission's decision against Mauritania.[62] In the case of most of the returnees who are agriculturalists, lack of land means lack of livelihoods. Yet as the population of Mauritania has grown over the past 20 years, and desertification has driven more and more pastoralists from the places of their previous livelihoods and into the more fertile parts of the country, the Senegal River Valley, the pressure on land has enormously increased. After the expulsions in 1989, many Haratines who had been 'freed' or who were dispossessed from their nomadic lifestyles were settled on land vacated by the expellees. While this may have been an injustice, it cannot now be undone without creating another group of dispossessed individuals whose citizenship may not be in doubt but whose livelihoods are severely jeopardized.

In many people's minds, access to citizenship and access to land are closely linked. Both citizenship and land ownership symbolize linkage with the country. The government can hand out documents far more easily than it can hand out parcels of arable land, and while the latest repatriations can be celebrated as an important step towards implementation of an historical legal decision and recognition of rights, seeds of a future conflict may already have been sown. Local administrative authorities must be more proactive in allocating land. Civil society organizations are proposing the creation of an independent commission charged with addressing the land issues in order to prevent latent conflict from exploding.

This is the double-edged sword of citizenship: individuals now have the right to live in Mauritania and fight for their rights, and this should be celebrated. But restoration of citizenship does not guarantee justice or peace.

NOTES

1. *Accord Tripartite, Mauritania-Senegal-UNHCR*, 12 November 2007, (hereinafter Accord Tripartite).
2. Ibid., Article 9.
3. Palmer (1959).
4. Palmer (1971), p. 69.
5. French Ministry of Foreign and European Affairs (n.d.).
6. Chastain (2004).
7. Upchurch (2002).
8. Anti-Slavery International (2009).
9. Handloff (1990).
10. Ibid. p. 42.
11. *Loi No. 1961-112; Loi portant code de la nationalité mauritanienne*, (hereafter *Code de la nationalité*), http://www.unhcr.org/refworld/docid/3ae6b5304.html.
12. The terminology employed to describe different types of citizenship is as yet not well developed. One important distinction is between citizenship that an individual has as a matter of right, and citizenship that she must apply for. In French, the term *'d'origine'* captures in one phrase the notion of citizenship as a matter of right from the moment of birth. In English, the terms 'citizenship from birth' or 'citizenship by birth' are not

so clear. For this reason, I follow Manby's importation of the term 'citizen of origin' to English Manby (2009c), pp.ix–x and p. 33 n.7.

13. Ibid., p. 30.
14. *Code de la nationalité, Article* 8.3.
15. Ibid., Article 9.2.
16. Ibid., Article 13.
17. 'Habitual residence' is neither defined in Mauritanian law nor in international law. In its *Draft Articles on Nationality of Natural Persons in Relation to the Succession of States*, the International Law Commission provides only that habitual residence is a test to determine the relationship of the individual to the state for determining the granting of nationality. Habitual residence is also used throughout the *Hague Convention on the Civil Aspects of International Child Abduction*, but no further definition is provided, although a standard is developing in US courts. *See Draft Articles on Nationality of Natural Persons in relation to the Succession of States with Commentaries* (1999); *Rapport Explicatif de Mlle Elisa Pérez-Vera* (1982); and Vivatvaraphol (2009).
18. *Code de la nationalité, Article* 18.
19. Ibid., Article 19.2.
20. *Ordonnance no. 91.022 du 20 Juillet 1991 portant Constitution de la République Islamique de Mauritanie.*
21. There were, especially in the colonial civil service, quite a few individuals who had been born in Senegal and who came to work in Mauritania when they had finished their education. Neither these individuals nor any children they had in Mauritania were automatically eligible for Mauritania citizenship under the law; however, they either became Senegalese citizens at the time of independence, or Mauritanian citizen by acquisition/naturalization under the five-year residence provision.
22. For example, the Nubians in Kenya had already been resident for generations at the time of Kenyan independence, but were denied Kenyan citizenship and remain of uncertain citizenship status today. See Manby 2009b); also Singo'ei, (2009), p. 38.
23. Although the term 'black Mauritanians' is inaccurate in the literal sense, in that the Haratines, who make up fully a third of the population, are also black, the term is a commonly employed shorthand to refer to all of the sub-Saharan African groups who live in Mauritania, who, although they speak a variety of different languages (as recognized in Article 19.2 of the citizenship law), share political interests, for example, an interest in maintaining the use of French language in official functions.
24. Handloff (1990), pp. 179–80.
25. Muslih and Norton (1991), p. 7.
26. Ibid.
27. Parker (1991), pp. 155–71, especially p. 164.
28. Refugees International (2007).
29. Kinne (2001), pp. 597, 602; Affidavit of N.M.K., 14, 22 July 2004, on file with the Open Society Justice Initiative.
30. Affidavit of H.A.B., 15, 26 June 2004, on file with the Open Society Justice Initiative.
31. Ibid.
32. Affidavit of I.B., 14 November 2006, on file with the Open Society Justice Initiative.
33. Affidavit of N.M.K. 15, 22 July 2004, on file with the Open Society Justice Initiative.
34. Affidavit of M.A.O., 27, 24 July 2004, on file with the Open Society Justice Initiative.
35. Affidavit of H.M., 9, 26 July 2004, on file with the Open Society Justice Initiative.
36. Affidavit of M.G.D., 13, 26 July 2004, on file with the Open Society Justice Initiative.
37. Noble (1989), section 1, p. 1, column 2.
38. Affidavit of M.H.S., 10, 24 June 2004, on file with the Open Society Justice Initiative.
39. Affidavit of F.B.G., 16, 24 July 2004, on file with the Open Society Justice Initiative.
40. Affidavit of F.O.T, 15 November 2006, on file with the Open Society Justice Initiative.
41. Interview with XX, 2004, on video, on file with the Open Society Justice Initiative.
42. Affidavit of IB., 14 November 2006, on file with the Open Society Justice Initiative.
43. UNHCR (2008).

44. Ibid. n. 49.
45. Affidavit of A.K., 14 November 2006, on file with the author.
46. Ibid.
47. *Code de la nationalité sénégalaise*, Article *29*.
48. *Loi no. 79 .01 du 4 Janvier 1979*, Article 12.
49. Malawi African Association and Others/Mauritania, (2000).
50. Ibid., Paragraph 126.
51. The African Commission's decision on Mauritania is groundbreaking in several respects. Foremost among these is the specificity of the recommendations it makes, which was unprecedented up to that time. The African Commission recommends specific policy and legislative action. Ibid., Recommendations 1–6.
52. Ibid., Recommendation 2.
53. In addition to tackling the issue of repatriations, the new government also began a legislative process that culminated in the adoption of detailed law setting out punishments for the ownership of slaves, including specifying compensation of those who were 'freed' by their former masters.
54. Accord Tripartite, Article 16.
55. Sagna (2009).
56. Souleymane Sagna interview with the author, 14 December 2009.
57. Accord Tripartite, Article 16.
58. From 1976 to the early 1980s, Mauritania was engaged in a military conflict in Western Sahara, which it had partially annexed upon agreement with Morocco once the Spanish withdrew.
59. XX, interviewed by Souleymane Sagna, 2009.
60. Ibid.
61. Ibid.
62. Malawi African Association and Others/Mauritania, Recommendation 2.

9. Statelessness, citizenship and belonging in Estonia

Raivo Vetik

After regaining independence in August 1991 and reintroducing the *Citizenship Act* of 1938 half a year later in February 1992, about one third of the population of Estonia became stateless. The 1992 law was based on the idea of the 'legal continuity' of the pre-war Estonian Republic, which means that only those persons who were citizens before Estonia's incorporation into the Soviet Union in 1940 and their descendants were entitled to automatic citizenship. Migrants from the Soviet period and their descendants, by contrast, had to go through the process of naturalization. The law required two years of residence before a person is entitled to apply for citizenship and a further one year waiting period before the applicant can be naturalized. The law also included a loyalty oath and restricts certain categories of people from gaining citizenship (military officers, foreign intelligence officers etc.). Last but not least, the law required knowledge of the Estonian language.[1]

This chapter examines the benefits of citizenship to formerly stateless people in Estonia. It analyses how the change in the legal status of the Russian-speaking minority population in Estonia, above all the acquisition of Estonian citizenship, has affected their socio-economic and socio-cultural adaptation. To this end, it draws upon two principal sources of information: evidence gathered in a public opinion poll on the integration of ethnic Russians in Estonia, conducted in spring 2008,[2] and in-depth interviews connected to the poll.[3] The chapter examines, first, the history of citizenship reform in Estonia and considers reasons why statelessness has persisted nearly 20 years after Estonia regained independence. Second, the chapter discusses the legal status of Estonian Russians and its connection to their socio-economic, socio-cultural and emotional adaptation in the independent state of Estonia.

PERSISTENCE OF WIDESPREAD STATELESSNESS OF ESTONIAN RUSSIANS

The most controversial consequence of the 1992 citizenship law lay in the fact that although it was presented in an ethnically neutral language, the law nonetheless principally affected the Russian-speaking minority, who had migrated to Estonia during the Soviet period. However, in spite of this law, the social rights enjoyed by the Russian-speaking minority were not remarkably different from those of the Estonian citizens who had only two (though important) additional rights – the right to vote and to run in the parliamentary elections as well as to apply for certain positions that are related to protecting the public interest.[4] The fact that non-citizens enjoyed the same social rights as those of citizens partly explains why the citizenship policy that most marginalized Estonian Russians did not bring about any significant ethnic mobilization, as might otherwise have been expected,[5] and why, over time, Russian-speakers considered other alternatives, including the adoption of Russian citizenship, on the one hand and even remaining as stateless non-citizens in Estonia, on the other.

In 1995 a new *Citizenship Act* was adopted in Estonia. In order to submit a citizenship application, the following criteria, defined in the new law, need to be met: a person must have been residing in Estonia before 1 July 1990 and possess a long-term or permanent residence permit at the time of submitting the request. If one of these requirements is met, the person applying for Estonian citizenship must also (a) have proficiency in the Estonian language on a day-to-day level; (b) be at least 15 years of age; (c) have lived in Estonia on the basis of a residence permit for at least eight years, at least five years permanently; (d) have knowledge of the Estonian Constitution and the *Citizenship Act*; (e) have permanent lawful income sufficient to support himself or herself and his or her dependents; (f) have a registered residence in Estonia; (g) be loyal to the state of Estonia; and, (h) take an oath of loyalty (*Citizenship Act* 1995).

Since 1995 the *Citizenship Act* has been amended several times in order to ease the requirements for obtaining citizenship for certain categories of non-citizens. For example, in 2004 the waiting period for naturalization was reduced to six months and a simplified naturalization procedure has been established for people with disabilities. In addition, stateless children who were born after 1992 may also obtain citizenship with a simplified procedure if both parents are stateless. According to Article 13, section 4 of the *Citizenship Act*, a simplified naturalization procedure can be sought for minors less than 15 years of age who were born in Estonia after 26 February 1992. This can be done by either of two parents, a single parent or an adoptive parent, who has or have, by the time of submitting the application, legally resided in Estonia for no less than five years and who are not considered as citizens by any other state (for example, persons with undetermined citizenship).

Compared to other countries, the naturalization requirements in Estonia can be regarded as rather liberal. However, what makes the Estonian citizenship law exceptional is that at the moment it was brought into force, it left a considerable part of the population without citizenship. The exclusive nature of the citizenship policy in Estonia should be considered in the context of the high level of mistrust between the Estonian majority and Russian-speaking minority population at the beginning of the transition into independent statehood. This can be illustrated, for example, by the fact that while in the 1991 independence referendum a majority of Estonians voted for Estonian independence from the Soviet Union, only 25 per cent of the Estonian Russians were in favour.[6] Thus only six months before actually regaining independence, Estonian society was fundamentally polarized over one of the most existential political issues, which inevitably evoked strong mutual fears regarding the future of the state and its mixed population.

As of 31 December 2009, there were 104 813 persons with undetermined citizenship in Estonia, including 2153 children under 15 years of age who held long-term residence permits and whose both parents had undetermined citizenship. This number is particularly glaring in a country with a population of less than 1.4 million and which has established procedures for the acquisition of citizenship. The core legal Act regulating the foundation of the non-citizens' status in Estonia is the *Law on Aliens* adopted in 1993. The law refers to both citizens of foreign states and stateless persons as 'aliens'. The Estonian legislation makes no distinction between these two categories of non-citizens. In general, non-citizens in Estonia enjoy the same rights and free access to social protection as citizens. For example, aliens with any type of residence permit are subjects of the *Law on Social Protection,*[7] *Law on Social Protection of Unemployed,*[8] *Law on Social Protection of Disabled,*[9] *Law on State Pension Insurance,*[10] and the *Law on State Support for Families,*[11] and so on.

While there was considerable demand for naturalization by stateless non-citizens in the first half of the 1990s, the pace has since slowed down. In 1999, the percentage of Estonian citizens within the population had risen to 80 per cent but over the next decade it had only increased slightly to 84 per cent in 2008. The current population of non-citizens now stands at 16 per cent of the total population of Estonia: of this 16 per cent, about half are stateless and the other half are citizens of other states, above all Russia. Thus, from 1992 to 2008 about 150 000 people have been naturalized in Estonia while another 100 000 people have become citizens of Russia.

A study of ethnic Russians conducted in April 2008 offered four explanations for the persistent and widespread statelessness among Estonian Russians. These include: (1) difficulties in learning the Estonian language and passing the citizenship test; (2) emotional aversion to applying for citizenship related to the fact that many Estonian Russians feel that, similarly to ethnic Estonians, they should have been granted citizenship automatically after independence was restored in Estonia; (3) preferring Russian citizenship due to better travel and other opportunities; and (4) lack of Estonian citizenship does not affect a person's daily life.

The non-citizen respondents considered difficulties with learning the Estonian language to be the most significant reason for not applying for citizenship. Six out of ten respondents in interview mentioned the language issue as one of the reasons for not obtaining Estonian citizenship thus far. The significance of the problems related to learning Estonian is also affirmed by the integration monitoring exercise, conducted in parallel with the in-depth interviews, in which over 90 per cent of Estonian Russians named difficulties with learning the Estonian language as the reason why many Estonian Russians do not yet have Estonian citizenship. The main obstacles mentioned in the interview study were the absence of contact with Estonians as well as the cost of the courses and their own sense that the lessons should be provided free of charge:

> I cannot speak Estonian sufficiently to pass the language exam. Estonian is very hard to learn, because there are so few contacts between the two ethnic groups in our country. Some people do communicate in Estonian at work, but I worked at a place where everybody was Russian. So, I use Estonian only in shops, about 5–10 minutes per day. But this is not sufficient . . . . We have not been provided with proper conditions for studying Estonian. That is the first reason why I have not applied for Estonian citizenship. (F, 37y, Tallinn).

She added:

> Estonian language courses cost an immense amount of money. I cannot afford to pay 1500–2000 kroons per month [US$135–$180] for them, because I have two children and one of them, besides, is ill. And so I am faced with a vicious circle: if I do not know Estonian, I cannot find a well-paying job, and therefore cannot pay for the courses. (F, 37y, Tallinn)

The second group of reasons is related to emotional aversion, which stems from the opinion that the citizenship policy of the Estonian state is unjust by its very nature. Many respondents felt bitter for not receiving citizenship unconditionally like most ethnic Estonians did at the beginning of the 1990s, despite being born and raised in Estonia and living there for their entire lives. The need to apply for citizenship was considered demeaning by most respondents, and, in their judgement, the state should care more about its residents and not give privileges to one ethnic group. During the integration monitoring, two thirds of the Russian-speaking respondents agreed with these types of claims explaining the reasons behind statelessness:

> But overall, it is all so strange that second or third generation people, born here, are not offered citizenship. In the USA, they offer citizenship even if a person was born in the airplane, provided that the airline was American. But overall, I think that our country is still young and the attitude towards citizenship is still not so serious. (F, 37y, Tallinn)

> We have not applied, and do not intend to apply for citizenship in the future. I was born here and have lived here for over 40 years. I already have two children here. And I consider applying for citizenship a big humiliation for myself. Nothing like this exists in any other state of the European Union. (M, 41y, Jõhvi)

In addition to the fact that applying for citizenship is considered by some to be demeaning and unfair, other respondents said that they feel they are second-rate persons in the eyes of Estonians and the Estonian state. Thus, they perceived the attitude of ethnic Estonians as hostile and this deters some Russian-speaking non-citizens from applying for Estonian citizenship:

> I have already applied for Russian citizenship, for I will no doubt receive it without problems, just like that. I actually do not care which citizenship I receive. If I had lived in the USA or England for a long time, I could have already become an American or Englishman. But our situation with these 'wolf' passports is atrocious. They have already made such a big deal out of their nationality that we are like flies to them with these gray passports. We were simply segregated from the very start. (M, 41y, Jõhvi)

> The second reason why I do not wish to apply for citizenship lies in the fact that I do not want to become a so-called second-rate citizen because I will be thought of as this person who became a citizen through naturalization. But why acquire citizenship then? Anyway, these feelings that I have now will remain the same, my attitude will not change. I seriously do not like this differentiation: you have received citizenship through naturalization, but I am a true citizen. Therefore we can speak of first and second-rate citizens. But we are all, in fact, equal . . . . All people must be regarded as equal. There is no sense in wasting time, money and emotions to become a citizen, if in the end you do not gain anything, because their attitude will stay the same. But the color of the passport

does not mean anything, if the attitude towards me stays the same. (F, 35y, Tallinn)

The third group of reasons for not choosing Estonian citizenship is related to preferring Russian citizenship. According to the integration monitoring data, this reason was mentioned by 70 per cent of the respondents.[12] It can be added that applying for Russian citizenship has abruptly increased in Estonia in recent years.[13] Reasons for this were explored in the interview study and categories of answers are identified below:

1. Applying for Russian citizenship is easier than applying for Estonian citizenship:

   Being a noncitizen is very difficult. Also, some people have relatives in Russia. Some take Russian citizenship because they have tried but not succeeded in obtaining Estonian citizenship. Some elderly people take up Russian citizenship only because they are unable to learn the language. (F, 35y, Tallinn)

2. Travelling to Russia is easier:

   Maybe, because it is cheaper and for business as well. The cigarettes and lots of other things, like children's clothes, are cheaper there. This is how many people probably reason. On the other hand, many have relatives on the other side. I also have relatives there. If you want to visit, you need to apply for a visa and so on. (M, 41y, Jõhvi)

3. The impact of the removal of the Bronze Soldier monument from the centre of Tallinn by the Estonian government:[14]

   I think that one of the motivating reasons for applying for Russian citizenship has been the April events. It was like a big blow to the Russians' self-respect. These events also brought about big changes. In these times, it was almost impossible to find work. My husband encountered it himself. Maybe some people think that their children would receive higher quality education in Russia. And even if people have worked hard with the Estonian language, they think that if they go to Russia, it will be easier for them to find work, but I doubt that. Because Russia is a rapidly developing state, it gives people more opportunities, for example, to find work. (F, 37y, Tallinn)

The fourth group of reasons has to do with the opinion that the lack of Estonian citizenship does not affect a person's daily life and this is why people do not want to make the effort required for obtaining citizenship. About three quarters of the respondents of the Integration Monitoring project suggested this was the case.[15] We encountered the following answers to the questions of whether not having Estonian citizenship affects their lives:

He [the interviewee's husband] does not intend to apply for Estonian citizenship, because he knows that he already came here at a more mature age and cannot learn Estonian language in any way. He doesn't apply for some other state citizenship because he also feels comfortable with the gray passport. My husband does not feel that he is discriminated here in any way. And he has also not encountered that. He has his own business here. He is very loyal to Estonia, but as his business here is doing well and the lack of citizenship does not bother him, he does not feel that applying for some country's citizenship is necessary. . . .

I think that those people who want citizenship do everything to receive it, but those who do not want it will never get it. Citizenship is not important to some, because they are satisfied with their lives and also have a good income. So they don't even have time to think about citizenship. (F, 33y, Tallinn)

The pragmatic reasons also include circumstances that are related to the difficulties of stateless parents in deciding on the future options of their underage children:

My second child is a boy. And I don't want anyone to send him into the army, no matter if it's the Estonian or Russian one, to fight in some strange place without him agreeing to it. I want to leave him the right to choose which country's citizenship he wants. (F, 37y, Tallinn)

My son wants to go study in Russia and that is hard to do with a Russian visa. The language barrier is also a problem. It's easier for him to study in Russian in his native language, than in Estonia in a foreign language. But my daughter is applying for Estonian citizenship, since she is planning on continuing her studies in Estonia (M, 41y, Jõhvi)

For older non-citizens, their desire not to acquire Estonian citizenship may also be understood as a form of complacency: there is a large share of older and retired people among the Russian citizens, who have lower expectations and, at the same time, enjoy the relatively high level of social security in Estonia, when compared to Russia.[16]

EFFECT OF CITIZENSHIP STATUS ON ADAPTATION OF ESTONIAN RUSSIANS IN ESTONIAN SOCIETY

The Integration Monitoring (IM) project referred to above was conducted four times during the past ten years (in 2000, 2002, 2005 and 2008). The IM project data show the trends in applications for citizenship along with the factors that explain any changes. Comparing the reasons why people did not apply for citizenship from 2000 and 2008, the research team identified explanations relating to the fulfilment of citizenship requirements, pragmatic reasons and participants' feeling of connection to Estonia.

In the 2008 monitoring exercise 34 per cent of Russian Estonians surveyed considered the inability to learn Estonian to be the primary reason for their refusal to naturalize in Estonia. A further 23 per cent stated that the reason why they opted against citizenship lies in the humiliating nature of the citizenship requirements. Participants noted that they still felt an attachment to Estonia and few claimed to have turned down the possibility of citizenship on the grounds that they did not have a sense of belonging to Estonia (10 per cent) or were disinterested in national politics (11 per cent). Very few rejected citizenship on the grounds of global irrelevance, given the size of Estonia (7 per cent).

The findings from the 2008 monitoring exercise, when compared with the earlier exercises, suggest that there has been a change in the intensity of the negative attitudes among the Estonian Russians towards the process of acquiring Estonian citizenship. More people appear to have come to appreciate the difficulty of learning Estonian, and this may also have discouraged them from applying for citizenship.[17] The findings also indicate a decline in the Estonian Russian's perception of the value of integration and the state's integrationist policies. This tendency is corroborated by comparing the data on citizenship preferences gathered during the four integration monitoring studies. In 2000, the preference for Estonian citizenship was on the rise, reaching its highest point in 2005 (at 74 per cent), but by 2008 the number of those who desired Estonian citizenship dropped to half (51 per cent). During the same time period, the desirability of Russian citizenship increased steadily from just 5 per cent in 2000 to 11 per cent in 2005 and to 19 per cent in 2008. These changes suggest a new protest identity among Estonian Russians, which has notably increased in recent years.[18]

As noted above, some participants stated during in-depth interviews that remaining a non-citizen did not have a profound effect on their daily lives and that they could not see any benefit to taking up Estonian citizenship. However, evidence from integration monitoring data suggests that even if ethnic Russians encounter societal discrimination, citizenship does make a difference. The integration monitorings (as well as other studies) record that in general the socio-economic situation of the Russian-speaking population in Estonia has gradually improved as evidenced by the steadily decreasing pay gap between the salaries of ethnic Estonians and Estonian Russians.[19] Education rather than ethnic identity now seems to be the main reason for the existing differences in earnings between the ethnic groups, as fewer Russian-speakers have access to higher education and hence are disadvantaged from taking up the best-paid jobs.[20]

Between the three groups among the Russian-speaking population there are some important differences in terms of human capital and adaptability, which are not based on nationality status. This is nonetheless important to consider: compared to Russian citizens and ethnic Russian non-citizens, Estonian Russians who hold Estonian citizenship tend to be younger, better educated, more proficient in Estonian and other languages and have a higher employment status. People who acquired Russian citizenship, by contrast, tend to belong to the older generation, have less education and their Estonian language skills are not as strong, mainly because they reside in Eastern Estonia where the population is mostly Russian-speaking. At the same time, their socio-economic situation is somewhat better than that of people with no citizenship at all.

The Russian-speaking citizens of Estonia are also characterized by a greater degree of social confidence compared to the stateless persons. They are more optimistic about their future. They do not feel inferior within the society, and they are prepared to protect their rights. While there is a marked difference between Estonian-speaking and Russian-speaking Estonian citizens in terms of the way they evaluate their economic situation, this gap is closing. Progress has been made over the past decade and as a result, those who seek to integrate by opting for Estonian citizenship are reportedly able to lead better lives than those who remain stateless non-citizens.

The data of the integration monitoring studies indicate that knowledge of the Estonian language among Russian-speakers has gradually improved over the last decade. However, it is important to differentiate between two opposing tendencies. First, the utilitarian significance of learning Estonian has become stronger, meaning that people feel that the Estonian language is important for them and that they need it to maintain good employment. On the other hand, the integrative potential of learning Estonian has decreased in the opinion of many Estonian Russians. This is confirmed by the fact that learning Estonian is considered less important for achieving mutual trust and an equal standing in society. For example, in the monitoring of 2005, the positive responses to the questions – does learning Estonian increase confidence and help one achieve an equal position in society – were 68 per cent and 64 per cent, respectively. In the monitoring survey of 2008, however, only 38 per cent and 23 per cent responded positively to the same questions.[21]

Thus it can be said that while structural integration of Estonian Russians has gradually improved, the indicators of identificational integration, understood in the context of national integration and the development of shared values and acceptance of national symbols, have worsened over recent years. In addition to what has already been mentioned, this is also affirmed by other data from the IM project 2008 – for example, the trust of the Russian-speaking population toward Estonian state institutions and the numbers of those who feel that they are part of the Estonian society have decreased remarkably over recent years.[22] In addition, Estonian Russians perceive the opportunities available to them in Estonia with mistrust. Poll data records that 80–90 per cent of Estonian Russians believe that the opportunities for ethnic Estonians are better in the labour market, the educational system and politics than they are for Estonian Russians. As a result, integration through naturalization and language acquisition is seen not so much as a socially valuable act that furthers adaptation and relations between the main ethnic communities but rather as an instrumental choice to improve individual's standard of living.[23] A closer look reveals that such sentiments have emerged quite recently. Until 2005, the attitudes of Estonian Russians regarding these issues were generally becoming more positive, but have now suffered an abrupt decline. In the literature, this has been explained mostly by the significant increase in the politization of the ethnic issue and conflicting historical memories of ethnic Estonians and ethnic Russians.[24]

CONCLUSION: CITIZENSHIP AND LOYALTY RECONSIDERED

The underlying ideology of Estonian citizenship policy assumes the statelessness issue in Estonia has to do with loyalty; that is, if a person successfully passes the Estonian language and citizenship exams, then that is presumed to prove his or her loyalty to the Estonian state making them worthy of Estonian citizenship. The logic behind such reasoning holds that those who acquire Estonian citizenship demonstrate through this formal legal act that they have successfully integrated into Estonian society by having adopted the so-called 'Estonian mindset'.[25]

In practice, however, for most Estonian Russians, obtaining Estonian citizenship is more of a pragmatic and instrumental step motivated foremost by seeking the socio-economic advantages that follow citizenship.[26] This claim is supported by the integration monitoring exercises as well as other studies cited above. Thus, acquiring citizenship and learning Estonian cannot be taken as a one-time solution regarding issues related to personal identity and social integration.[27]

The Russian-language population in Estonia is in large part not satisfied with the citizenship policy the Estonian state has pursued as it is perceived to be unfair towards their group. The obligation to apply for citizenship, as a result of the legalistic citizenship policy introduced at the beginning of the 1990s, is viewed as demeaning to those people who have lived in Estonia all their life. Perceptions of unfairness as well as difficulties in learning the Estonian language and passing the citizenship exam are the main reasons for the Estonian Russians' refusal to acquire Estonian citizenship. In addition, pragmatic personal calculations and the ease with which Russian-speakers may obtain Russian citizenship, as well as efforts of the Russian state to engage its diaspora, are important additional factors in persuading people to abandon their pursuit of Estonian citizenship.

One of the main findings of this study is that there are measurable benefits associated with the acquisition of citizenship by formerly stateless ethnic Russians in Estonia. This conclusion is, however, set against a particular context: namely, the unusually strong non-discrimination provisions recorded in law and Estonia's geo-political situation. In particular, the proximity to Russia and the possibility of obtaining Russian citizenship while simultaneously benefiting from residency in a European Union member state has made Estonian citizenship less desirable today than when independence was restored in 1991. While Estonian citizenship offers more advantages, there are benefits associated with the acquisition of Russian citizenship too. By contrast, stateless non-citizens expressed comparatively more feelings of rejection, inferiority and passivity. They fare worst of all in the labour market. In this context then, citizenship is indeed important.

NOTES

1. Kionka and Vetik (1996).
2. 'Integration Monitoring 2008' was carried out by this author and his colleagues at Tallinn University and Tartu University in the form of a statewide poll, where oral interviews and the proportional random cohort method were used to question 1505 people aged 15–74 in March and April 2008. Among the respondents, 83 per cent had Estonian citizenship, 8 per cent had Russian citizenship, 2 per cent citizenship in another state and 7 per cent of the cohort was stateless. In the cohort, there were 992 Estonians and 513 other nationalities; among the latter 51 per cent had Estonian citizenship, 23 per cent were Russian citizens, 5 per cent citizens of another state and 21 per cent were stateless persons. In compiling the socio-demographic characterization of the model, population statistics data from 1 January 2008 were used. To reduce the differences that arose when comparing the model and the representativeness of the poll results, the results obtained were considered according to the following socio-demographic features: place of residence, gender, age, religion and education.
3. The research team conducted ten in-depth interviews with ethnic Russians who had children below 15 years of age with undetermined citizenship. Five interviews were carried out with respondents from Tallinn, two from Narva and one each from Jõhvi, Sillamäe, and Kohtla-Järve. In Tallinn, people from different parts of town were interviewed (three from Lasnamäe, one from Õismäe and one from the city centre area).

The sample was chosen from an anonymized list provided by the State Chancellery and which included Estonian residents with undetermined citizenship who also had children below 15 years of age. The full list included 2437 cases. The gross sample was determined to be ten times bigger, and the stratified sample ($n = 100$) chosen from the total population was divided into strata on the basis of residence areas and the children's age. In each stratum, simple random sampling was employed after that. The people included in the sample were sent contact letters, introducing them to the research and asking for their consent for participation. Eighteen people demonstrated their willingness to take part in the study, of whom ten where chosen for the interview according to the initially stipulated condition for residential variety, as well as accounting for variety in gender, age and one's status as a single or joint parent.

4. *Public Service Act*, 25 January 1995; *Riigikogu Election Act*, 12 June 2002.
5. Kolsto and Melberg (2002); Smith et al. (1998).
6. Vetik (1993).
7. Law on Social Protection, Article 4.
8. Law on Social Protection of Unemployed, Article 2.
9. Law on Social Protection of Disabled, Article 3.
10. Law on State Pension Insurance, Article 4.
11. Law on State Support for Families, Article 2.
12. Ibid.
13. Kase (2008).
14. The so-called 'Bronze Soldier crisis' in April 2007 culminated in massive protests against the removal of the Soviet era war memorial from downtown Tallinn by young Russians. The confrontation with police grew into vandalizing in Tallinn's old town, as a result of which over 1000 people were arrested.
15. 'Integration Monitoring 2008'.
16. Lauristin (2008).
17. In 2000 the percentage of Estonian Russians who considered their inability to learn Estonian to be a reason for not naturalizing was 34 per cent; in 2008 it was already 53 per cent.
18. Burch and Smith (2007); Hackmann and Lehti (2008); Wertsch (2008).
19. Leping and Toomet (2008).
20. Kasearu and Trumm (2008).
21. Vihalemm (2008).
22. Vetik (1993).
23. Ibid.
24. Ibid.
25. Steen (2006).
26. Lauristin (2008); Vihalemm (2008).
27. Vetik (1993).

10. Arabia's Bidoon

Abbas Shiblak

The word Bidoon is an Arabic term meaning 'without'. It is used in Arabia and the Gulf States for those who are without nationality.[1] Most of the Bidoon are people who have been long settled in Kuwait and nearby states, and the majority of them are Bedouins of nomadic origin. However, these categories are not coterminous and one should not confuse the term Bidoon with that of Bedouin. It has been estimated that the number of Bidoon in Kuwait before the Iraqi invasion of 1990 was between 240 000 and 250 000, but (although the full scope of the problem in the region is unknown) that figure is estimated to have been cut in half in the aftermath of the invasion to approximately 80 000–120 000 persons.[2]

This chapter focuses on the situation of the Bidoon in countries the researcher visited in 2009 – Kuwait, Bahrain and Oman. In addition, the researcher gathered desk information and conducted interviews with human rights experts and exiles in Europe to learn more about other Gulf States that the team was not able to visit.

Focusing primarily on Kuwait because of the size of the population, the research examines the causes of the phenomenon of statelessness in a lightly populated but rich oil-producing country where issues of security and the place of foreign migrant workers remain highly sensitive. The first section describes Kuwait's nationality law while the second part examines the human impact of restrictions imposed on the Bidoon community. This is followed by an assessment of efforts made by the government to deal with this community of stateless persons who for decades were considered part and parcel of the Kuwaiti society. The situation of Bidoon in other states is then also addressed.

LITERATURE SURVEY

There are a limited number of studies on the Bidoon in Kuwait and else-where in the region. A small booklet published in 1994 by Rasheed Al-Anezi, a respected Kuwaiti scholar and expert on international law, offers a legal analysis focused on the residency status of the Bidoon in Kuwait.[3] This study appeared at a time when the Kuwaiti authorities started to review the state's policy towards the Bidoon against the backdrop of the invasion of Kuwait by Iraq, the liberation of 1991 and the backlash against the Bidoon that followed. Hassan A. El-Najjar, [4] a Palestinian American sociologist has also written on the history of the Bidoon and their fate following the 1991 Gulf War.[5]

Human Rights Watch released a report in 1995 that provided insight into the way that the Bidoon were treated during that crucial period.[6] The short but concise reports issued by Refugees International were perhaps the only unofficial reports that have shed light on the Bidoon status during the last few years.[7]

At least two Kuwaiti scholars wrote about the Bidoon but never published their work. The first was written in 2003 by Ghanim Al-Najjar, a Kuwaiti academic who became involved in an earlier internal study by the Kuwait parliament that was completed in 1996.[8] The second was a doctoral dissertation recently completed by a Kuwaiti student at Sorbonne University.[9] The author has made use of these studies to understand the evolution and the complexity of the Bidoon issue and to provide context for the more recent developments.

Kuwaiti media reports, especially printed articles, broadly keep pace with the ongoing debate and developments in relation to the Bidoon issue. The Kuwaiti press also publishes official statements, interviews with parliamentarians, reader comments and in some cases self-censored stories by Bidoon themselves.

The author also consulted a number of websites on the Bidoon of Kuwait (also known as *Muntadayat*, an Arabic word for debates) that include news, articles and comments.[10] While these sites give free space especially for the young to engage in and tell their own stories, the *Muntadayat* are accountable to the state security agency and those who manage the sites tend to be careful not to offend anybody or engage in politics. They are, therefore, of limited research value. Finally, the author consulted recent reports on Bahrain, Oman and the United Arab Emirates (UAE) regarding nationality and human rights issues published by monitoring bodies as well as personal accounts that appeared in the press.[11]

METHODOLOGY

Interviews in Kuwait were arranged by members of the Bidoon community in the United Kingdom (UK) and carried out with concerned parties including family members and close associates in order to understand the benefits to those who attained citizenship. Informal questions were asked to establish the strength of links with Kuwait, their treatment there, their socio-legal status, documentation, work, education, health care and housing situation.

All participants interviewed asked not to have their identities disclosed for fear of reprisals by the authorities. Even those who have settled in the UK are afraid of measures that might be taken against friends and relatives in Kuwait and of losing their own opportunity to visit the country.

Two interviews regarding the stateless in Bahrain (one in Bahrain and one in the UK) were conducted with activists, one of whom was later detained. At the time of the interviews in Bahrain, there was a tense political situation (stand-off) between the government and the opposition groups.

In Oman, the researcher relied on interviews conducted with officials from the Foreign Ministry in charge of the Omani communities abroad. Further, the interviewer met participants from the UAE in Oman who reported that there is currently a review process underway, but in the absence of official documentation, the researcher was advised that the only way forward in his quest for information on the effects of changes in the naturalization procedures was through informal and unofficial channels.

LEGAL FRAMEWORK

Kuwait's 1959 *Nationality Law* was issued when it was still a British protectorate and before the country became independent in 1961. The law defined Kuwaiti nationals as persons who were settled in Kuwait prior to 1920 and maintained normal residence there until the date of publication of the law. As noted above, the Bidoon are mainly descendants of indigenous Bedouin tribes who lived in the northern part of Arabia before states were created.

Extended tribes such as Shammar, Anezi and Mtair roamed freely across what are present day borders. The Bidoon ancestors, members of these tribes, had lived their nomadic way of life for centuries. They were not pleased by the idea of belonging to any specific place. Most of the time they were on the move in the 'Badiya,' the desert on the borders of present day Syria, Iraq, Jordan, Kuwait and Saudi Arabia.

Nationality was a foreign concept for the semi-nomadic societies of Arabia. For the majority of the population, citizenship (or any other official documents issued by the newly established central government at the time) did not have the significance it does now. The structure and processes of the central government were still in their basic form and undergoing refinement. In addition, illiteracy was quite common among Bedouins and means of communication among the scattered communities was poor. Radio was a rare commodity and many did not hear of nor follow the actions of the central government. Others did not bother to register in the population census nor did they apply for a passport. Regardless, it is widely understood that the ruling family and its allied founding families determined citizenship arbitrarily.

Al-Najjar (2003) argues that when the 1959 nationality law was issued, it was estimated that approximately one-third of the population was recognized as having *Jinseya Asliyah* (genuine nationality) and were bona fide citizens. These included the so-called founding families of the country. Another third had *Jinseya Tajnees* (granted nationality) by naturalization. These were granted partial citizenship rights. The remaining third was classified as *Bidoon jinsiya* which means without nationality.[12] AL-Najjar did not specify whose estimation it was, but there is reason to believe that such estimates were probably made in the parliament study of 1996 on which his study is based.

From the time of Kuwait's independence in 1961 until the late 1960s, there was no strict border control, and the Bedouin tribes continued to move freely across the Kuwait-Saudi and Kuwait-Iraqi borders. According to Al-Anezi (1994) and Al-Najjar (2003), the Kuwaiti government not only tolerated the presence of the Bidoon but also offered them a financial incentive to settle and work in Kuwait due to the need for greater manpower following the discovery of oil. Al-Anezi argues that this is why the Bidoon were not considered to be foreign residents or guest workers and why they were exempted from visa restrictions.[13]

The Bidoon were treated very much as Kuwaiti citizens until the mid 1980s. They had full civil, social and economic rights with access to government services including housing, work, education and medical care, although they did not enjoy political rights. At one stage they constituted 80 to 90 per cent of the Kuwaiti Army[14] as well as the bulk of the police force. They filled the lower ranks while command was left to the sons of the ruling family and other founding families.[15]

According to Al-Anezi, the Bidoon believed that equality would prevail and eventually their government would extend them citizenship. He argues that withdrawing these rights from the Bidoon after four decades had no legal or moral justification.

THE SECURITY DIMENSION: NATIONALITY VERSUS LOYALTY

Over the last three decades, modernization has transformed Gulf societies at an unexpectedly rapid rate. The region's countries have become magnets for foreign workers. Numbers vary, but they seem to constitute approximately 30 per cent to 85 per cent of the worker populations in Gulf Cooperation Council (GCC) countries. Initially, the largest numbers of workers were from Arab countries, but were gradually surpassed by Asians. Population figures for Kuwait in 2008 show that foreign workers, mainly individuals of Asian origin, equal about two-thirds of the overall population which is approximately 3 399 637.[16] This introduction of non-nationals into the loyalty and security conscious states of Arabia raises sensitive issues, since newcomers are thought to challenge state security and identity as well as society and culture.

In most of the Gulf States, nationality is still largely associated with loyalty, and it has been treated more like a gift granted by the head of state rather than as a human or constitutional right. Loyalty is an important matter in traditional tribal societies and throughout Arabia where it is the informal criterion for naturalization. It should be noted that Al-Saud rulers of Saudi Arabia once expelled their tribal opponents, mainly al-Rashid and their allies (then Shammar or Eneza). As a result, these tribes were denied citizenship and until very recently none of these tribes was allowed to join the army or hold public office.[17] More recently the Qatari Emir denationalized an entire tribe of Murrah (5000–6000 members) loyal to his ousted father because they refused to grant loyalty to the son who arranged the *coup d'état* against his father.[18]

An important consequence of the priority given to loyalty as a means of participation in the state has been the breakdown of tribal arrangements. The tribe as a form of social bond was replaced by a new order based on groups of individuals who aspire to wealth and power. Privileges are largely determined by closeness to the centre of power represented by the ruling family. It is no longer tribal affiliation but rather an individual's loyalty that matters. Thus, one may find Kuwaiti nationals and Bidoon in the same tribe, even within the same family.[19]

The political turbulence that swept the Gulf region as a result of the Iraq–Iran War from 1980 to 1988 created a climate of fear and suspicion towards irregular residents whether Bidoon or foreign workers. In the context of the conflict, the Bidoon who are mostly Shiites (and in the view of the authorities, originated mainly from southern Iraq) were sometimes seen by the authorities as Iranians and sometimes as Iraqi supporters.

Following an assassination attempt on the life of the Emir in 1986, the situation became even more uneasy. It is not clear who was behind the event, but some pointed to Iran while others thought Iraq was responsible. Finally it was reported that Bidoon were among the perpetrators, though it later became evident that a number of Bidoon were actually among those guarding the Emir and that some died or were injured protecting the Emir.

As a result of the prevailing political turbulence and the assassination attempt, the Kuwaiti government began to review Bidoon status and to impose restrictions against them that denied their civic social and economic rights. Employment and access to government services, including health and education gradually were restricted or withdrawn. From all appearances, the government seemed to have embarked upon a policy to dispel the notion that the Bidoon would be ultimately granted citizenship. When the population census was carried out in 1995, Bidoon were excluded for the first time.

The six-month Iraqi occupation from August 1990 to January 1991 made Bidoon residency even more uncertain. Some Bidoon who sought shelter in neighbouring countries, as did many Kuwaitis, were not allowed to return.[20] The government issued a series of measures to keep them out and to force those left behind to leave the country. Families were split up, dispersed and forced into exile. Official estimates put the number of those remaining after the invasion at some 102 000[21]–111 693.[22]

The Iraqi invasion generally increased mistrust within Kuwait. In this atmosphere it was easy for the Kuwaiti government, which was reinstated in February 1991 by the US-led multinational forces, to exacerbate anger against the Bidoon and other non-Kuwaiti Arab communities by accusing them of supporting the Iraqi Army.[23] Hundreds of non-Kuwaitis were summarily killed or disappeared during and following the expulsion of the Iraqi Army.[24]

Those who stayed were threatened with deportation, jail or high fines if they did not prove their identity. In desperation, some of the Bidoon felt compelled to buy counterfeit passports from countries they had never set foot in such as Somalia, Nigeria, Eritrea and the Dominican Republic. They did this in order to be allowed to stay as foreign guest workers.[25] A report by Human Rights Watch at the time suggested that Kuwaiti officials had become involved in the forged passport trade.[26] The government later bowed to international pressure and stopped imposing fines or jailing the Bidoon, though harsh treatment designed to push them out of the country continued.

In contrast to the official argument, numbers of lawmakers and scholars in Kuwait question whether the policy of exclusion of the Bidoon is the right one to pursue. They argue that denial of basic human rights for the Bidoon is not only short-sighted and morally wrong but that it also carries a great degree of risk. Creating a deprived community in the midst of a prosperous society is a recipe for resentment, social destabilization and further insecurity. One Member of Parliament has described the present situation as a 'human bomb ready to explode at any time'.[27]

ANTI-BIDOON ACTIONS

Measures taken against the Bidoon continue to affect their daily social
and economic life as well as their overall well-being. Since 1991 the Bidoon
have been denied most of their basic rights and have been subjected to acts
of discrimination and persecution by authorities. They were dismissed en
masse from working in government agencies, especially in the military and
the police. They have been denied their rightful claim to pursue Kuwaiti
citizenship, and they have been denied education provided free of charge in
government schools. They are denied formal employment and civil services
in addition to state health services (offered free of charge to Kuwaiti nationals), social security and other social services. Bidoon previously dismissed
from their jobs cannot collect their severance pay unless they produce a
passport, either Kuwaiti or foreign, or unless they leave the country.

Bidoon are harassed by the police, rounded up at checkpoints and
tortured – a 'normal' practice in police stations. They are not permitted to own property or, until recently, to register a vehicle in their own
name. The term 'Bidoon' has been replaced, first with the designation
'non-Kuwaiti' and then with the official label 'illegal residents'. The term
'Bidoon' is, however, still in use as the common designation for this group
classified as stateless.[28]

Today the Bidoon are estimated to number between 80 000 and 140 000.
The majority of them live in virtual exile in squalid housing projects in
Sulaibiya and Jahra, in Ahmadi and the rundown neighbourhood of Jilib
ash-Shuyukh.[29] A 2005 Parliamentary Committee report[30] described the
Bidoon situation as follows:

> The Kuwaiti government exerts security, economic and social pressures on
> more than 120,000 Bidoons to force them to either reveal their native nation-
> alities or to sign affidavits admitting to foreign nationality for modification of
> their legality status and for depriving Bidoons of the freedom of movement and
> freedom to travel except on rare occasions. Bidoons are not employed by the
> public sector and their employment in the private sector has been restricted.
> They are not allowed to get driving licenses or any other form of identifica-
> tion from governmental offices. Bidoons do not have the right of ownership of
> property or even cars. They are also deprived of any rights of possession of per-
> sonal identity or anything to prove their legal residence. They cannot register
> births, marriages, divorces and deaths. It is in breach of the law for a Bidoon
> to get married without official approval. All these practices are considered as
> contradicting Islamic Sharia law and violating human rights and international
> conventions, which Kuwait is obliged to follow as it has signed them.

Fourteen years after the Iraqi invasion and the restoration of the
Kuwaiti government, the Parliamentary Committee for Defending Human

Rights in Kuwait criticized the government approach that continues to deal with the Bidoon as a security matter regardless of the human side of the problem.

ACCESS TO EMPLOYMENT, EDUCATION, MEDICAL CARE AND HOUSING

In Kuwait, like other small oil-producing countries in the Gulf such as the UAE and Qatar, there are financial benefits attached to citizenship. Kuwait's oil revenues were estimated in 2008 to be above US$111 billion for a country with a population estimated to be 1.05 million citizens. Kuwait offers its citizens generously subsidized education, medical care, grants and soft long-term loans for housing, jobs and social security. Low wage earners would not be independently able to match the cost of living in Kuwait. Unlike the Asian labour force, which is mainly young, single and mobile, the Bidoon have the responsibility of large families compared to the average family size of Kuwaiti nationals. Having to further divide the economic pie into a greater number of slices is an oft-given reason for not solving the stateless problem of the Bidoon. Such socio-economic factors impact the lives of the Bidoon in countless ways.

In principle, the Bidoon are not allowed to work in the public sector. Working in the private sector officially requires work permits similar to those issued to foreign workers but which are generally denied to the Bidoon. Hiring firms and supermarkets have to pay a fine of 30 KD (about US$240) each time a Bidoon is caught working for them, and the employer generally deducts the cost from the salary of the Bidoon worker. As the size of the fee increases each time a Bidoon is caught, he is left with no choice but to leave his employment.[31]

Fewer than 5000 Bidoon have been recruited to work in the army or the police during the last few years, and those jobs were acquired because of 'wasta' (personal favours) or because they were the children of national Kuwaiti mothers. Such positions usually include what the authorities consider 'privileges'. These may include the right to send their children to government schools, the possibility of registering civil matters and having their rent paid by the army. However, these 'privileges' are normally terminated at the end of service. In one case brought to the author's attention while in Kuwait, a Bidoon soldier who had been allowed to pay minimal rent for a house as part of his benefits was killed in a car accident. The authorities were quick to ask the family to pay full rent or leave the house – even before the man was buried.[32]

Because they are not officially allowed to work, many Bidoon work under black market conditions and are exposed to various forms of exploitation, including low wages (less than a quarter to a third of the Kuwaiti national labourer's average wage) and are subject to daily police harassment. It is important to emphasize here that they are harassed not because they work illegally but because they are working which is not allowed. Abu Muhammad (49) spoke about his experience:

> I spent more time looking for work than in work. Last time I found work in a local supermarket. They promised to give me KD 150 (US$520). I worked there for six months but I was paid for three only. I have six children and I have to feed them and pay KS 100 (US$350) for the house rent (2 rooms). I could not afford a school for my elder son. He is working to help me. He is selling vegetables in the street as many of Bidoon do. The problem is that the police never leave him in peace. They harass him and detain him from time to time. Each time I have to ask Kuwaiti friend to get him out. I see no future for us.[33]

With no access to subsidized government services offered to Kuwaiti nationals, including education and medical care, the only option left for the Bidoon families is to send their children to private schools, which they cannot afford. They may have limited assistance from some charitable foundations that offer financial help with private school fees for families with children at primary level. These schools operate commercially but do not provide quality instruction. The class size in these private schools is 47 to one compared with 26 to one in government's schools and 23 to one in al-Namuzajiyah (or grammar schools). It has been suggested that these schools are owned by government employees working for the Ministry of Education to enable them to earn additional income. A number of these schools closed amid complaints of both poor standards and resources.[34]

There are also two main foundations that help with medical care: Sandouq Re'ayet Al-Marda 'Patients' Help Foundation' that covers medical costs for the most needy families and Beit Al-Zakat or 'Al-Zakat Foundation' which helps to pay medical insurance costs.

However, interviewees stated that not all the Bidoon seem to benefit from this help as they suffer from both the lengthy bureaucratic process and a lack of resources. The majority of the Bidoon still have to pay KD 50 (US$150) per person annually for medical insurance. They also have to pay privately KD 5 (US$17) for each appointment at a clinic and KD 10 (US$35) to be seen by a consultant or to go to a hospital emergency unit. These fees are separate from the actual treatment and pharmaceutical costs.

Interviewees also said that unlike Kuwaiti nationals, the Bidoon are frequently told that their medicine is not available in the hospital pharmacy, where it is offered without cost. Instead they are advised to acquire it privately outside the hospital at their own expense. Some hospitals refuse to accept Bidoon patients, citing a lack of capacity.[35]

Each Kuwaiti national is entitled to either free housing or a low interest mortgage. In the 1970s the government built low quality two-bedroom houses for the Bidoon in interior suburbs such as al-Jahra. They were leased for minimal rent to the Bidoon families whose bread earner was employed by the government, mainly as policemen or in the army. As these families grew and the space became less adequate, housing became an acute problem for the new generation of Bidoon. They now pay about KD 120–150 per month (US$420–520) for a two-room house. This may have been reasonable when the Bidoon were working and earning on average KD 600 per month (US$2000), but today paying rent is simply beyond the capability of the Bidoon whose average income is no more than KD 200 (US$700), if they are working at all.

While it may be understandable that Kuwaiti authorities exaggerate the impact of assistance, it nevertheless seems that the government's figures lack clarity.[36] What is perhaps of greater concern is that the UK Home Office and the US State Department seem to accept in good faith the Kuwaiti official accounts of the status of the Bidoon regarding their human rights.

The Home Office's *Country of Origin* (COI) report of 2009 on Kuwait stated, for instance, 'that only the documented Bidoon (that is, the guest workers or the foreigners) have access to health care which is dependent on payment of fees'.[37] Although it is true that foreigners are required to pay for medical care in Kuwait, foreign domestic workers pay less for their medical care than do the Bidoon. Medical insurance is paid by employers of foreign workers, and those workers pay the lower fee of KD 1 (US$3.50) for a clinic appointment and KD 2 (US$7) for a hospital appointment and for medicine.[38]

The 2007 US *Country Report on Human Rights Practices 2006* also seems to have unquestioningly accepted that 10 600 Bidoon were granted citizenship 'in the last few years'.[39] This number has not been scrutinized or supported by any independent body, including the Kuwaiti Committee for Human Rights and the Popular Committee defending the Bidoon.

DOCUMENTATION, CIVIL REGISTRATION AND BURDEN OF PROOF

The authorities have set up a special unit within the Ministry of Interior known as the Executive Committee for Illegal Residents' Affairs (ECIRA)[40] to be in charge of the Bidoon. The main task of the ECIRA is to register, monitor and deal with almost every aspect of Bidoon affairs, making the hardships faced by the Bidoon community a matter of security rather than a matter of social, humanitarian or legal issues. The bureau is primarily staffed by military and security personnel. The Bidoon must now complete *Qayed Amni* (security clearance) not only for their naturalization application but also to request assistance with school fees and medical care, or to request the temporary *laissez-passers* (the Article 17 passport) required before being allowed to travel abroad even under the strictest conditions.

An ECIRA-issued Reporting or Attendance Card (RC) had been commonly known as a 'Green Card' because of its colour. The plastic, wallet-sized documents were used to keep official records of and to monitor individual members of this stateless community. These were not considered ID cards and should not be confused with the IDs issued to Kuwaiti nationals. They, however, have been replaced recently by multi-coloured cards. The new RC is nearly the same as the previous one and states the following: 'It is not considered as an identity card and used only for the purpose for which it was issued' that is, a RC. The main differences between the new and the old green card are its colours (yellow and grey) and more importantly the addition of a column added to the left of the photo. The new column is for a 'civil number' and an invisible stamp meant to speed up the process of accessing the personal details of the holder and to ensure the authenticity of the card.

As a result the Bidoon have no Kuwaiti national number. They do not have an ID or a passport. A relatively few possess an Article 17 passport. This document used to be issued to foreigners employed by the government to facilitate their travel abroad when they were on official assignment. As Kuwait became less dependent on foreigners in senior posts, it issued fewer Article 17 passports for foreigners. The Kuwaiti authorities now use a provision in the law to issue Article 17 passports to elderly Bidoon going to Mecca for pilgrimage, for serious medical treatment or for a university education.

During the past few years, the Kuwaiti authorities have started issuing Article 17 passports with later expiration dates. The Director of the Nationality and Travel Documents has acknowledged that in most situations acquiring a passport takes a lot of '*wasta*' from someone in power. [41] The new version of the Article 17 passport features a change of colour to brown from the previous grey/blue. It is not easy to distinguish between the former and the latter, and some foreign embassies have complained. The procedure for issuing a visa for Article 17 passport holders is far more restricting than is the procedure in place for the Kuwaiti nationals. [42] Many applicants have been refused visas even when they have all the required papers.

Bidoon are barred from registering civil matters, including marriages. To get around this, some desperate young Bidoon try to obtain court rulings rather than official marriage certificates to prove their marital status. The couple marries first according to the Islamic Shari'a law by going to the Sheikh or Ma'zoon who conducts a marriage ceremony in accordance with the religious requirement. This takes place in the presence of the bride's *Wakeel*, or family member (who acts on her behalf and with her consent), the groom and two witnesses. After the Sheikh reads some verses from the Koran and asks the bride's *Wakeel* and the groom a few questions, they and the religious Sheikh sign the marriage document. The marriage document is then taken to the Department of Civil Affairs where it should be recognized by the authorities. It is at this step, however, that the registration of the document is denied. While the religious marriage allows the couple to live together and to be accepted as husband and wife in their community, their marriage is not officially recognized by the government and as such they remain single in the view of the authorities. As a result, any children born from this union will be unable to obtain a birth certificate issued by the Ministry of Health.

Some young Bidoon realize they can acquire an official marriage certificate when their wives become pregnant. The husband must first initiate a case against himself in the courts. By doing so, he can make use of a provision in the law (Islamic Shari'a law) that Kuwait still applies to family matters. The law forces the individual who has committed rape against a woman to marry his victim or to face long years in detention.

The court ruling is not a registration of marriage, but it is the only official document a Bidoon couple can use to show that they are married. It does not constitute grounds to issue a birth certificate for their children. This messy state of affairs demonstrates the extraordinary lengths that the Bidoon must go to in order to receive civil recognition. A Kuwaiti ex-judge recently called for an end to this practice that he described as 'an acrobatic and inhuman piece of legislative blunder that needs to be scrapped' so that the Bidoon can register their marriages officially.[43]

No new driving licences have been issued to Bidoons since the 1980s, and the few who had previously obtained them are now characterized as 'illegal residents.'[44] Those who acquired marriage, birth or death certificates in the past are now denied replacements if these documents are lost or if they have become illegible. A newborn child cannot have a birth certificate but rather may receive an unofficial reporting form or declaration signed by the midwife or the hospital. A copy of this form should be endorsed by the Ministry of Health who would then issue the birth certificate. It is during this process that the Bidoon are again barred and consequently denied birth certificates.[45]

What is perhaps most significant is that the authorities put the burden of proof in civil matters exclusively on the Bidoon. In some cases people who were interviewed said they were told that the original documents they sent to the ECIRA with their naturalization application had been lost and that the authorities then washed their hands of trying to find them.[46] They were, therefore, refused replacement documents.

GENDER-BASED DISCRIMINATION

Marginalization is often based on discriminatory structures and practice in various areas of society. These may be referred to as institutional and structural exclusion. In the case of Kuwait, as in many other states, there is also an important gender dimension that has not been addressed by the reform of naturalization procedures. Women in Kuwait who are married to Bidoon (and any of their children) are subject to discrimination on the basis of national origin.

Kuwait's nationality laws still adhere to the principle of *jus sanguines* (nationality law by blood or descent) on the father's side. Consequently, the children of a Kuwaiti woman and a Bidoon husband are also Bidoon. Other Arab countries, such as Algeria, Egypt, Morocco and Tunisia, have amended their nationality laws to allow mothers to pass on their nationality to their children if the father is stateless. This policy has not been endorsed by Kuwait or by any of the Gulf States in order to bar Bidoon children from being naturalized.[47] One Kuwaiti mother noted, 'How could it be fair that an illegal child has better chance to be granted nationality than mine, simply because his father is Bidoon?"

The Kuwaiti government has promised that it will offer 'privileges' to the children of Kuwaiti mothers. The privileges, however, remain vague and are selectively applied. For instance, the authorities promised to employ some of these children to work for the army or the police, thus giving them some access to free schooling and health care. It seems though that those recruited have Kuwaiti mothers with husbands who come mostly from other Gulf States. These recruits are not the offspring of Bidoon from Kuwait. In addition, the so-called privileges ordinarily come with the job and are not specially conferred because the recruits are the children of Kuwaiti mothers. It should be noted that only 500–600 persons were accepted into these services.[48]

Two mothers of Kuwaiti nationality married to Bidoon husbands were interviewed. Both denied any differentiation in treatment between their children and other Bidoon children. Um Salem (47), living in Tayma neighbourhood in al-Jahra, whose husband is an unemployed Bidoon said:

I have nine children. My nationality is of no use to them. Their rights are denied including going to government schools, having a driving license or having free of charge medical care. I see my children growing up as my responsibility towards them too. I see that my brother's and sister's children who are Kuwaiti nationals as myself. Their children have no problems because of this damned paper they call it Jinsiye/nationality. I feel helpless. My elder son is 29 years old but did not marry as my brother's son who is 24. Our house is two-bedroom house and we can't afford to have a new person living with us. My son leaves the house looking for work. He carried a copy of my passport but this is of no help. He is still stateless Bidoon.[49]

On 16 May 2005, the Kuwaiti parliament extended political rights to women. Observers hoped that this step would help Kuwait bring domestic legislation in line with Kuwait's international obligations included in the international conventions that Kuwait acceded to, in particular those related to citizenship rights such as the *International Covenant on Civil and Political Rights* (ICCPR) of 1966. Article 24 states that 'every child has the right to acquire a nationality'. The 1989 *Convention on the Rights of the Child* (CRC) stipulates that children have the right to acquire a nationality and that they shall acquire that of the state of birth if they will otherwise be stateless.[50] The 1979 *Convention on the Elimination of all Forms of Discrimination against Women* (CEDAW) bars all forms of sex discrimination, including in matters of nationality. Article 9 specifically provides that "state party shall grant women equal rights with men in respect of the nationality of their children".[51]

All these conventions bar gender-based discrimination and affirm in clear and definite terms the right of children to a nationality. Nevertheless, it is common knowledge that Kuwait is moving in the opposite direction from its international obligation concerning the right of all persons to a nationality. The *Nationality Law* of 1959 has been amended 14 times since and with almost every amendment, it has become more restrictive. For example, the 1959 law (Article 3) granted citizenship to the children of Kuwaiti mothers when at least one of four circumstances existed: the father was unknown paternity could not be proven, the father's nationality was unknown or he was stateless. When amended in 1980, the mention of unknown nationality and statelessness was omitted. Also the *Nationality Law* of 1959 stated that residents in Kuwait who complete their education to the *Tawjihi* level (equal to Baccalaureate or A level in the UK) be granted Kuwaiti citizenship. A number of young Bidoon benefited from this until it was later revoked.[52] Perhaps this is the reason why there is growing recognition among legal scholars and human rights bodies both regionally and abroad that Kuwait has to take necessary measures to harmonize all aspects of its domestic legislation according to the principles and provisions of the international conventions.

NATURALIZATION

Nationality is deemed a sovereign matter in Kuwait. Unlike in other countries, though, Kuwaiti courts of law are not allowed to review sovereign actions of the state.[53] However, the combined efforts by some parliamentarians, along with international and local human rights organizations, led the Kuwaiti government to issue *Law 22* in the year 2000. The law is aimed at granting nationality to the Bidoon but allows for the annual naturalization of only 2000 persons. It is estimated that not more than 20 per cent have been able to fulfil the restrictive conditions laid out by this law that require, for example, registration in the 1965 census. The number of those registered in the census taken recently by the government is 43 777.[54]

The majority of individuals who applied were refused nationality without any clear reason; it seems that very few of those registered benefited from the law. The government could use *Qayed Amny*, a required conditions for naturalization, to exclude any applicant without giving reason. There was no clear guideline on how the law applied. Determinations were left to the discretion of the ECIRA, which was accused of making arbitrary decisions and accepting '*wasta*'. In short, the process lacked transparency and accountability, and there was no appeal process.[55] At least three individuals interviewed were registered in the 1965 census, but their applications for naturalization were thrown out without explanation.[56]

Saad (60) said all his relatives have *Jinseya Asliyah* making them bona fide citizens. When he and his family applied for naturalization, they showed proof that they were registered in the 1965 census and that his father had worked in Al-Ahmadi since 1948 and had never left the country to live anywhere else:

> Our situation deteriorated dramatically since 1990. This has put enormous pressure on me and the whole family. I go to ask in the ECIRA if there is any development regarding our naturalization application. They demonize us and let us wait in the burning sun for hours. I was insulted and treated badly each time I went there. Last time I was there, one of the officers told me: You are following Sarab [Arabic for mirage]. I stopped going there for more than a year now. My grandfather waited and passed away, my father waited and passed away, I have been waiting for 37 years now. What future remains for us to be normal citizens?[57]

It is difficult to know how many Bidoon were naturalized in accordance with the 2000 law. Government sources claim that prior to 2007 the number was 7827.[58] This figure has not been supported by any independent body. It has, instead, been rejected by human rights activists who believe that the figure does not exceed 2300.[59] According to credible sources among the Bidoon community, the majority of cases wherein nationality was granted were heard before 2003 when the law was altogether shelved. Figures offered by the government in fact include naturalized foreigners, mainly wives of Kuwaitis who were not indigenous Bidoon.[60]

In early 2008, the Kuwaiti government decided, in accordance with two Emiri Decrees, to grant nationality to a list of about 600 Bidoon.[61] Ten days later, 27 names were withdrawn from the list with no explanation. The majority of those granted nationality were in fact the children and families of Bidoon soldiers who sacrificed their lives defending the late Emir during an assassination attempt as well as others who lost their lives during the fighting with the invading Iraqi Army in the summer of 1990.

IMPACT OF CITIZENSHIP ON THE BIDOON

According to interviewees, the main barrier to the realization of full citizenship in Kuwait is not the introduction of specific laws but rather the restrictive criteria that have been used to exclude individuals from receiving citizenship at all. Those Bidoon who have been granted Kuwaiti nationality were mostly older residents who formerly enjoyed extensive social and economic rights in Kuwait before 1990 and have now had those rights restored. For other Bidoon who have received Kuwaiti citizenship, there have been some important changes. Not only are they entitled to obtain birth certificates for their children, but they also may obtain driving licences and business permits. Many are self-employed as traders. A small number of high-profile individuals have received documents and are able to work in sports or the arts. A few well-educated professional Bidoon, mainly medical doctors, have returned to work and live in Kuwait after acquiring foreign citizenship. Less than 5 per cent of naturalized Bidoon have been allowed back to serve in the army or the police.

The author was unable to personally interview Bidoon granted Kuwait nationality but did obtain accounts from relevant third parties. For example, a Bidoon woman who married a Bidoon and was without citizenship talked about how her sister who had married a Kuwaiti national enjoyed the benefits of citizenship in Kuwait. She noted the contrast between her situation and her sisters: "Citizenship has driven us apart. We hardly see each other. Our children took separate paths one for the fortunate and another for the less fortunate the deprived. It is hard and unfair."[62]

Her account and information gathered from those interviewed suggest that the few Bidoon who have managed to obtain Kuwaiti citizenship are enjoying most of the benefits offered to Kuwaitis, other than the political rights for which the naturalized person needs to wait a period of 15 years.

People who are naturalized are allowed to work, be granted soft loans for housing, and enjoy the right to send their children to government schools free of charge and to seek free medical care and social benefits.

Some Bidoon have taken citizenship in a second country. The challenge of establishing oneself as a non-citizen in Kuwait has deterred Bidoon ex-patriates from returning. Since 1990, many Bidoon, especially young men, have sought asylum in countries such as Canada, Australia and throughout Europe, especially the UK. Their number is difficult to assess as there are no records available in Kuwait or in the receiving countries, but based on the official Kuwaiti figures recorded between 1992 and 2001, an estimated 30000 Bidoon left Kuwait and sought asylum beyond the Arab region.[63] When those who settled in the UK and acquired British nationality were asked if they would go back and live in Kuwait, only two out of 18 said they would return to live in Kuwait as foreigners. One was a medical doctor who practised a few years in Kuwait before he came to specialize in the UK prior to the Iraqi invasion. The second is an electrician married to a Kuwaiti woman who could work as a foreigner with partial state benefits due to the fact that his wife is Kuwaiti. They feel that they are more protected by having British citizenship.

The rest of those interviewed said they were not willing to go back to live in Kuwait. They had suffered from their lack of education and opportunities in Kuwait. They now have large families and feel they have passed the age to pursue education in their newly adopted country. They are the lost Bidoon generation of the 1990s. Though the majority of them travelled to Kuwait to see their family and friends after they acquired a British passport, they do not see Kuwait as a place for them to live in anymore. They resent the notion of being guest workers/foreigners in their own country. They refuse to live with the uncertain status of guest workers where the authorities can put an end to their residency at any time. One of them summarized the situation by borrowing an Arabic proverb "The injustice by someone close is more severe than that by foreigners. . . . One can't afford to be an alien in his own country but he can in foreign land." He added: "Here in the UK we are equal with others before the law. In Kuwait we have been demonized. We are the only ones who are both Kuwaitis and foreigners as well."[64]

PURSUING CITIZENSHIP FOR BIDOON IN BAHRAIN, OMAN AND THE UNITED ARAB EMIRATES

In June 2002, the King of Bahrain issued a decree allowing citizens of the GCC to take up Bahraini nationality while keeping their original nationality. Six years later in November 2008, Bahrain announced that it had comprehensively resolved the issue of the Bidoon.[65] The prospect of holding dual nationality opened the door to the possible correction of the problem of statelessness. In May 2009, the Minister of Interior claimed that Bahrain had also given passports, unlike many other Arab states, to stateless families and children of Bahraini mothers married to foreigners.

However, the number of beneficiaries is unknown. According to press reports, the Minister of Interior, Sheikh Rashid bin Abdullah Al Khalifa, clarified that Bahraini passports were only given to those who could fulfil certain criteria, including a good knowledge of the Arabic language and the completion of 15 years of residency in the country for Arabs and 25 years for non-Arabs. He also announced that the process for those applying for citizenship could require a personal interview. In spite of these requirements, the Minister affirmed that 7012 persons were naturalized in the last five years. Of those granted citizenship in Bahrain, the largest group were non-Arabs from Asian states (3599), followed by Arabs (2240), GCC citizens (1095) and immigrants from 78 other countries.

Independent and opposition groups acknowledged that there had been some progress in Bahrain but estimated that around 5000 Bidoon were left behind despite the government claims to the contrary.[66] They also pointed out that the Bahraini government is using the recent naturalization measures as a political tool by granting nationality to thousands of Sunni Arabs who hold other nationalities in an attempt to change the demography to the detriment of the Shiite majority of the island.[67] The issue of demographic engineering has brought attention to the management and rationale of the naturalization process and has even encouraged citizens to reapply for citizenship.[68] A young Bidoon interviewed by Refugees International in 2009 described the case of an older brother who had been able to secure nationality in Bahrain. "His life is different in all aspects. At his job, he got a raise. He feels safe and secure." Via phone, the new citizen articulated the change from being stateless to having a nationality: "We were like birds. We could eat but never fly. Now we have the sky.'

In Oman, the researcher relied on interviews conducted with officials from the Foreign Ministry in charge of the Omani communities abroad. No women were interviewed. The researcher was assured that there is no longer a problem of stateless or non–documented indigenous communities – amid official reports that Oman had offered nationality to all expatriate Omanis who choose to return to the country from East Africa or Asia. However, not all Omani returnees have been accounted for – primarily those who settled in the wealthy oil-producing countries in the region such as the UAE. This failing in the naturalization policy has caused some Bidoon to move to the UAE in the hope of being naturalized there.

It is also not clear how many Bidoon have been naturalized in the UAE since a registration campaign was introduced at the end of 2008. The UN Human Rights Council reported that 1294 stateless persons had been naturalized by the UAE government in the previous year, but this figure did not single out Bidoon, and it was therefore difficult to gauge reform.[69] Other reports suggest that 51 people were naturalized in the first half of 2009. The issue of citizenship is still considered a sensitive topic in the UAE and among its neighbours. The interviewer met participants from the UAE in Oman who reported that there is currently a review process underway, but in the absence of official documentation, the researcher was advised that the only way forward in his quest for information was to pursue both informal and unofficial channels.

CONCLUSION

Promises of reform have not improved the lives of the vast majority of Bidoon. Despite the fact that the Bidoon were part and parcel of Kuwaiti society before Kuwait got its independence in 1960 and had been treated as Kuwaiti nationals enjoying full civil, social and economic rights, the Kuwaiti government gradually began to withdraw the Bidoon's rights, imposing restrictions on them since the 1980s and embarking on a policy to push them out of the country following the Iraqi invasion of 1990. Half of the estimated 220 000–250 000 Bidoon who fled the country during the war, like other Kuwaitis, were not allowed back and are still stranded in neighbouring countries.

Some 30 000 to 40 000 Bidoon are believed to have sought asylum in countries such as Australia and Canada but have mainly settled in Europe. And although Kuwait issued a law in 2000 allowing gradual naturalization of 2000 Bidoon annually, very few benefited from the scheme, which was subsequently shelved by the government in 2003. Furthermore, Kuwait remains reluctant to take steps to reduce statelessness, such as allowing women to extend their nationality to their children.

While this study suggests that the few Bidoon who were granted nationality enjoy the same rights as Kuwaiti citizens – even if they have to wait a long time before enjoying any political rights – the problem of statelessness among the Bidoon is so significant that none of the reforms introduced by the Kuwaiti government, above all the passage of *Law 22* in 2000 which was supposed to permit the flow of naturalizations, are having much positive effect. Only a handful of Bidoon have been able to meet the restrictive conditions laid out by this law. In this context, any discussion of the benefits of citizenship remains academic. Genuine reform is needed before the Bidoon can enjoy their human rights in Kuwait.

Equally, the stated change of policy in Bahrain has not been applied in a comprehensive or consistent manner, and many Bidoon there remain excluded and under suspicion. Until the Gulf States treat the Bidoon issue as a matter of human rights rather than as a security threat, the Bidoon will continue to be the victims of both official and societal discrimination.

NOTES

1. The term Bidoon should not be confused with Bedouin, from the Arabic word *Badawi*, meaning nomad.
2. Refugees International (2008c).
3. Al-Anezi (1994)
4. El-Najjar(2001). See in particular Chapter III, 'Discrimination Against Immigrants', available at http://www.gulfwar1991.com/Gulf%20War%20Complete/Chapter%203,%20Discrimination%20Against%20Immigrants,%20By%20Hassan%20A%20El-Najjar.htm.
5. Ibid.
6. Human Rights Watch (1995).
7. Refugees International (2007b).
8. Al-Najjar (2003), unpublished presentation given in the regional workshop organized by the author on statelessness in the Arab region, Cyprus, 2–5 November 2001.
9. Al-Wogayyan (2009).
10. Among these links: http://www.bedoon.cc/, http://www.tkbedoon.org/, http://www.bedoon.net/.
11. For a personal account regarding life in the UAE, see Ghazal (2008) and Atwood (2008).
12. Al-Najjar (2003).
13. Al-Anezi (1994).
14. The Foreign and Commonwealth Office (FCO) estimated recently that 80 per cent of the Kuwaiti Army in 1980s were Bidoon, unpublished British Embassy in Kuwait, November 2007. The Bidoon community sources put even higher figures of 90 per cent but not within the senior officers' ranks, interview with Chair of Bidoon Community in the UK, 17 November 2008.
15. See El-Najjar (2001) for a discussion of the role of the Bidoon in the police and armed forces.
16. Estimated Population (June 2008): 3399637 including approximately 1.05 million Kuwaiti citizens and 2.34 million non-Kuwaiti nationals, US State Department, June 2008. The number of foreigners was higher in the 1980s.
17. See Al-Rashid (2007), Madawi and Loulouwa (1996).
18. Swissinfo.ch, 21 October 2008.
19. Conversation with Kuwaiti academic Faris Mattar, Kuwait, 22 Dececember 2008.
20. Parliamentary Committee for Defending Human Rights in Kuwait estimated in 2005 that about 100000 were set to be stranded in Iraq since 1991 as *de facto* stateless with disputed citizenship as neither Kuwait nor Iraq would accept them as their citizens.
21. Agence France Press, 19 September 2000, quoted unnamed official sources.
22. Estimates given by Interior Minster Muhammad Khaled al-Sabah, *Al-Quds al-Arabi* daily, London, 19 September 2000.

23. Those, namely citizens of Arab States, viewed by the Kuwaiti government, rightly or wrongly, as taking the side of Iraq in the conflict include Palestinians, Jordanians, Sudanese and Yemenis.
24. Kuwait Human Rights Committee (2007).
25. US Department of State (2007).
26. Human Rights Watch (1995).
27. MPs Ahmad al-Sadoun, Muhammad Khaleefa and and Al-Hureithi criticized on various occasions the government policy towards the Bidoon and warned against its repercussions on the Bidoon community, and Kuwait standing in the international community, *al-Qabas* daily, 30 November 2008 and 31 July 2009.
28. Refugees International (2007b).
29. Refugees International (2007c).
30. The Parliamentary Committee for Defending Human Rights in Kuwait (2005).
31. Interview with the Ayed, Mohammed and Salim: street traders and Bidoon activist member of the Bidoon Popular Committee, Kuwait, March 2009.
32. Interview, MA, Kuwait, 22 June 2009.
33. Abu Mohammad interview, Kuwait, 20 March 2009.
34. Interview with Abu Ahmad ex-Bidoon teacher and seven primary level students, Kuwait and London, March and June 2009.
35. See, for instance announcement made by Al-Ahmadi Hospital in *Al-Rai al Am* daily and *Al-Jarida* electronic daily, 5, April 2009, cited 17 July 2009, http://www.aljarida.com/aljarida/Article.aspx?id=54102.
36. Case studies, Ghanim, July 2009.
37. Home Office (2009), paragraph 20.12.
38. Interview with Abu Nasser, Kuwait, 11 June 2009.
39. US Department of State (2007).
40. The name initially was the 'Central Committee for Illegal Residents' Affairs' (CCIRA) but was later changed to the 'Executive Committee for the Illegal Residents' Affairs' (ECIRA).
41. See interview with General Faisal Al-Nawaf Al-Sabah, the General Director of the "Department of Nationality and Travel Documents" in *Al-Qabas* Kuwaiti daily, 5 July 2009.
42. Ibid.
43. *Al-Rai Am* Kuwaiti Arabic daily, 25 July 2009.
44. Refugees International (2007b).
45. Information gathered in Kuwait interviews conducted on 21 December 2008 and later with two elderly Bidoon asylum women who confirmed that the situation remain the same, interviewed in London, 3 August 2009.
46. Interview with Bidoon community activist, London, 22 May 2009.
47. Joseph (2000).
48. Interview with the Head of the Bidoon Community in the UK, 22 May 2009.
49. Interview, Um Salem, Kuwait, March 2009.
50. See Articles 7 and 8 of the 1989 CRC.
51. CEDWA, UN, GA Resolution 34/180, UN Declaration A/34/46, Article 9, adopted 18 December 1979, entry into force 2 September 1990.
52. Al-Najjar (2003)
53. Castles Davidson (2000).
54. Unpublished British Embassy report on the Bidoon in November 2007.
55. US Department of State (2007).
56. Kuwait interview nos 7 and 8, 4 April 2009.
57. Saad interview, Kuwait City, 18 March 2009.
58. Unpublished British Embassy report on the Bidoon in November 2007.
59. Approximately 1600 of those were granted nationality during the first three years following the issuing of the *Law 22* of 2000 and up to 2003. See UK Home Office, Operational Guidance Notes, Country Assessment, Kuwait, August 2005. A further

600 family members of Bidoon military personnel who sacrificed their lives during the assassination attempt on the Emir's life on 1986 and others who sacrificed their lives defending Kuwait against the Iraqi invasion were granted nationality after years of lobbying by some parliamentarians.

60. Interview with the Head of the Bidoon Community in the UK, London, 24 February 2008.
61. UNHCR, Regional Operation Plan 2008; Kuwait and other GCC countries.
62. Interview with Um Ayyed, Kuwait, 21 March 2009.
63. This is based on the official estimates of Bidoon that suggest that 117604 were registered with the General Commission of Civil Information in the year 1992 and their number in 2001 as suggested to be 87320 in 2001 according to the Ministry of Interior, quoted by Najjar (2003). An unknown number has to be added for those who sought asylum after 2001.
64. Interview with Ghani, London, 6 February 2009.
65. Al-Sayegh (2008).
66. IRC, 10000–15000. Interview with Bahraini academic and political activist put the figures not more than 5000, interview no. 1, Bahrain, 23 December 2008.
67. See US Department of State (2009).
68. See Saldanha (2009).
69. See UN General Assembly (2007b).

11. Summary and conclusions

Maureen Lynch and Brad K. Blitz

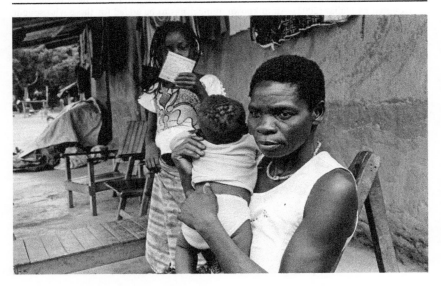

Source: © UNHCR/Greg Constantine 2010.

Figure 11.1   In the Cote d'Ivoire, the definition of who is 'Ivorian' and who isn't has influenced issues relating to documentation, nationality, land ownership and voting rights. Many people born of foreign parents or in the north of the country face difficulty claiming their right to nationality.

RECOGNIZING AND RESOLVING THE GLOBAL PROBLEM OF STATELESSNESS

More than 60 years after the international community embedded the right to nationality in the human rights architecture that we rely on today, approximately 12 million people around the world remain stateless.

194

These are people who struggle to exist, much less enjoy protection of their human dignity. Statelessness also cuts across a host of other issues that operate not just at the level of the state but at the sub-national and global levels. While the global problem of statelessness is commonly associated with political and territorial upheaval, displacement, migration, population growth, trafficking and climate change, it is sustained by the absence of the rule of law and by weak and undemocratic systems of governance. Statelessness is further institutionalized in systemic discrimination in the form of gender inequality and racist and ethnocentric policies.

The premise for this study is that, in spite of the challenges noted above and the complex issues that give rise to statelessness, a small number of states have made measurable progress in helping individuals acquire or regain citizenship. The current project was designed to take stock of positive developments in eight of those countries, and more importantly, to explore the benefits of citizenship as well as the broad array of human rights now enjoyed by formerly stateless populations. The goal was to then illustrate if and how citizenship has made a qualitative difference in the lives of formerly excluded groups and to examine barriers that still prevent individuals from the full enjoyment of citizenship.

The literature review highlighted the convergence between the rights of citizens and non-citizens under international law. It also noted that statelessness itself exposes the hollowness of international human rights law as a means of influencing domestic reform; hence, the absolute importance of national actions for effective protection and the rationale for this research project. While the focus of the research was to investigate the degree to which the granting of citizenship really does remove some of the 'unfreedoms' that Sen speaks of and to which he attributes the horrors of 'want and fear,' the literature also highlighted that there are a multitude of domestic factors that undermine the possibility of protection and that one of the by-products of weak governance and societal discrimination is the fragmentation of citizenship into different classes and entitlements that vary greatly, depending on one's place in the hierarchy of privilege.

As with qualitative studies in general, the empirical data may illustrate particular trends and tensions but can rarely be considered representative or indeed establish claims of causality. In the context of this study, the reliance on some 120 interviews conducted with formerly stateless individuals and representatives of social service organizations across Bangladesh, Estonia, Kenya, Kuwait, Mauritania, Slovenia, Sri Lanka and Ukraine can only offer some selected insights into an issue of global proportions. For that reason, the research was designed with a strong exploratory focus.

The project was set back by some particular limitations. Both anticipated and unexpected mitigating factors affected the research process, which the team attempted to correct when once aware. The team recognized the challenges of vulnerable populations and, therefore, sought out community bodies, social service organizations and personal contacts in the human rights field that were able to identify potential interviewees. However, in some cases, early transcripts demonstrated a lack of clarity in expectations. As a result, the editors additionally requested that research team members complete a questionnaire about their findings to help harmonize the responses.

SUMMARY OF FINDINGS

While the exact number of individuals granted citizenship is not clear – figures for Slovenia, Ukraine, Bangladesh and Sri Lanka seem to be more concrete – some people have benefited from reform. In light of this fact, country data were studied to identify common themes, patterns and trends. A brief survey of both state-specific and common findings follows.

Research from Kenya indicated that the situation for the Nubians has generally changed for the better but has not brought full relief. It was noted that in the aftermath of the presidential promise of 2007, government initiatives to accelerate the distribution of identity cards to members of the Nubian community appeared to be effective. And while the Kenyan government recently established a process to address the challenge of documenting the citizenship status of the Nubian community in Kenya, it was estimated that, in this case, at least half of the approximately 100 000 members do not yet have citizenship.

Positive effects of citizenship include the fact that more people are obtaining registration documents and passports, which has facilitated their entry into the labour market, mostly in the private sector. There has also been an increase in political participation. Participants reported that their ability to vote during the elections of December 2007 represented to them their most important civic contribution.

Negative effects, however, include state capture and further manipulation of the Nubians' precarious status by authorities. At the administrative level, there are barriers that undermine the provision of official documents, including birth certificates, identity cards and passports. One participant described how the loss of identity documents was met with onerous demands to prove Kenyan birth. There has been no improved access to housing rights, sanitation, water or education. While there has been some improvement, the granting of nationality has still not addressed the wider recognition of the group as birthright citizens nor has there been progress in the social economic rights issues, particularly for children.

In the case of Slovenia, theoretically at least, individuals who regained permanent residency can claim a series of rights, including education, health insurance, employment inclusive of the right to start a business, family unity, social assistance and free legal aid, as well as freedom of movement and protection from expulsion or detention. In addition, those who subsequently became citizens have political rights (to vote and stand for national and European elections). In some cases they can even purchase apartments they have lived in since 1991. In practice, however, the above rights have not been easily accessed.

The public awareness campaigns for the 'erased' in Slovenia have been successful in empowering those affected and in bringing the issues of exclusion, exploitation and injustice to the public agenda. However, a number of erased persons who regained their permanent residence status are not in a position to acquire Slovene citizenship – mostly because they still lack the 'proof of the permanent means to support themselves'. The reforms also did not address underlying societal problems of exclusion and exploitation, and the above-mentioned political campaigns saw greater polarization. The net result might be categorized as further stigmatization of the erased and harassment of individual activists. Current legislation fails to compensate for the period of 'stolen years', and there is no sense at this time that the erased will receive an official apology or be exonerated by the Slovenian state.

According to field research in Sri Lanka, participants generally felt that the citizenship campaign initiated by the government and the UNHCR was a good attempt to solve the problem of stateless 'Upcountry' or 'Plantation Tamils' who at the time of the 2003 campaign were estimated to be 300 000 in number. A total of 190 000 individuals were registered as citizens during the naturalization campaign and of those, 72 000 *de facto* stateless persons have received 'special declarations' that record a formal acknowledgement of their status from the immigration authorities.

The benefits for these individuals so far include the right of nationality and the provision of national identification documents; greater political participation, including the right to vote and the right to stand as a candidate in local elections; and improved basic rights for their children who now have the right to receive a birth certificate. One development is the expansion of political bargaining over their rights to protection and assistance in the economic development of their communities. Nonetheless, the interviews record several challenges. A number of individuals cannot be registered on voters' lists and there are still administrative barriers (including fees) that need to be overcome. Moreover, the extension of citizenship to former stateless Plantation Tamils has not yet been able to address broader problems, including poverty reduction. For this reason, the Estate Tamils remain disadvantaged relative to the wider population.

The most notable benefits of the campaigns in Ukraine included a greater degree of confidence and assertiveness among the Crimean Tatar community, which has been formally recognized after years of marginalization. This was due in part to the large numbers of returnees and the active leadership of the Crimean Tatar community, which prompted the Ukrainian authorities to adopt a new law for the use of proportional representation that guaranteed their presence in local self-government and the Verkhovna Rada of the Autonomous Republic of Crimea. For individuals, there were some personal benefits, for example the possibility of finding employment in public service, which is traditionally secure. Individuals can participate in the privatization schemes of public property and, in theory, have a greater possibility of becoming landowners.

Granting of nationality status enabled individuals to receive valid travel documents that permitted them to travel not just in the former Soviet Union but also to other parts of Europe and Turkey. More important for younger persons was the possibility of entering public universities and not having to pay high tuition fees. The only perceived negative effect was compulsory military service, which took them out of the labour market.

The citizenship campaigns of the 1990s could not, however, solve the issue of legislative rehabilitation nor address some of the systemic problems of unemployment, the lack of decent housing and public infrastructure, high levels of morbidity and the lack of access to sufficient medical care, limited social integration, or the restoration of property rights and the multiple challenges involved in the allocation of land. These challenges undermine the full inclusion of the Crimean Tatars in Ukraine and suggest that further reforms are needed to ensure their rights are fully respected.

The case of Bangladesh provides important lessons regarding successful advocacy for nationality rights, yet at the same time demonstrates that ending statelessness does not always resolve all of its consequences or eliminate all of its causes. Interviewees' assessments of their situation since obtaining national identity cards are not resoundingly enthusiastic, though the success of the Urdu-speakers in confirming their citizenship rights through the courts is unquestionably significant. Some Urdu-speakers appear to have taken advantage of the country's progress, pursuing higher education and obtaining jobs. Others report that discrimination continues, particularly regarding access to public schools, government jobs and passports, and the little change in the slum-like conditions in urban settlements about half of the community has lived in since the early 1970s. Poverty, resulting in part from years of statelessness, continues to hinder upward mobility, in contrast to other citizens.

The remaining challenge to genuinely ending statelessness among the

Urdu-speakers of Bangladesh is to remove the final political, social, economic and administrative obstacles that frustrate implementation of the group's rights as citizens. Effort must be made to help the government see the Urdu-speakers as part of the population, while still allowing the community to retain its linguistic traditions. It should also continue to raise with Pakistan the rights of certain individuals to reunite with family members.

While thousands of individuals have been able to return to Mauritania and obtain proof of a tie to the country, the current research highlighted the difficulties faced by returnees who have not received identity cards, whether they came 'spontaneously' or in the current wave. It also noted that they face vulnerability to charges that they are not Mauritanian and hence may be politically disenfranchised. Such threats are particular to the returnees and reveal that their human rights are not secure. Interviewees also indicated that as a result of lack of documentation there is the difficulty in freedom of movement.

The return of property is also a current and potentially explosive problem. In the case of most of the returnees who are agriculturalists, lack of land means lack of livelihoods. The population of Mauritania has grown over the past 20 years, and desertification has driven more and more people out of their previous livelihoods as pastoralists and into the more fertile parts of the country, the Senegal River Valley, so pressure on land has greatly increased.

One of the main findings of the research in Estonia was that there are measurable benefits associated with the acquisition of citizenship by formerly stateless ethnic Russians in Estonia, though it was noted there are benefits associated with the acquisition of Russian citizenship as well. By contrast, non-citizens expressed feelings of rejection, inferiority and passivity and fare worst of all in the labour market.

The case study on Estonia also showed that preference for citizenship might fluctuate due to local and external conditions. Following Estonia's admission to the European Union, citizenship became a less popular option for those who preferred Russian citizenship, while enjoying rights afforded to EU residents. Growing social distance between the two main ethnic groups and the failure to address the sensitivities of the Russian-speaking minority have, however, undervalued citizenship as a tool of integration. Hence, both benefits and limitations of citizenship are identified.

The situation of the Bidoon in Arabia was also examined, though less successfully than originally planned. It is notoriously difficult to conduct interview research of a sensitive nature in the Gulf States and, regretfully, insufficient evidence was gathered to permit conclusions to be drawn about the current situation of Bidoon who received citizenship status. The data provided did, however, suggest that the problems of exclusion and denial of nationality have seen little change, with the exception of perhaps Bahrain where independent and opposition groups acknowledged that there had been some progress with naturalization campaigns. Sources estimated that around 5000 Bidoon in Bahrain are still stateless despite government claims to the contrary.

In Kuwait, official sources estimate that approximately 6000 Bidoon were naturalized, but this figure has been contested by human rights groups that claim the number is not much higher than 2000. Secondary sources recorded that for those who received Kuwaiti citizenship, there have been some notable changes. Not only are they now entitled to birth certificates for their children, but they may also obtain driving licences as well as business permits.

In Oman, interviewees indicated that there was no longer a problem of naturalization but that poor economic conditions had caused many Bidoon to move to the UAE in the hope of being naturalized there instead. The researcher was provided with no information about the nature of any positive or negative developments post-naturalization and the matter requires further investigation.

COMMON THEMES

A comparative review of the findings outlined above reveals a number of common themes as well as some disturbing patterns. In no case was there a blanket remedy for the entire stateless group nor did reversal of their situation occur in rapid order. Rather, numbers of individuals appeared to benefit from state action over time or at some point became able to access more rights than were previously available to them.

Six of the eight researchers articulate the importance of receiving identification documentation. However, in each case there are numbers of persons who have not received formal recognition of their legal status. Interviewees who had secured identification documents mentioned that they now live without being harassed by police or other authorities; that they are basically safe and secure.

Obtaining a nationality triggered a wide range of feelings among interviewees that includes ambivalence, uncertainty, fear, confusion, relief, belonging, greater confidence and optimism about the future. One noted that they are now 'treated as a human being', another said, 'I exist' and a third mentioned that their group was able to 'recover their pride and self-respect'.

Somewhat surprisingly, reference was made to political rights or voting in just five of the cases. In Kenya, Slovenia, Ukraine and Bangladesh the possibility for political participation was noted, whereas in Sri Lanka there were problems getting to vote.

In each of the case studies, there have been varying degrees of improvement in access to the labour market. This was most evident in Kenya where individuals went from not having worked because they were stateless to finding employment in the government sector, though the overall results were mixed. Interviews noted improvements in accessing jobs in Slovenia, Sri Lanka, Ukraine and Bangladesh. In Sri Lanka and Slovenia, former stateless people enjoyed considerably more benefits with regard to internal and international travel.

The matters of property ownership, housing and living conditions were highlighted in the cases of Kenya, Sri Lanka, Slovenia and Ukraine. In each situation the problem has yet to be resolved for the larger community. In only two situations, Slovenia and Ukraine, was any positive reference made to getting a residence or the acquisition of property. In the situation of Bangladesh, camp conditions have not changed for the better, and it is not clear what the housing rights of the Urdu-speaking population are. The challenge of land acquisition in Mauritania is serious in its own right, but is clearly linked to lack of access to employment because of the large number of individuals who formerly worked in the agriculture sector. As this study demonstrates, there is a marked need to address nationality rights comprehensively and that includes guaranteeing that property rights are simultaneously addressed.

Far less attention was paid to matters of education, health care or access to social assistance – typically common elements of complaint among stateless persons. Research from Slovenia and Ukraine indicated that access to education improved when individuals were able to regularize their status. This was not the case in Kenya. With regard to health care, data suggest that only Slovenia's formerly stateless persons had greater access. In two instances, reference was made to the improvement in the situation of children, how achieving nationality would be useful and that the next generation would 'lead a better life'.

Systemic problems of poor living conditions, poverty, underdevelopment and corruption have undermined the potential benefit of citizenship and many excluded people remain without basic services. This is particularly acute in poor states such as Bangladesh, Kenya and Sri Lanka and also in the Republic of Crimea in Ukraine. Interviewees in two of these cases highlighted the need for rehabilitation or need of development activities.

In two situations, Sri Lanka and Ukraine, the United Nations played a vital role in instituting fruitful campaigns. In the final instance, regarding the ongoing challenges facing the Bidoon, government initiatives played a primary role – though with limited results and in only one state (Bahrain) out of a group of countries that hosts Bidoon populations.

With the exception of Ukraine, where the problems of statelessness took place inside a wider context of political transition and the reorganization of nationality across the former Soviet Union, the protracted nature of statelessness was, in each situation, solved in part but not in whole, over the course of decades. In all of the cases presented in this study, pockets of affected people remain in limbo until now.

The passage of time as a push factor is unclear. There was no lurch towards democracy, no natural or even normative evolution in state thinking: rather, in each case, specific domestic and external pressures held greater explanatory weight for the changes in nationality and related laws that opened the doors to the fortunate few. While national governments were sensitive to external pressure, and each government is to be commended for the positive steps taken to date, the persistence of statelessness and discrimination, especially in Slovenia and Kuwait, and the failure to address it comprehensively over many decades, suggests that states do not perceive themselves to be truly vulnerable to external criticism.

Seven of the eight researchers identified discrimination or marginalization as ongoing problems. Described as stigmatization, stereotypes or disenfranchisement, one interviewee simply said, 'We are not immune to discrimination.' Only in the case of Estonia did one person say, 'We do not feel inferior.' Related is the fact that generally younger people profited more from acquiring their nationality than did older individuals. Great care must be taken to avoid ageism in facilitating the nationality rights and integration of stateless persons.

A related and particularly disturbing discovery is that, where mentioned, the underlying problem or cause of statelessness was at best swept under the carpet and at worst further frustrated by the process of acquiring nationality in practically every case. For example, Nubians have still not been assured of their right to Kenyan nationality at birth and must continue to go through a challenging process (though certainly less harsh than it was previously). Slovenia's 'erased', while able to get the underlying issues of exclusion and discrimination on the public agenda, are still at risk. The perceived issues of security and economic threat are two of the sticking points that continue to prevent the Bidoon from resolving their situation.

Researchers called attention to the fact that interviewees sought to regain lost ground or in some way seek recompense for their lost lives. An interviewee in Slovenia said there had been no compensation for the lost years; one in Bangladesh said they don't know how to seek compensation. A Crimean Tatar said they were compensated for travel and luggage expenses. Perhaps most significantly, an individual expelled from Mauritania said that returning to the country and getting nationality was a 'symbolic undoing of wrong'.

The important role of courts, national or regional, should be noted here. In the majority of the cases, rule of law played a role in establishing the status of the populations at risk.

Other benefits noted in individual case studies included receiving a pension, being able to open a bank account or purchase stock, ability to acquire licences or business permits, and not being detained or deported due to statelessness. The only two negative affects mentioned were compulsory military service and ongoing high levels of morbidity.

Overall, this research provides further evidence of the reassertion of state sovereignty at the expense of human rights and the protection of human dignity – a finding which supports Goldston's claim that the discrimination between citizens and non-citizens, including stateless people, is primarily 'a problem of lapsed enforcement of existing norms'.

THE BENEFITS OF CITIZENSHIP

While it might be premature in some cases to draw conclusions and comparisons regarding benefits of citizenship in this context, each case example already provides lessons learned or best practices for the efforts of other states. Despite gaps and limitations, this study illustrates that the granting of citizenship offers some very real and important material and non-material benefits at both the community and individual levels. In general terms, one may state that the benefits of citizenship include the fundamental right to obtain identification documents; the right to be represented politically, to access the labour market beyond the informal sector or underground economy; and to move about freely. The potential for property ownership was also noted. Regaining citizenship ends isolation and empowers people, collectively and personally. Such political and personal changes are of considerable importance to the advancement of a human rights regime based on dignity and respect.

This research also makes a contribution to the theoretical debates over the value of citizenship and the need to investigate further the relationship between the 'unfreedoms' that Sen describes and that featured in the *Human Development Report [1994]* on human security. It affirms the importance of studies produced by Refugees International and organizations on the ground that can inform our understanding of the ways in which repression and the denial of human rights affects individuals not only in law but also in practice and what must be done to change the situation.

Irrespective of trends in international law, the granting of citizenship itself is not sufficient to ensure the protection of human rights and to act as a unifying force for social integration. Indeed, the findings of this research study call into question some of the claims made by cosmopolitan scholars – most of whose work is based on European investigations and studies from advanced economies – over the potency of citizenship. The ending of direct discrimination on the basis of nationality does not undo structural effects or other modes of discrimination. Fragmentation and division occur both before and after the granting of citizenship. Hence, there is a need for both better historically informed studies and micro-level investigations of the way in which repression and the denial of human rights affects individuals on the ground.

Equally important, the interplay between domestic actors and agendas, as suggested by Bauböck in his study on acquisition and loss of nationality, is borne out by the above findings and suggests that the process of nationality reform is a highly contested process in which stateless people may play a pivotal role. Just as pro- and anti-immigrant forces have defined the situation for non-citizens in Bauböck's European model, the above findings from Kenya, Mauritania, Bangladesh and Ukraine suggest that large stateless populations have considerable agency and may set agendas for reform, even if they are challenged by xenophobic forces.

In spite of the relatively small sample, the research provides further insight into the modalities of domestic political reform and some mechanisms which under favourable circumstances may influence change in the protection and promotion of human rights. Six premises to advance future policy-relevant research on the prevention and reduction of statelessness are offered.

1. Documentation is essential to the realization of human rights: all of the field researchers referenced the importance of acquiring documents in the form of passports, civil identification documents, birth certificates or even licences. As noted in the findings from Slovenia, Sri Lanka, Mauritania and Kenya, documentation offered formerly stateless persons a means to civil and political participation as well as better access to services; conversely, those who lacked documentation were liable to abuse, including deportation. The realization of the rights to citizenship may be advanced by the establishment of flexible policies regarding the provision of and recognition of official documentation.

2. Demographics matter: in countries where there were a large number of stateless people relative to the overall population, there was a clear political interest in regularizing the status of individuals who lacked citizenship. In Kenya, the large Nubian community was perceived as a potentially captive political constituency. In Ukraine, the numbers of Crimean Tatars returning from Central Asia forced the government to acknowledge this minority and, in an attempt to prevent inter-ethnic tension and division, grant it formal recognition. Thus, the presence of the community had a bearing on the eventual granting of minority rights as a matter of expediency. There were other negative aspects that came with communities' new founded political influence. The research team recorded how states had manipulated the situation of specific minorities and groups for political though not necessarily societal benefit, for example in Slovenia. Given the potential currency of stateless people as potential constituents, regions with large stateless populations may also become sites of new citizenship campaigns and will require further assistance from the UNHCR and close monitoring of the treatment of minorities during periods of political reform and development.

3. The benefits of citizenship are not evenly distributed: in each of the above case studies, there have been varying degrees of improvement in access to the labour market. This was most noted in Kenya and Sri Lanka where individuals went from being stateless to having the opportunity of working in the state sector. In several cases, the granting of documentation enabled young people to acquire a university education and then enter jobs in secure sectors, including the government and health service. In Sri Lanka and Slovenia, former stateless people enjoyed considerably more benefits with regard to internal and international travel; this change in the right to travel again favoured the young who were better placed to relocate to cities and large towns, especially in Sri Lanka. The granting of citizenship does not absolve state responsibility to ensure all persons can access and enjoy their human rights.

4. Setting the nationality agenda may move the reform process forward: once stateless groups organized themselves, asserted their social identities as well as their claims to nationality, and, in some cases, attained the restoration of their social and economic privileges, they saw a marked change in their respective situations. In four examples, Kenya, Slovenia, Mauritania and Bangladesh, stateless persons themselves were key actors and initiated the resolution of their plight. The case of Slovenia also raises the important point regarding the individualization of rights and the way in which former *de facto* stateless

   people have been able to engage in the wider polity (both in Slovenia
   and in the European Union) and access European institutions such
   as the European Court of Human Rights. Arguably, by defining their
   rights and the parameters of the exclusion they experienced, they were
   well placed to press for change.

5. Recognition and exoneration have important implications: the fact
   that participants sought to be exonerated by the state and public and
   achieve some recognition for the abuse they suffered at the hands
   of the state is central to the pursuit of dignity and, as evidenced in
   Slovenia, Ukraine and Mauritania was a major motivating factor in
   their struggle for citizenship.

6. Populations with a recognized ethno-national identity are more easily
   integrated: a shared understanding of the historical relationship of
   the state concerned to the respective populations affected appears to
   determine the degree and manner in which they have been integrated
   following periods of statelessness. For example, while the origins
   of the Bidoon, Bihari and the erased are neither uniform nor free
   from ambiguity, the terms themselves relate to people's status not
   their national or ethnic identities. There is little denying the historical attachment of the Plantation Tamils or the Crimean Tatars in Sri
   Lanka or Ukraine, respectively. In spite of inter-ethnic tension and
   long-standing discrimination against the Crimean Tatars, especially
   during the height of Stalinism, the fact of their deportation from the
   Crimea and their historical connection to Ukraine is undeniable. By
   contrast, the erased in Slovenia, the Bihari in Bangladesh and the
   Bidoon in the Gulf region are still viewed as foreigners who have not
   been well integrated and are the victims of suspicion.

CONCLUSION

It can be said that the eight cases outlined in the present study demonstrate
that there are a number of important benefits associated with acquisition
of nationality. As anticipated, some of the most notable changes acted to
reverse the deprivation of rights suffered by stateless persons, sometimes
for decades. Yet stateless people are not the only beneficiaries when statelessness ends. States also gain greater legitimacy and improved standing
in the international community: the resolution of the Crimean Tatar
situation and the fate of the erased in Slovenia have both been central
to discussions between the European Union, Council of Europe and the
governments of Ukraine and Slovenia, respectively.

   Because ensuring the right to nationality is a foundation of human rights and a deterrent to displacement and disaffection, state action to reduce the number of individuals who are *de jure* or *de facto* stateless also benefits that state, its region and the global community by increasing global stability and security. The number of persons at risk of being trafficked is potentially reduced. The rule of law gains sway. New citizens contribute their voices to politics, strengthen a nation's labour pool and pay taxes. The list goes on.

The fact that the granting of citizenship ameliorates many, but not all, of the complex problems that have roots in economic inequality, systemic discrimination and other forms of injustice, points to the need to incorporate greater care to ensure the underlying causes are addressed by citizenship campaigns. Moreover, it is important to recognize the need to sustain integration initiatives and, in some cases, development aid for as long as deemed necessary. State responsibility does not end with the granting of citizenship status, as important as such action is. Proactive steps to educate officials and stateless persons as well as to ensure and enhance protection are required.

States studied in the current project along with representatives of countries such as Nepal and Latvia, all of which have worked to end statelessness, should be brought together to identify, systematically and comprehensively, lessons learned and best practices that can be utilized by others seeking to do so. Meanwhile, states desiring to uphold nationality rights can draw points from the present study to guide their initiatives.

The absence of citizenship has a human cost, which can be prevented but not renewed. Timely and serious steps must be taken to avoid statelessness before it strikes – through birth registration for all children, gender equality in nationality laws and other types of reform.

The research also calls attention to a number of additional avenues for future investigation. There is a vast opportunity to evaluate the often-overlooked impacts of statelessness. Little is known about the psycho-social implications of statelessness and much could be gained by measuring life expectancy, socio-economic status, public health risks and educational trajectories of stateless persons. Furthermore, additional comparative analyses as well as compilations of individual case studies identifying cause, effect and remedy might prove helpful. Longitudinal studies could prove indicative as well.

In the end, individual and collective human rights are no less important today than they were 60 years ago. The good news is that solutions for some of the world's most persistent human rights problems are finally within reach. Globalization, along with the development of vast social networks, increasingly visible civil society organizations and innovative technology, now make it possible for the global community to advance meaningful change where it was not possible before. The time is ripe for a more active human rights agenda.

Effective strategies to end the injustice of statelessness must not only involve fundamental changes in laws and norms that allow these human rights violations to continue but must be partnered with focused, ceaseless and well-timed advocacy. A few countries have made measured strides in reducing statelessness. The United Nations response has improved. Non-governmental agencies, legal experts and affected individuals are joining forces. Media attention has increased, but progress is limited and slow. Bolder and more creative efforts to uphold nationality rights for all – a foundation of identity, dignity, justice, peace and security – must be identified and relentlessly pursued until every person has access to their right to a nationality.

12. Epilogue

James A. Goldston

Source: © Greg Constantine 2010.

Figure 12.1   Most Rohingya men in Bangladesh are exploited as labourers. Several thousand work as bonded labourers and are trapped into debt to local Bangladeshi boat owners. A group of Rohingya men in southern Bangladesh push their fishing boat out for another day's work.

As many as 175 million people worldwide are not citizens of the countries in which they reside. A sizeable percentage of them, an estimated 12 million, have been denied or deprived of a legal status – citizenship – that serves, in practice, as a precondition to the enjoyment of many rights, including voting, property ownership, health care, education and travel outside one's own country.

Ill-treatment of non-citizens, arbitrary denial of citizenship and statelessness are twenty-first century problems that implicate fundamental questions of state sovereignty, human rights and non-discrimination. While international law grants non-citizens virtually all rights to which citizens are entitled, except the rights to vote, hold public office and exit and enter at will, in reality, citizenship creates a giant loophole in the international framework. As a result non-citizens remain among the most vulnerable segments of humanity.

States improperly deploy the concept of citizenship to carve out significant exceptions to the universality of human rights protection in two ways: through deprivation of, and/or restrictions on access to, citizenship; and through the imposition of distinctions between citizens and non-citizens. When taken together, the powers to deny citizenship and treat non-citizens differently can – particularly when employed arbitrarily – lead to tragic consequences. Entire groups of native-born residents may be excluded from access to public benefits; citizens suddenly stripped of their status may be physically expelled; long-term residents may be fearful of deportation and denied the vote; and acts of violence and discrimination against non-citizens may be abetted or allowed to go unpunished.

The divide between citizens and non-citizens is primarily a problem of lapsed enforcement of existing norms. But those provisions are little known and rarely applied. The challenge is to use human rights law to combat the worst effects of citizenship denial and the ill-treatment of non-citizens. Existing international mechanisms must be activated to provide effective protection for non-citizens.

By contrast, combating citizenship deprivation and denial requires the clarification and articulation of new legal norms that stipulate the boundaries of state prerogative. Eventually, international law must not simply set forth the individual right to a nationality: it must specify states' obligations to provide it. Over time, the broad discretion that states enjoy over citizenship questions must be narrowed by the incorporation of human rights concerns, including the prohibition against racial discrimination, into international legal rules on citizenship.

The resulting new or modified norms should be rooted firmly in the evolving body of international human rights law giving primacy to the principle of human dignity. Even as longer-term objectives are pursued – on the one hand, better implementation of the rights of non-citizens; on the other, new and refined standards governing access to, and deprivation of, citizenship – advocates should intensify their use of existing legal tools on behalf of non-citizens. The most comprehensive, well known and generally accepted of these are the *jus cogens* rules of international law that prohibit discrimination on the basis of race.

Given that states themselves have no incentive to enforce regulations that diminish their discretion, four major tasks confront those concerned with the human rights consequences of citizenship denial and the ill-treatment of non-citizens: first, improvement of documentation and education of the broader public; second, institutional reform; third, clarification and distillation of legal standards related to citizenship; and fourth, enforcement of existing norms. A central objective underlies each: to transform public understanding so as to render politically unacceptable the abuse of non-citizens and arbitrary denial and deprivation of citizenship.

DOCUMENTATION AND PUBLIC AWARENESS

There is a need for improved documentation and public education concerning the extent, and human rights and security consequences, of discriminatory access to citizenship and the ill-treatment of non-citizens. Gaps in the provision of citizenship are often both reflections and causes of political instability and conflict. States and intergovernmental bodies must be persuaded of their own long-term interests in filling these gaps more systematically and expeditiously. Citizenship denial and statelessness must increasingly be seen not as arcane legal matters but as the human tragedies, political problems and security threats they are.

Governments should also improve outreach efforts to ensure that all persons are registered and have a legal identity, including a valid birth certificate. We have seen that affirmative registration efforts can have real impact. In the Democratic Republic of Congo in 2006, UN agencies succeeded in registering more than 25 million persons to vote in national elections. They used planes, boats, trucks, canoes and carts to distribute registration kits and reach persons in outlying communities. Since 2004, NGOs have gone door to door to deliver free birth registrations to people's homes in Cambodia, resulting in many more legally registered persons. A UNICEF-backed programme in Bangladesh pursued a similar strategy, and also joined birth registration with child health vaccinations. The effort resulted in registration of 12 million births in the past decade. Similar programmes in South Africa and other countries have undertaken large-scale birth registrations in public hospitals and at public schools. These examples demonstrate what can be done.

INSTITUTIONAL REFORM

Issues of citizenship access must increasingly be mainstreamed into human rights reporting mechanisms, including those of the United Nations.

Recent reforms of the UN human rights architecture, including the creation of a Human Rights Council, are likely to give them enhanced authority and resources to address these problems. UN bodies can do more.

The UN High Commissioner for Refugees (UNHCR) should enhance its field capacity to address statelessness, expand its training for government officials and build on its important efforts to quantify the number of stateless persons worldwide, including by improving its methodology to collect data on statelessness.

While the UNHCR has done admirable work with scarce resources in addressing statelessness, it cannot do the job alone. There currently exists no international supervisory body tasked with monitoring and enforcing the proper treatment of the stateless, in accordance with the 1954 *Convention relating to the Status of Stateless Persons*. A UN working group or Inter-Agency Task Force, directed by and/or working closely with the UNHCR, should be established to address the situation of the stateless and those with uncertain citizenship status. This body should elaborate guidelines on statelessness and citizenship status, and should mainstream nationality denial and statelessness issues throughout the UN institutional framework, through information exchange and cross-agency coordination on policy development and implementation.

The UN Human Rights Council should create a Special Rapporteur for the Rights of Non-citizens that includes statelessness and access to citizenship as a priority within its mandate. UN treaty bodies should monitor issues of access to nationality, statelessness and treatment of non-citizens in country reports and, where appropriate, in individual complaints.

The Office of the High Commissioner for Human Rights should establish a senior-level staff position to deal specifically with issues of nationality and statelessness, and should include citizenship and statelessness in all monitoring, reporting, training and protection activities.

The UN Children's Fund should apply more widely its birth registration programmes, intensify monitoring of Article 7 of the *Convention on the Rights of the Child* and increase its activities on behalf of stateless children. Correspondingly, the UN Development Fund for Women should dedicate more attention to stateless women, including through monitoring of Article 9 of the *Convention on the Elimination of Discrimination against Women*.

CLARIFICATION OF NORMS

More work is required to translate the end-goals of Article 15 of the *Universal Declaration of Human Rights* and related norms into concrete, realizable benchmarks against which action to prevent and resolve stateless-ness can be measured. As international law articulates a 'right' to national-ity which no individual state is required to secure, legal uncertainties will continue to serve – consciously or not – as an excuse for state inaction.

Three areas of uncertainty stand out for attention and clarification: (1) the concept of '*de facto*' statelessness; (2) the legal obligations of states, not just not to deprive or deny, but affirmatively to grant, nationality absent an objective and reasonable basis not to; and (3) the particular procedural safeguards, consistent with international due process standards, necessary to guarantee a minimum of fairness whenever a state employs administra-tive or judicial mechanisms to address an individual's citizenship status.

The trend of gradually incorporating the sphere of citizenship within the expanding corpus of human rights law must be accelerated and intensified so that, over time, statelessness, arbitrary denationalization and discrimi-natory access are eliminated. International norms governing access to nationality deprivation of nationality and the prevention of statelessness must be clarified, disseminated, and more widely ratified and applied by national governments. As part of this process, guidelines for citizenship access should be developed that adequately take account of, on the one hand, a democratic society's right to determine its membership, and, on the other, universal human rights norms, including non-discrimination.

Many recommendations may be drawn from, and/or built upon, exist-ing international standards. Gathering all relevant provisions into one document would be important, because to date their dispersion in differ-ent materials has contributed to their lack of effective force. One possibil-ity would be for the UN treaty bodies collectively to generate a unified general comment that addresses access to citizenship and treatment of non-citizens.

Such a general comment might include the following principles:

- In order to effectuate the principle that 'everyone has the right to a nationality', nationality should be granted by the state of birth if the person at issue does not clearly enjoy the right to another nationality.
- States should be under an affirmative duty to ensure adequate documentation capable of establishing citizenship is afforded to all persons within their jurisdiction. Children should be registered immediately after birth, and provided with necessary documenta-tion simultaneously.
- In the ordinary course, persons continually resident in a state for a reasonable period of time – perhaps five years – should be entitled to citizenship.

- The process and criteria for obtaining citizenship should be further elaborated so that they are readily accessible and transparent in all countries. Cases of contested citizenship should be resolved either by the courts or a special administrative mechanism independent of the executive branch of government. The government should bear the burden of persuasion with respect to citizenship status.
- Citizenship should be withdrawn only where such withdrawal is prescribed by law, is non-discriminatory and is accompanied by procedural due process, including the opportunity for appeal and review by a judicial organ. It should be clear that any withdrawal of citizenship that results in statelessness is unlawful.
- Access to citizenship should not be denied arbitrarily or apportioned on the basis of race, ethnicity, religion, gender, sexual orientation, political opinion or any other criterion that would be inadmissible grounds for distinctions among citizens.

While it would be useful to work toward the adoption of an international legal instrument that expressly incorporates the above principles, in the meantime, these norms should be enforced by UN treaty bodies, such as the Human Rights Committee, empowered to review country reports and decide upon individual communications. Governments should be encouraged to amend national legislation in conformity with these standards, and to ratify the 1954 and 1961 statelessness conventions, which provide important if limited protection to stateless persons. Finally, regional bodies should consider the adoption of region-wide nationality legislation, such as the European Convention on Nationality. Supervisory mechanisms and/or monitoring bodies should oversee implementation of such legislation.

ENFORCEMENT OF LEGAL NORMS

Training for judges, lawyers and relevant government administrative officials is necessary to make clear that existing anti-discrimination laws may be applicable to citizenship issues and that governments have a responsibility to address discriminatory citizenship patterns. Senior officials should publicly underscore the unacceptability of discrimination and violence against non-citizens, and the importance of adequately implementing legal protections. This is a more controversial undertaking in some countries than it might seem at first glance, given the scarce political benefits and the often substantial political costs that come with defending the rights of people who generally don't vote. Complaints of abuse should be acted upon swiftly, professionally and effectively. Where state oversight agencies do not exist or are under-resourced, international donor assistance should be channelled for such purposes.

Much can be done simply by changing the way that lawyers and others think about discrimination in relation to non-citizens. Examples of innovative uses of anti-discrimination principles already exist. They must be publicized, and, in some cases, reconceived in the context of citizenship.

Government-sponsored legal aid offices, university-based legal clinics and NGOs should explicitly include non-citizens within their target client base and access to citizenship among their areas of focus. In addition, non-citizens' rights advocates working with counsel should seek to identify suitable cases that may be brought before national, constitutional and regional tribunals or UN treaty bodies to secure concrete legal remedies for racial discrimination against non-citizens, including in access to citizenship.

With respect to each of these tasks, a major challenge is that the principal constituency for any action – persons who are not citizens of the states where they reside – is not a unified political force. To the contrary, non-citizens are dispersed geographically; are divided by language, religion and ethnicity; and are intimidated by the threat of arrest and deportation. Identity, a crucial variable for policy on so many other questions, is equally important.

Building a movement aimed at expanding both citizenship access and effective rights protection for non-citizens requires developing alliances among a broad range of potential constituencies. As there are few NGOs composed by and for stateless people or non-citizens as such, a movement to promote the rights of these persons will have to enlist NGOs working on minority rights, race relations, women's rights, children's rights and many others. Advocates will have to tailor their articulation of what is at stake to different contexts. A major goal must be to reconceptualize what at first seem to be locally specific matters, whether it's schooling for Hill Tribe people in Thailand or surveillance of Arab and Muslim immigrants in the USA and western Europe – as a global issue of non-citizens' rights.

Bibliography

Abdul Khaleque v. The Court of Settlement, 44 DLR 273.

Abid Khan and Others v. Government of Bangladesh, 55 DLR 318 (2003).

Ablyatifov, R.M. (2004), 'The Resettlement, Adaptation and Integration of Formerly Deported Crimean Tatars in Ukraine: Evaluation of the Governmental Programme Impact in 2002', Paper presented at the 12th NISPAcee Annual Conference, Central and Eastern European Countries Inside and Outside the European Union: Avoiding a New divide, Vilnius, Lithuania, 13–15 May, http://www.nispa.sk/_portal/files/conferences/2004/papers/200405311210200.Ablyatifov-final.doc.

Accord Tripartite, Mauritania-Senegal-UNHCR, 12 November 2007, http://www.ihrda.org/Repatriation2.asp?pagename=Repatriation2.asp.

Adam, D. (2009), 'Sea Level Could Rise More Than a Metre by 2100, Say Experts', *Guardian*, 11 March, http://www.guardian.co.uk/environment/2009/mar/11/sea-level-rises-climate-change-copenhagen.

Adaptation of Existing Bangladesh Laws Order, Preamble (1972).

Adejumobi, S. (2001), 'Citizenship, Rights and the Problem of Conflicts and Civil Wars in Africa', *Human Rights Quarterly*, 3, 148–70.

Adjami, M. and J. Harrington. (2008), 'The Scope and Content of Article 15 of the Universal Declaration of Human Rights', *Refugee Survey Quarterly*, 27(3), 93–109.

Affidavit of A.K., 14 November 2006, on file with the author.

Affidavit of F.B.G., 16, 24 July 2004, on file with the Open Society Justice Initiative.

Affidavit of F.O.T, 15 November 2006, on file with the Open Society Justice Initiative.

Affidavit of H.M., 9, 26 July 2004, on file with the Open Society Justice Initiative.

Affidavit of H.A.B., 15, 26 June 2004, on file with the Open Society Justice Initiative.

Affidavit of I.B., 14 November 2006, on file with the Open Society Justice Initiative.

Affidavit of M.A.O., 27, 24 July 2004, on file with the Open Society Justice Initiative.

Affidavit of M.G.D., 13, 26 July 2004, on file with the Open Society Justice Initiative.

Affidavit of M.H.S., 10, 24 June 2004, on file with the Open Society Justice Initiative.

Affidavit of N.M.K., 15, 22 July 2004, on file with the Open Society Justice Initiative.

Affidavit of N.M.K., 14, 22 July 2004, on file with the Open Society Justice Initiative.

African Commission on Human and Peoples' Rights (2006), *Institute for Human Rights and Development in Africa, Open Society Justice Initiative and Center for Minority Rights Development (On Behalf of the Nubian Community in Kenya) v. Kenya* (decision pending). Communication 317/2006, African Commission on Human and Peoples' Rights, Banjul, the Gambia.

Al-Anezi, R.H. (1994), *The Residency Status of the Bidoon in International Law* [Kuwait:] (Al-Qertas Publishing House in Arabic).

Al-Jarida electronic daily, (2009), 5 April http://www.aljarida.com/al jarida/Article.aspx?id=54102.

Al–Najjar, G. (2003) Revised version of unpublished presentation given in the regional workshop on statelessness in the Arab region, Cyprus, 2–5 November 2001.

Al-Rashid, M. (2007), 'Critical Relations: The Tribe and the State in Saudi Arabia', *Al-Quds al-Arabi*, Tuesday, 28 August, http://www.biyokulule. com/view_content.php?articleid=2273.

Al-Sayegh, M. (2008), 'بــدون الخليــج... مواطنـون بـلا وطـن' (Without the Gulf ... Citizens Without Homeland)', Arab Information Centre, 9 November, http://www.arabinfocenter.net/index.php?p=42&id=71728.

Al-Wogayyan, F.M. (2009), *Citizenship in Kuwait: Its Political, Legal Aspects and the Current Challenges*, Kuwait: Centre for Strategic Studies, Kuwait University.

Aleinikoff, T.A. (1986), 'Theories of Loss of Citizenship', *Michigan Law Review*, **84**(7), 1471–503.

Aleinikoff, T.A. and D. Klusmeyer (eds) (2000), *From Migrants to Citizens: Membership in a Changing World*, Washington, DC: Carnegie Endowment for International Peace.

Ali, Y. (2006), 'Stateless and Citizenship Rights in the Middle East: The Case of Kuwait', *DOMES*, **15**(1), 62–76.

Aljazeera Television (2007), 'Kenya's Nubians Fight for Rights: Interview of Youssef Abdalla', 12 August, http://english.aljazeera.net/news/africa/ 2007/08/200852517380140544.html.

Amis, P. (1984), 'Squatters or Tenants: The Commercialization of Unauthorized Housing in Nairobi', *World Development*, **12**(1), 87–96.

Amnesty International (2000), 'Bhutan: Nationality, Expulsion, Statelessness and the Right to Return', AI Index: ASA, 14 January

(London: Amnesty International), http://www.unhcr.org/refworld/docid/3b83b6df7.html.

Amnesty International (2004), 'Myanmar – The Rohingya Minority: Fundamental Rights Denied', AI Index: ASA, 16 May 2004 (London: Amnesty International), http://www.amnesty.org/en/library/asset/ASA16/005/2004/en/dom-ASA160052004en.pdf.

Anderson, A.B. (2005), 'Missing Boundaries: Refugees, Migrants, Stateless and Internally Displaced Persons in South Asia', *Pacific Affairs*, **78**(2), 320–1.

Andreev, S. (2003), 'Making Slovenian Citizens: The Problem of the Former Yugoslav Citizens and Asylum Seekers Living in Slovenia', *Southeast European Politics*, **4**(1), 1–24.

Ansley, F. (2005), 'Constructing Citizenship Without a License: The Struggle of Undocumented Immigrants in the USA for Livelihoods and Recognition', in N. Kabeer (ed.), *Inclusive Citizenship Meanings and Expressions* (London: Zed Books), pp 199–218.

Anti-Slavery International (2009), 'Slavery in Mauritania', http://www.antislavery.org/english/what_we_do/antislavery_international_today/award/2009_award_winner/slavery_in_mauritania.aspx.

Arakan Project (2008), 'Issues to be Raised Concerning the Situation of Stateless Rohingya Women in Myanmar (Burma). Submission to the Committee on the Elimination of Discrimination Against Women (CEDAW) For the Examination of the Combined 2nd and 3rd Periodic State Party Reports', CEDAW/C/MMR/3)-MYANMAR-October, http://www.burmalibrary.org/docs6/CEDAW_Myanmar_AP_Submiss ion-Final-Web.pdf.

Arendt, H. (2004), *The Origins of Totalitarianism*, New York: Schocken Books.

Associated Press (2007), 'Muslim Minority May Decide Kenyan polls', *Taipei Times*, 26 December, http://www.taipeitimes.com/News/world/archives/2007/ 12/26/2003394181.

Atwood, K. (2008), 'I Belong Here, It is My Home', *The National*, 21 October, http://www.karenattwood.co.uk/index.php?option=com_cont ent&view=article&id=74: i-belong-here-it-is-my-home&catid=38: travel &Itemid=56.

Aurescu, B. (2007), 'The 2006 Venice Commission Report on Non-citizens and Minority Rights: Presentation and Assessment', *Helsinki Monitor*, **18**(2), 150–63.

Avebury, E. (2009), 'Britain Must Resolve Issue of Stateless People', *South China Morning Post*, 14 March, http://ericavebury.blogspot. com/2009/03/letter-in-south-china-morning-post.html.

Bahar, A. (2007), 'Issues Related to Minorities and Deprivation of

Citizenship', Paper presented at the UN Experts Consultation Conference, UN Office of the High Commissioner for Human Rights, Geneva, 6–7 December.

Bajt, V. (2003), 'From Nation to Statehood: The Emergence of Slovenia', PhD thesis, Faculty of Social Science, University of Bristol, Bristol.

Baluarte, D. (2006), 'Inter-American Justice Comes to the Dominican Republic: An Island Shakes as Human Rights and Sovereignty Clash', (Washington, DC: Washington College of Law, American University), http://www.wcl.american.edu/hrbrief/13/2baluarte.pdf?rd=1.

Bangladesh v. Professor Golam Azam, 46 DLR (AD) 192 (1994).

Bangladesh Citizenship (Temporary Provisions) Order, 1972 (Bangladesh), No.149 of 1972, 26 March 1971, http://www.unhcr.org/refworld/docid/3ae6b51f10.html.

The Bangladesh Abandoned Property (Control, Management and Disposal) Order, 1972, President's Order No. 16 of 1972, 28 February 1972.

Barbieri, P. (2007), *About Being Without: Stories of Stateless in Kuwait*, Washington, DC (Refugees International, http://www.refugees international.org/sites/default/files/Kuwait_statelessrpt.pdf.

Barrington, L. (1995), 'The Domestic and International Consequences of Citizenship in the Soviet Successor States', *Europe-Asia Studies*, 731–63.

Bartolomei, L., E. Pittaway. and E.E. Pittaway. (2003), 'Who Am I? Identity and Citizenship in Kakuma Refugee Camp in Northern Kenya', *Development*, **46**(3), 87–93.

Batchelor, C.A. (1995), 'Stateless Persons: Some Gaps in International Protection', *International Journal of Refugee Law*, **7**(2), 232–59.

Batchelor, C.A. (2006), 'Transforming International Legal Principles into National Law: The Right to a Nationality and the Avoidance of Statelessness', *Refugee Survey Quarterly*, **25**(3), 8–25.

Bauböck, R. (ed.) (2006), *Migration and Citizenship: Legal Status, Rights and Political Participation*, Amsterdam: Amsterdam University Press.

Bauböck, R. (2007), 'The Rights of Others and the Boundaries of Democracy', *European Journal of Political Theory*, **6**(4), 398–405.

Beckman, L. (2006), 'Citizenship and Voting Rights: Should Resident Aliens Vote?', *Citizenship Studies*, **10**(2), 153–65.

Benhabib, S (2004), *The Rights of Others: Aliens, Residents, and Citizens*, Cambridge: Cambridge University Press.

Berezina, E. (2004), 'Children as Refugees: Abuse of Child Refugees in Foreign Detention Camps', (Washington, DC: Youth Advocate Program International), http://www.yapi.org/rpchildrenasrefugees.pdf.

Bernstein, R.J. (2005), 'Hannah Arendt on the Stateless', *Parallax*, **11**(1), 46–60.

Bernstein, R.J. (2008), 'Are Arendt's Reflections on Evil Still Relevant?' *Review of Politics*, **70**(1), 64–76.

Beznec, B. (2008), 'The Impossible is Possible. An Interview with Aleksandar Todorović', in Jelka Zorn and Uršula Lipovec Čebron (eds), *Once upon an Erasure. From Citizens to Illegal Residents in the Republic of Slovenia* (Ljubljana: Študentska založba), pp 19–31.

Bhabha, J. (1998), 'Enforcing the Human Rights of Citizens and Non-citizens in the Era of Maastricht: Some Reflections on the Importance of States', *Development and Change*, **29**(4), 697–724.

Bhabha, J. (2003), 'The Citizenship Deficit: On Being a Citizen Child', *Development*, **46**(3), 53–59.

Blitz, B.K. (2005), 'Refugee Returns, Civic Differentiation and Minority Rights in Croatia 1991–2004', *Journal of Refugee Studies*, **18**(3), 362–86.

Blitz, B.K. (2006), 'Statelessness and the Social (De)Construction of Citizenship: Political Restructuring and Ethnic Discrimination in Slovenia', *Journal of Human Rights*, **5**(4), 453–79.

Blitz, B.K. (2008), 'Democratic Development, Judical Reform and the Serbian Question in Croatia', *Human Rights Review*, **9**(1), 123–35.

Blitz, B.K. (2009a), 'Advocacy Campaigns and Policy Development', *Forced Migration Review*, **32**, 25–26.

Blitz, B.K. (2009b), 'Statelessness, Protection and Equality', UK Department of International Development and University of Oxford Refugee Studies Centre Policy Brief, September, http://www.rsc.ox.ac.uk/PDFs/RSCPB3-Statelessness.pdf.

Blitz, B.K. and M. Otero-Igtesias. (2010), 'Stateless by Any Other Name: Refused Asylum Seekers in the United Kingdom', *Journal of Ethnic and Migration Studies* (forthcoming).

Bowring, B. (2008a), *The Degradation of the International Legal Order? The Rehabilitation of Law and the Possibility of Politics*, London: Routledge/Cavendish.

Bowring, B. (2008b), 'European Minority Protection: The Past and Future of a Major Historical Achievement', *International Journal on Minority and Group Rights*, **15**(2–3), 413–25.

Boyden, J. and J. Hart. (2007), 'The Statelessness of the World's Children', *Children and Society*, **21**(4), 237–48.

British Nationality Act (1948), http://www.opsi.gov/acts/acts1948/pdf/ukpga_19480056_en.pdf.

Brock, G. and H. Brighouse. (2005), *The Political Philosophy of Cosmopolitanism*, Cambridge: Cambridge University Press.

Brouwer, E. (2003), 'Immigration, Asylum and Terrorism: A Changing Dynamic Legal and Practical Developments in the EU in Response to the Terrorist Attacks of 11.09', *European Journal of Migration and Law*, **4**, 399–424.

Brownlie, I. (1963), 'The Relations of Nationality in Public International Law', *The British Year Book of International Law*, **39**, 284–364.

Bryce, J. and A.J. Toynbee. (2000), *The Treatment of Armenians in the Ottoman Empire, 1915–1916: Documents Presented to Viscount Grey of Falloden by Viscount Bryce (Uncensored Edition)*. *Also Known as 'The Blue Book'* (Reading: Taderon Press).

Buck, T. (2005), *International Child Law*, London: Routledge/Cavendish.

Burch, S. and D.J. Smith. (2007), 'Empty Spaces and the Value of Symbols: Estonia's War of Monuments from Another Angle', *Europe-Asia Studies*, **59**(6), 913–936.

Camerota, S. (2005), 'Immigrants at Mid-decade: A Snap-shot of America's Foreign-Born Population in 2005', Washington, DC: Center for Immigration Studies, http://www.cis.org/articles/2005/back1405. html.

Carens, J. (2005), 'On Belonging: What We Owe People Who Stay', Boston : Somerville, http://bostonreview.net/BR30.3/carens.html.

Castles, S. and Davidson, A. (2000), *Citizenship and Migration; Globalization and the Politics of Belonging*, London: Macmillan.

Centre on Housing Rights and Evictions (2006), 'Listening to the Poor', (Geneva: Centre on Housing Rights and Evictions), http://www.cohre. org/kenya.

Chastain, J. (2004), 'Senegal in 1848 in Encyclopedia of 1848 Revolutions, http://www.ohio.edu/chastain/rz/senegal.htm.

Chinyama, V. (2006), 'Kenya's Abolition of School Fees Offers Lessons for Rest of Africa', http://www.unicef.org/infobycountry/kenya_33391. html.

Chowdhury, R.Abrar (1998), 'Issues and Constraints in the Repatriation/ Rehabilitation of the Rehingya and Chakma Refugees and the Biharis', Paper presented at the Conference of Scholars and other Professionals Working on Refugees and the Displaced Persons in South Asia, Dhaka, Bangladesh, February.

Chubarov, R. (2002), *Vybory 31 bereznia 2002 roku v. Avtonomniy Respublitsi Krym* (Elections of 31 March, 2002 in the Autonomous Republic of Crimea), Information bulletin, Krymski Studii Nos.3–4.

Cohen, R. (1989), 'Citizens, Denizens and Helots: The Politics of International Migration Flows in the Post-war World', *Hitotsubashi Journal of Social Studies*, **21**(1), 153–65.

Constitutional Court of Slovenia (1999), *Decision No. U-I-284/94*, Constitutional Court of Slovenia, http://www.unhcr.org/refworld/ docid/3ae6b74a10.html.

Constitution of the People's Republic of Bangladesh (1972). http://www.pmo.gov.bd/constitution/contents.html.

Coventry Peace House (2008), *Statelessness: The Quiet Torture of Belonging Nowhere* (Coventry: Coventry Peace House).

Craven, M. (2000), 'The International Law of State Succession', *International Law Forum du Droit International*, **2**(23), 202-205.

Crush, J. and W. Pendleton. (2007), 'Mapping Hostilities: The Geography of Xenophobia in Southern Africa', *South African Geographical Journal*, **89**(1), 64-82.

The Dhaka Declaration, Summit of SPGRC 1, 5 November 2009.

Daily Nation (2006), 'Kenya; Uproar as MPs Allege Bias Against Muslims', *Daily Nation*, 17 November, http://www.propertykenya.com/news/439028-uproar-as-mps-allege-bias-against-muslims.php.

Daily Star (1993), 'Over 300 Stranded Pakistanis Nationals Go Home Today', *Daily Star*, 10 January.

Dankwa, E. (1987), 'Working Paper on Article 2(3) of the International Covenant on Economic, Social and Cultural Rights', *Human Rights Quarterly*, **9**, 239-40.

Dedić, J., V. Jalušic. and J. Zorn. (2003), *The Erased: Organized Innocence and the Politics of Exclusion*, Ljubljana: Peace Institute.

Dell'Olio, F. (2005), *The Europeanization of Citizenship: Between the Ideology of Nationality, Immigration and European Identity*, Aldershot: Ashgate.

Detrick, S. (1999), *A Commentary on the United Nations Convention on the Rights of the Child*, The Hague: Kluwer Law International.

Diène, D. (2007), 'Report by the Special Rapporteur on Contemporary Forms of Racism, Racial Discrimination, Xenophobia and Related Intolerance, Addendum –Summary of Cases Transmitted to Governments and Replies Received', A/HRC/4/19/Add.1, 5 June.

Doebbler, C.F. (2002), 'A Human Rights Approach to Statelessness in the Middle East', *Leiden Journal of International Law*, **15**(3), 527–52.

Doek, J.E. (2006), 'The CRC and the Right to Acquire and to Preserve a Nationality', *Refugee Survey Quarterly*, **25**, 26–32.

Donner, R. (1994), *The Regulation of Nationality in International Law* (Ardsley, NY: Transnational Publishers).

Draft Articles on Nationality of Natural Persons in relation to the Succession of States with Commentaries at 40, 1999 Y.B. International Law Communication, Vol. II, Part Two.

El-Najjar, H.A. (2001), The *Gulf War Overreaction and Excessiveness: How America was Dragged into Conflict with the Arab and Muslim Worlds* (Daton, EA: Amazone Press), http://www.gulfwar1991.com.

Elles, D. (1980), *International Provisions Protecting the Human Rights of Non-citizens: Study*, New York: United Nations.

Elman, R.A. (2001), 'Testing the Limits of European Citizenship: Ethnic Hatred and Male Violence', *NWSA Journal*, **13**(3), 49–69.

Equal Rights Trust (2009a), 'The Protection of Stateless Persons in Detention Under International Law', ERT Legal Working Paper, Equal Rights Trust, London, http://www.equalrightstrust.org/ertdocument bank/ERT%20Legal%20Working%20Paper.pdf.

Equal Rights Trust (2009b), 'The Protection of Stateless Persons in Detention', ERT Research Working Paper, Equal Rights Trust, London, http://www.equalrightstrust.org/ertdocumentbank/ERT%20 Research%20Working%20Paper.pdf.

European Court of Human Rights (1999), *Slavov v. Sweden*, Application No. 44828/98, European Court of Human Rights, Strasbourg, 29 June.

European Court of Human Rights (2001),*Okonkwo v. Austria*, Application No. 35117/97, European Court of Human Rights, Strasbourg, 22 May.

European Court of Human Rights (2002), *Al-Nashif v. Bulgaria*, Application No. 50963/99, European Court of Human Rights, Strasbourg, 20 June.

European Court of Human Rights (2007), *Tatishvili v. Russia*, Application No. 1509/02, European Court of Human Rights, Strasbourg, 22 February.

Farooqui, M.I. (2000), *Law of Abandoned Property*, http://www.stateless peopleinbangladesh.net/law_abandoned_property.php, pp 25–29.

Farzana, K.F. (2008), 'The Neglected Stateless Bihari Community in Bangladesh: Victims of Political and Diplomatic Onslaught', *Journal of Humanities and Social Sciences*, **2**(1), 1–19.

Fehervary, A. (1993), 'Citizenship, Statelessness and Human Rights: Recent Developments in the Baltic States', *International Journal of Refugee Law*, **5**(3), 392–423.

Feldman, I. (2008), 'Waiting for Palestine: Refracted Citizenship and Latent Sovereignty in Gaza', *Citizenship Studies*, **12**(5), 447–63.

Foreign and Commonwealth Office (2007) *The Bidoon of Kuwait*, British Embassy, Kuwait, November.

Frelick, B. and M. Lynch. (2005), 'Statelessness: A Forgotten Human Rights Crisis', *Forced Migration Review*, **24**, 65–66.

French Ministry of Foreign and European Affairs (n.d.) 'France and the Abolition of Slavery', http://www.diplomatie.gouv.fr/en/france_159 /history_6813/dossiers_6938/france-and-the-abolition-of-slavery_8095. html.

Gelazis, N.M. (2004), 'The European Union and the Statelessness Problem in the Baltic States', *European Journal of Migration and Law*, **6**(3), 225–42.

Ghazal, R. (2008) 'The Frustration of Being a "Bidoon"', *The National*, 7 November, http://www.thenational.ae/article/20081106/NATIONAL /693483381/1010 November 07. 2008.

Ginsburgs, G. (1966), 'Soviet Citizenship Legislation and Statelessness as a Consequence of the Conflict of Nationality Laws', *International and Comparative Law Quarterly*, **15**(1), 1–54.

Ginsburgs, G. (2000), 'The "Right to a Nationality" and the Regime of Loss of Russian Citizenship', *Review of Central and East European Law*, **26**(1), 1–33.

Goldston, J.A. (2006), 'Holes in the Rights Framework: Racial Discrimination, Citizenship, and the Rights of Noncitizens', *Ethics and International Affairs*, **20**, 321–47.

Government of Sri Lanka (1948), *Citizenship Act No. 18*, 15 November. http://www.unhcr.org/refworld/docid/3ae6b50414.html.

Government of Sri Lanka (2003), *Grant of Citizenship to Persons of Indian Origin Act*, No. 35 of 2003, Colombo, Sri Lanka: State Printing Department.

Grant, S. (2005), 'International Migration and Human Rights', Paper prepared for the Policy Analysis and Research Programme of the Global Commission on International Migration,' Global Commission on Migration, Geneva, http://www.gcim.org/attachements/TP7.pdf.

Green, S. (2000), 'Beyond Ethnoculturalism? German Citizenship in the New Millennium', *German Politics*, **9**(3), 105–24.

Groenendijk, C.A. and B.D. Hart. (2007), *Multiple Nationality: The Practice of Germany and the Netherlands*, Den Haag: T.M.C. Asser Press.

Gyulai, G. (2007), *Forgotten Without Reason: Protection of Non-refugee Stateless Persons in Central Europe*, Budapest: Hungarian Helsinki Committee.

Hackmann, J. and M. Lehti. (2008) 'Introduction: Contested and Shared Places of Memory. History and Politics in North Eastern Europe', *Journal of Baltic Studies,* **39**(4), 377–9.

Handloff, R.E. (ed.) (1990), *Mauritania: A Country Study*, 2nd edn, (Washington, DC: US Government), http://countrystudies.us/ mauritania/.

Hansen, R. (2000), *Citizenship and Immigration in Post-war Britain: The Institutional Origins of a Multicultural Nation*, Oxford: Oxford University Press.

Hansen, R. and P. Weil. (2000), *Dual Nationality, Social Rights and Federal Citizenship in the U.S. and Europe: The Reinvention of Citizenship*, New York: Berghahn Books.

Hanzek, M. (2007), 'When Will Words Become Actions? Reflections On Hate Speech in Slovenia', *Eurozine*, 20 July, http://www.eurozine.com/pdf/2007-07-20- hanzek-en.pdf.

Hegland, C. (2007), 'How Other Countries Detain Terrorist Suspects', *National Journal*, **39**(31), 24–25.

Helton, A.C. (1996), 'Stalin's Legacy of Statelessness', *Christian Science Monitor,* 5 June.

Hess, J.M. (2006), 'Statelessness and the State: Tibetans, Citizenship, and Nationalist Activism in a Transnational World', *International Migration*, **44**(1), 79–103.

High Court of the Republic of Kenya (2003), *Yunus Ali and Others (On behalf of the Nubian Community) v. Attorney General of the Republic of Kenya and Others*, Civil Application No. 256/2003, Nairobi High Court, Nairobi.

Hodgson, D. (1993), 'The International Legal Protection of the Child's Right to a Legal Identity and The problem of Statelessness', *International Journal of Law Policy Family*, **7**(2), 255–70.

Home Office (2009), *Country of Origin Information*, February, http://rds.homeoffice.gov.uk/rds/country_reports.html.

Home Office UK Border Agency (2009), *Kuwait Operational Guidance Note v.5* (dated 3 May 2007), Asylum Policy Directorate, Home Office, March, http://www.ukba.homeoffice.gov.uk/sitecontent/documents/policyandlaw/countryspecificasylumpolicyogns/kuwaitogn?view=Binary.

Hughes, J. (2005), 'Exit in Deeply Divided Societies: Regimes of Discrimination in Estonia and Latvia and the Potential for Russophone Migration', *Journal of Common Market Studies*, **43**(4), 739–62.

Human Rights Committee (1989), *Guye et al. v. France*, Comm. No. 196/1985, Decision of the Human Rights Committee Under Article 5 (4) of the Optional Protocol to the International Covenant on Civil and Political Rights, 35th Session, Geneva.

Human Rights Watch (1995), *Report on the Bidoon of Kuwait*, New York: Human Rights Watch.

Human Rights Watch (2002), *'Illegal People': Haitians and Dominico-Haitians in the Dominican Republic*, (New York.Human Rights Watch), http://www.unhcr.org/refworld/docid/3cf2429a4.html.

Human Rights Watch (2003), *The Horn of Africa War: Mass Expulsions and the Nationality Issue (June 1998–April 2002)*, New York: Human Rights Watch, http://www.hrw.org/sites/default/files/reports/ethioerit0103.pdf.

Human Rights Watch (2010), 'Stateless Again: Palestinian Origin Jordanians Deprived of their Nationality', 2 February, 1-56432-575-x, available at http://www.unhcr.org/refworld/docid/466ac5702.html.

Human Security Commission (2003), *Human Security Now: Protecting and Empowering People* (New York: Commission on Human Security), http://www.humansecurity-chs.org/finalreport/English/FinalReport. pdf.

Hussain, K. (2009), 'The End of Bihari Statelessness', *Forced Migration Review*, **32** April, 30–1, http://www.fmreview.org/FMRpdfs/FMR32/ FMR32.pdf.

Hussein Adam, A. (2009), 'Kenyan Nubians: Standing up to statelessness', *Forced Migration Review*, **32**, 19–20.

Ilias, A. (2002), *Biharis: The Indian Émigrés in Bangladesh: An Objective Analysis*, Faridpur, Bangladesh: Shamsul Haque Foundation.

Inter-American Court of Human Rights (2005), *Yean and Bosico v. Dominican Republic*, Series C, Case 130, 8 September, Inter-American Court of Human Rights, San José, Costa Rica.

International Labour Organization (1958), *ILO Convention No. 110 Adopted in 1958* (Geneva: International Labour Organization).

International Law Commission (2006), *Report of the Work of its 58th Session*, UN General Assembly Official Records, 61st Session, Supplement No. 10, A/61/10, 1 May–9 June and 3 July–11 August (New York: UN General Assembly).

International Law Commission (2001), 'Articles on the Nationality of Natural Persons in relation to the Succession of States', in annex of *Resolution adopted by the General Assembly(on the report of the Sixth Committee (A/55/610)), 55/153. Nationality of Natural Persons in relation to the Succession of States*, New York: United Nations, http://www. un.org/ga/search/view_doc.asp?symbol=A/RES/55/153.

Inter-Parliamentary Union (2005), *Nationality and Statelessness: A Handbook for Parliamentarians*, Geneva: Inter-Parliamentary Union.

IPCC (2008), Climate Change 2007: Impacts, Adaptation and Vulnerability, (Geneva: Intergovernmental Panel on Climate Change), http://www.ipcc.ch/pdf/assessment-report/ar4/wg2/ar4-wg2-intro.pdf.

Islami, R. (1992), *Survey of Stranded Pakistanis Conducted by Pakistan High Commission*.

Jalušič, V. and J. Dedić. (2008), '(The) Erasure – Mass Human Rights Violation and Denial of Responsibility: The Case of Independent Slovenia', *Human Rights Review*, **9**(1), 93–108.

Joseph, S. (ed.) (2000), *Gender and Citizenship in the Middle East*, (Contemporary Issues in the Middle East), Syracuse: Syracuse University Press.

Jubat, A. and B. Ongeri. (2009), 'Kenya's Citizenship on Sale', *East African Standard,* 30 September, http://www.standardmedia.co.ke/mag/ InsidePage.php?id=1144025169&cid=459&.

Kamto, M. (2005), *Preliminary Report on the Expulsion of Aliens*, Prepared for the International Law Commission, A/CN.4/554 (New York: UN General Assembly).

Kareithi, A. (2006), 'Nubians Prepare for Battle to Acquire Citizenship', *East African Standard,* 9 October, http://www.propertykenya.com/news/028841-nubians-prepare-for-battle-to-acquire-citizenship.php.

Kase, K. (2008), 'Vene kodakondsus peibutab Eesti omast rohkem' (Russian Citizenship is More Alluring than Estonian), *Postimees*, 20 October.

Kasearu, K. and A. Trumm. (2008), 'The Material Situation and Life Satisfaction of the Estonian- and Russian-speaking Population', in *Integration Monitoring of the Estonian Society 2008,* (Tallinn: Integration Foundation and Bureau of Population Minister), pp. 7–23.

Kelley, N. (2009), 'Ideas, Interests and Institutions: Conceding Citizenship in Bangladesh', *University of Toronto Law Journal*, 60.

Kemp, C. and A. Little (1987), 'People in Plantations: Means or Ends', *IDS Bulletin*, April, **18**(2).

Kenya Anti-Corruption Commission (2006), *An Examination Report of the Systems, Policies, Procedures and Practices of the Ministry of Immigration and Registration of Persons (April 2006)*, Nairobi: Kenya Anti-Corruption Commission 2006, http://www.kacc.go.ke/default.asp?pageid=86.

Kenya Human Rights Commission (2000), Forgotten People Revisited: Human Rights Abuses in Marsabit and Moyale, Nairobi: Kenya Human Rights Commission.

Kenya Human Rights Commission (2009), *Foreigners at Home; the Dilemma of Citizenship in Northern Kenya,* (Nairobi: Kenya Human Rights Commission), http://khrc.or.ke/images/2009-12/Foreigners%20at%20home.pdf.

Kenya Law Reports (1967), *Kenya Citizenship Act (Chapter 170 Laws of Kenya)*, http://www.kenyalaw.org/kenyalaw/klr_app/frames.php.

Kenya Law Reports (1969a), *Registration of Persons Act (Chapter 107 Laws of Kenya),* Article1, http://www.kenyalaw.org/kenyalaw/klr_app/frames.php.

Kenya Law Reports (1969b) *National Assembly and Presidential Elections Act (Chapter 7, section 4A (2) Laws of Kenya)*, http://www.kenyalaw.org/kenyalaw/klr_app/frames.php.

Kenya Law Reports (2006), 'Statistics Act, 2006, Schedule I', http://www.kenyalaw.org/kenyalaw/klr_app/frames.php.

Kerber, L.K. (2005), 'Toward a History of Statelessness in America', *American Quarterly*, **57**(3), 727–49.

Kerber, L.K. (2007), 'The Stateless as the Citizen's Other: A View from the United States', *American Historical Review*, **112**(1), 1–34.

Khan, M.H. (1993), 'Hopes Run High among Returnees to Pakistan', *Daily Star*, 10 January.

Khan, N. (2004), 'Stranded Pakistanis of Adamjee Nagar in Limbo', *Voice of Stranded Pakistanis*, 4.

Kinne, L. (2001), 'The Benefits of Exile: The Case of FLAM', *Journal of Modern African Studies*, **39**, December, 597–621.

Kionka, R. and R. Vetik. (1996), 'Estonia and the Estonians', in G. Smith (ed.), *The Nationalities Question in the Post-Soviet States*, (London and New York: Longman, pp 129–46.

Kirk, C. (1987), *People in Plantations: A Literature Review and Annotated Bibliography*, (London: IDS).

Knudsen, A. (2009), 'Widening the Protection Gap: The "Politics of Citizenship" for Palestinian Refugees in Lebanon, 1948–2008', *Journal of Refugee Studies*, **22**(1), 51–73.

Kogovšek, N. (2008), 'The Erasure: The Proposal of a Constitutional Law as the Negation of the Rule of Law', in J. Zorn and U. Lipovec Čebron (eds), *Once Upon an Erasure. From Citizens to Illegal Residents in the Republic of Slovenia* (Ljubljana: Študentska založba), pp. 196–210.

Kolsto, P. and H.O. Melberg. (2002), 'Integration, Alienation and Conflict in Estonia and Moldova at the Societal Level: A Comparison', in P. Kolsto. (ed.), *National Integration and Violent Conflict in Post-Soviet Societies, the Cases of Estonia and Moldova* (Rowman and Littlefield), pp 31–70.

Korovkin, T. (2008), 'The Colombian War and "Invisible" Refugees in Ecuador', *Peace Review*, **20**(3), 321–29.

Kotyhorenko, V. (2004), *Etnichni protyrichchya i konflikty v suchasnii Ukraini, (Ethnic tensions and conflicts in contemporary Ukraine: a political concept)*, (Kyiv: Svitohlyad).

Kuwait Human Rights Committee (2007), Report of 10 April 2007.

Lauristin, M. (2008), 'Citizens and Non-citizens: The Different Integration Categories and Tendencies of the Russian-speaking Population', in *Integration Monitoring of the Estonian Society 2008*, (Integration Foundation and Bureau of Population Minister) Tallinn: 2008, pp 142–163.

Louristin, M. and J. Vihalemm (2008), *RIP 2008–2013. Vajadus ja teostatavusuuringu lõpparuanne. Uuvingute raamistik, integratsiooni olemuse ring sihtühmade täpsustamine* [State Integration Programme 2008–2013. Final report of the necessity and feasibility study. The framework of research, specification of integration nature and target groups], Taiwan: Estonian Ministry of Finance.

Law (of Estonia) on Social Protection of Disabled, Article 3.

Law (of Estonia) on State Pension Insurance, Article 4.

Law (of Estonia) on State Support for Families, Article 2.

Law (of Estonia) on Social Protection, Article 4.

Law (of Estonia) *on Social Protection of Unemployed*, Article 2.

League of Nations (1930), *Protocol Relating to a Certain Case of Statelessness* (League of Nations: The Hague, 12 April), Pacific Islands Treaty Series, http://www.paclii.org/pits/en/treaty_database/1930/3. html.

Leclerc, P. and R. Colville. (2007), 'In the Shadows', *Refugees Magazine*, **147**(3), 4–7.

Lee, T.L. (2005), *Statelessness, Human Rights and Gender: Irregular Migrant Workers from Burma in Thailand*, Leiden: Martinus Nijhoff.

Leibovici, M. (2006), 'Apparaitre et Visibilité: Le Monde Selon Hannah Arendt et Emmanuel Levinas', *Journal of Jewish Thought and Philosophy (1053699X)*, **14**(1/2), 55–71.

Leping, K.–O. and O. Toomet (2008), 'Emerging ethnic wage gap: Estonia during political and economic transition', *Journal of Comparative Economics*, **36**, 599–619.

Lewa, C. (2007), 'Issues Related to Minorities and Deprivation of Citizenship', Paper presented at the UN Experts Consultation Conference, UN Office of the High Commissioner for Human Rights, Geneva, 6–7 December.

Linde, R. (2006), 'Statelessness and Roma Communities in the Czech Republic: Competing Theories of State Compliance', *International Journal on Minority and Group Rights*, **13**(4), 341–65.

Lipovec Čebron, U. (2008), '"Without a Health Insurance Card, You're Nobody": An Interview with the Physician Aleksander Doplihar', in J. Zorn and U. Lipovec Čebron (eds), *Once Upon an Erasure. From Citizens to Illegal Residents in the Republic of Slovenia* (Ljubljana: Študentska založba), pp. 89–93.

Loewenfeld, E. (1941), 'Status of Stateless Persons', *Transactions of the Grotius Society*, **27**, 59–112.

Loi no. 61-70 du 7 mars 1961, Code de la nationalité sénégalaise, Article 29.

Loi no. 79 .01 du 4 Janvier 1979, Article 12.

Loi portant code de la nationalité mauritanienne (Loi No. 1961-112), http://www.unhcr.org/refworld/docid/3ae6b5304.html.

London Detainee Support Group (2007), *Difficulties in Removal of Undocumented Iranian Nationals*, (London: London Detainee Support Group), http://www.ldsg.org.uk/files/uploads/dossierssummaries0708. pdf

London Detainee Support Group (2008), *Difficulties in Removal of Undocumented Algerian Nationals*, London: London Detainee Support

Group, http://www.ldsg.org.uk/files/uploads/dossierssummaries0708.
pdf.

London Detainee Support Group (2009), *Detained Lives: The Real
Costs of Indefinite Immigration Detention*, London: London Detainee
Support Group, http://www.detainedlives.org/wp-content/uploads/
detainedlives.pdf.

Lonsdale, J. and Odhiambo, A.E. (2003), Man Man and Nationhood:
Arms, Authority and Narration, 2.

Lynch, M. (2005), *Lives on Hold: the Human Cost of Statelessness*,
Washington, DC: Refugees International.

Lynch, M. (2008), *Futures Denied: Statelessness Among Infants, Children,
and Youth*, Washington, DC: Refugees International, http://www.refu-
geesinternational.org/sites/default/files/Stateless_Children_FINAL.pdf.

Lynch, M. and P. Ali. (2006), *Buried Alive: Stateless Kurds in Syria*,
(Washington, DC: Refugees International), http://www.refugeesinter-
national.org/sites/default/files/BuriedAlive.pdf.

Lynch, M. and D. Calabia. (2006), 'Bangladesh: Stateless Biharis
Grasp for a Resolution and Their Rights', *Refugees International*,
23 March, http://www.refintl.org/policy/field-report/bangladesh-state
less-biharis-grasp-resolution-and-their-rights.

Lynch, M. and T. Cook. (2006), *Citizens of Nowhere: Stateless Biharis
of Bangladesh*, Washington, DC: Refugees International, http://www.
refugeesinternational.org/sites/default/files/Bihari.pdf.

Madawi, Al-R. and Al-R. Loulouwa. (1996), 'The Politics of
Encapsulation: Saudi Policy Towards Tribal and Religious Opposition',
Middle Eastern Studies, **32**(1), January, 96–119.

Mascarenhas, A. (1971), *The Rape of Bangladesh*, New Delhi: Vikas
Publications.

Mascarenhas, A. (1986), *Bangladesh: A Legacy of Blood*, Arnold Overseas.

Magocsi, P.R. (1997), 'Mapping Stateless Peoples: The East Slavs of the
Carpathians', *Canadian Slavonic Papers*, **39**(3/4), 301–331.

Majina Ufanisi. (2007), 'Kibera Integrated Water, Sanitation & Waste
Management Project (K-WATSAN)', http://www.majinaufanisi.org/
projects/k-watsan.htm.

Makoloo M. (2005), *Kenya: Minorities, Indigenous People and Ethnic
Diversity* (London: Minority Rights Group International), http://www.
minorityrights.org/download.php?id=147.

Malawi African Association and Others/Mauritania (2000), African
Commission on Human and Peoples' Rights. Commission Nos 54/91,
61/91, 98/93, 164/9, 196/97 and 210/98, 11 May, http://www.ihrda.
org/images/54-91,%2061-91,%2098-93,%20164-197,%20210-98%20
Mauritania.pdf.

Manby, B. (2009a), 'Citizenship the Most Important Right of All', *African Arguments*, http://africanarguments.org/2009/10/citizenship-the-most-important-right-of-all/.

Manby, B. (2009b), *Struggles for Citizenship in Africa*, London: Zed Books.

Manby, B. (2009c), *Citizenship Law in Africa*, (Dakar, Senegal: Open Society Institute), http://www.soros.org/initiatives/justice/focus/equal ity_citizenship/articles_publications/publications/citizenship_20091009.

Mavroudi, E. (2008), 'Palestinians in Diaspora, Empowerment and Informal Political Space', *Political Geography*, 27(1), 57–73.

Mayoyo, P. and E. Otieno (2009), 'Long-standing Struggle for Migingo to be Discussed', *Daily Nation*, 11 March, http://www.nation.co.ke/News/-/1056/544676/-/u34cmv/-/index.html.

McKinsey, K. (2007) 'The Biharis of Bangladesh', *Refugees Magazine* 147, 10 September, http://www.unhcr.org/46dbccb42.html.

Medved, F. (2007), 'From Civic to Ethnic Community? The Evolution of Slovenian Citizenship', in R. Bauböck, B. Perching and W. Sievers (eds), *Citizenship Policies in the New Europe*, Amsterdam: Amsterdam University Press, pp 305–38.

Mekina, B. (2008), 'A Monument to the Erased', in J. Zorn and U. Lipovec Čebron (eds), *Once Upon an Erasure: From Citizens to Illegal Residents in the Republic of Slovenia*, Ljubljana: Študentska založba, pp. 44–51.

Mekina, Igor (2004), 'Izgnani, deložirani, izbrisani' (Expelled, evicted, erased) in *Mladina*, 22 November.

Menkhaus, K. (1998), 'Somalia: Political Order in a Stateless Society', *Current History*, 97(619), 220–4.

Menkhaus, K. and J. Prendergast. (1995), 'The Stateless State', *Africa Report*, 40(3), 22–5.

Mežnarić, S. (1986), *'Bosanci': A Kuda Idu Slovenci Nedeljom?*, Ljubljana: Krt.

Minahan, J. (2002), *Encyclopaedia of the Stateless Nations: Ethnic and National Groups Around the World*, Vols, four, A–Z, Santa Barbara: Greenwood Press.

Minorities at Risk Project (2007), 'Chronology for Biharis in Bangladesh', Minorities at Risk Project, University of Maryland, 10 January, http://www.cidcm.umd.edu/mar/chronology.asp?groupId=77103.

Mukhtar Ahmed v. Government (of Bangladesh), 34 DLR (1982) 29.

Muslih, M. and A.R. Norton (1991), 'The Need for Arab Democracy', *Foreign Policy*, 83, Summer.

Mutua, M. wa (1995), 'The Banjul Charter and the African Cultural Fingerprint: An Evaluation of the Language of Duties', *Virginia Journal of International Law*, 35, 339–80.

Mydans, S. (2009), 'Thailand is Accused of Rejecting Migrants', *New York Times,* 17 January.

Nadesan, S. (1993), *A History of Up-Country People in Sri Lanka*, Hatton, Sri Lanka: Nandalala Publication.

National Archives of Kenya (1933), *Kenya Land Commission Report*, Evidence,'Vol.1, (Nairobi: Kenya National Archives), p. 170.

National Assembly of Kenya, *Report of the Parliamentary Commission on Ethnic Clashes (Chaired by Kenneth Kiliku, 1993–1997)*, Nairobi: National Assembly of Kenya.

National Assembly of Slovenia (1991), *Transcripts of the National Assembly Sitting No 19*, 9, 15, 21, 22, 30 May and 3, 5 June, (Ljubljana: National Assembly of Slovenia).

National Land Policy Secretariat (2007), *Draft National Land Policy*, Ministry Of Lands, Nairobi, Kenya, http://www.ilegkenya.org/pubs/docs/DraftNationalLandPolicy.pdf.

Noble, K. B. (1989), An African Exodus with Racial Overtones, *New York Times*, 22 July.

Nyo, N. (2001), 'Burmese Children in Thailand: Legal Aspects', *Legal Issues on Burma Journal*, **10**, 51–56.

OBAT Helpers, Inc. (2009), 'Urdu-speaking People Should Have Equal Rights: Says US Ambassador', Diplomatic Correspondent, *Newage Bangladesh*, 24 November.

OBAT Helpers, Inc. (n.d.), http://www.obathelpers.org/index.html.

Odhiambo, A.E.S. and J. Lonsdale. (2003), *Mau Mau and Nationhood: Arms, Authority and Narration*, Athens, OH: Ohio University Press.

Official Gazette of the Republic of Slovenia (1991), 'Citizenship of the Republic of Slovenia Act', *Official Gazette of the Republic of Slovenia*, No. 1/1991, English version (Ljubljana: Republic of Slovenia), http://www.mnz.gov.si/fileadmin/mnz.gov.si/pageuploads/EN/enDUNZ/ZDRS-Eng.doc.

Official Gazette of the Republic of Slovenia (1997), 'Temporary Asylum Act', *Official Gazette of the Republic of Slovenia*, No. 20/1997.

Official Gazette of the Republic of Slovenia (1999), 'Act Regulating the Legal Status of Citizens of Former Yugoslavia Living in the Republic of Slovenia', *Official Gazette of the Republic of Slovenia*, No. 61/1999

Official Gazette of the Republic of Slovenia (2000), 'Passports of the Citizens of the Republic of Slovenia Act', *Official Gazette of the Republic of Slovenia*, No. 65/2000.

Official Gazette of the Republic of Slovenia (2003a), 'Decision of the Constitutional Court of Slovenia U-I-246/02-28', *Official Gazette of the Republic of Slovenia*, No. 36/2003.

Official Gazette of the Republic of Slovenia (2003b), 'Housing Act', *Official Gazette of the Republic of Slovenia*, No. 69/2003.

Official Gazette of the Republic of Slovenia (2004a), 'Social Assistance Act,' *Official Gazette of the Republic of Slovenia*, No. 36/2004.

Official Gazette of the Republic of Slovenia (2004b), 'Free Legal Aid Act', *Official Gazette of the Republic of Slovenia*, No. 96/2004.

Official Gazette of the Republic of Slovenia (2006a), 'Employment and Work of Aliens Act', *Official Gazette of the Republic of Slovenia*, No. 4/2006, English version (Ljubljana: Republic of Slovenia), http://www.mddsz.gov.si/fileadmin/mddsz.gov.si/pageuploads/dokumenti__pdf/zz dt_upb1_en.pdf.

Official Gazette of the Republic of Slovenia (2006b), 'Health Care and Health Insurance Act of the Republic of Slovenia', *Official Gazette of the Republic of Slovenia*, No. 72/2006.

Official Gazette of the Republic of Slovenia (2006c), 'Elementary School Act', *Official Gazette of the Republic of Slovenia*, No. 81/2006.

Official Gazette of the Republic of Slovenia (2006d), Gimnazije Act', *Official Gazette of the Republic of Slovenia*, No. 115/2006.

Official Gazette of the Republic of Slovenia (2006e), Higher Education Act', *Official Gazette of the Republic of Slovenia*, No. 119/2006.

Official Gazette of the Republic of Slovenia (2006f), National Assembly Elections Act', *Official Gazette of the Republic of Slovenia*, No. 109/2006.

Official Gazette of the Republic of Slovenia (2007), 'International Protection Act', *Official Gazette of the Republic of Slovenia*, No. 111/2007.

Ogola, B.D. (1996), 'Land Tenure System', in C. Juma and J.B. Ojwang (eds), *Land We Trust: Environment, Private Property and Constitutional Change* (Nairobi and London: Initiatives Publishers and Zed Books), pp. 85-116.

Open Society Justice Initiative (2006), 'Human Rights and Legal Identity: Approaches to Combating Statelessness and Arbitrary Deprivation of Nationality–Thematic Conference Paper', http://dev.justiceinitiative. org/db/resource2/fs/?file_id=17050.

Open Society Justice Initiative and Afrimap (2009), *Citizenship Laws in Africa* (New York: Open Society Institute).

Ordonnance no. 91.022 du 20 Juillet 1991 portant Constitution de la République Islamique de Mauritanie, Journal Officiel du 30 Juillet 1991, P.446), Titre II: Du Pouvoir Exécutif, Article 26, 'Est éligible à la Présidence de la République, tout citoyen né mauritanien jouissant de ses droits civils et politiques'.

Organization of African Unity (1990), *African Charter on the Rights and*

Welfare of the Child, 11 July, CAB/LEG/24.9/49, http://www.unhcr.org/refworld/docid/3ae6638c18.html.

OSI (2004), *Africa Citizenship and Discrimination Audit*, New York: Open Society Institute.

Pakistan Citizenship Act, 1951(Pakistan),13 April, http://www.unhcr.org/refworld/docid/3ae6b4ffa.html.

Palmer, R.R. (1959), *The Age of the Democratic Revolution: The Challenge*, Princeton: Princeton University Press.

Palmer, R.R. (1961), *The World of the French Revolution*, New York: Harper and Row.

Parekh, S. (2004), 'A Meaningful Place in the World: Hannah Arendt on the Nature of Human Rights', *Journal of Human Rights*, 3(1), 41–53.

Parker, R. (1991), 'The Senegal-Mauritania Conflict of 1989: A Fragile Equilibrium', *Journal of Modern African Studies*, 29(1), 155-171.

Parliamentary Committee for Defending Human Rights in Kuwait (2005), *Report by The Parliamentary Committee for Defending Human Rights in Kuwait*, June, 9th section.

Parveen, S. (2008) 'Citizenship Debate Comes to End But Doubts and Worries Remain', *Daily Star* 26 May, http://www.thedailystar.net/pf_story.php?nid=38148.

Pattie, C., P. Seyd and P. Whiteley (2004), *Citizenship in Britain: Values, Participation and Democracy*, Cambridge: Cambridge University Press.

Paulsen, E. (2006), 'The Citizenship Status of the Urdu-speakers/Biharis in Bangladesh', *Refugee Survey Quarterly*, 25, 54–69.

Peace Institute (2007), 'The Erased Residents of Slovenia: A Challenge for a Young Democratic State', http://www.mirovni-institut.si/Projekt/Detail/si/projekt/Izbrisani-prebivalci-Slovenije-Izziv-za-mlado-drzavo/.

Peled, Y. (2005), 'Restoring Ethnic Democracy: The Or Commission and Palestinian Citizenship in Israel', *Citizenship Studies*, 9(1), 89–105.

Peled, Y. (2008), 'The Evolution of Israeli Citizenship: An Overview', *Citizenship Studies*, 12(3), 335–45.

Pension and Disability Insurance Institute of the Republic of Slovenia, 'Kako do Državne Pokojne?, (How to Obtain a State Pension) (ZPIZ–Zavod za pokojninsko in invalidsko zavarovanje Slovenije, Ljubljana: The Institute of Pension and Invalidity Insurance of Slovenia, http://www.zpiz.si/src/pravice/drzavna.html.

Perara, S. (2007), 'Sri Lankan Success Story', *Refugees Magazine*, 147, September, 20–23.

Perić, T. (2003), 'Personal Documents and Threats to the Exercise of Fundamental Rights of Roma in Europe', *Roma Rights*, 3, 7–16.

Phadnis, U. (1967), 'The Indo-Ceylon Pact and the "Stateless" Indians in Ceylon', *Asian Survey*, 4(4), 226–36.

Pistotnik, S. (2008), 'Chronology of the Erasure 1990–2007', in J. Zorn and U. Lipovec Čebron (eds), *Once Upon an Erasure. From Citizens to Illegal Residents in the Republic of Slovenia*, Ljubljana: Študentska založba, pp. 222–60.

Plender, R. (ed.) (1988), *Basic Documents on International Migration Law* The Hague: Martinus Nijhoff.

Pohorilko, V. and V. Fedorenko (2006), *Konstitutsiine pravo Ukrainy* (*Constitution Law of Ukraine*), Kyiv: Naukova Dumka.

Presidential Press Services (2007), 'A Special Committee Appointed to Address Muslims' Issues', 17 October, http://www.kbc.co.ke/story. asp?ID=45789.

Prybytkova, I. (1999) *Pravovyye i gumanitarnyye problemy reintegratsii ranyeye deportirovanykh v Krymu* (*Legal and Humanitarian Problems of the Formerly Deported Persons in Crimea*), Kyiv: Glossariy.

Public Service Act (of Estonia), 25 January 1995, *State Gazette* I, 16, 228.

Rapport Explicatif de Mlle Elisa Pérez-Vera (*Explanatory Report by Elisa Pérez-Vera*) (1982), in 3 Conférence de la Haye de Droit International Privé, actes et documents de la Quartorziéme session, enlévement d'enfants (Hague Conference on Private International Law, Acts and Documents of the Fourteenth Session, Child Abduction).

Refugee and Migratory Movements Research Unit (2007), 'Accessing Rights as Citizens: The Camp-based Urdu Speaking Community in Bangladesh', Policy Brief 2 September.

Refugee and Migratory Movements Research Unit (2008), 'Demand for Rehabilitation with Dignity for the Dwellers of 116 Camps in Bangladesh', Press Release, 1, 25 August.

Refugees International (2004), *Stolen Futures: The Stateless Children of Burmese Asylum Seekers*, Washington, DC: Refugees International.

Refugees International (2007a), 'Senegal: Voluntary Repatriation Critical for Protecting Stateless Mauritanians', 9 February, http://www. refintl.org/policy/field-report/senegal-voluntary-repatriation-critical-pro tecting-stateless-mauritanians.

Refugees International (2007b), 'Kuwait: State of Exclusion', 25 July.

Refugees International (2007c), 'About Being Without: Stories of Stateless in Kuwait', October, http://www.refugeesinternational.org/files/10235_ file_Kuwaitstatelessrpt.pdf.

Refugees International (2008a), *Rohingya: Burma's Forgotten Minority*, Washington, DC: Refugees International, http://www.refugeesinterna-tional.org/sites/default/files/RohingyaDec19.pdf.

Refugees International (2008b), Kenya Voices: A Nubian Elder's Reflections on Ending Statelessness, Washington, DC: Refugees

International, http://www.refugeesinternational.org/blog/refugee-story/
  refugee-voices-nubian-elder%E2%80%99s-reflections-ending-statelessness.
Refugees International (2008c), 'Kuwait: Honor Nationality Rights of
  Bidoon',   17   September,http://www.refinth.org/policy/field-report/
  kuwait-honor-nationality-rights-bidyn.
Republic of Kenya (2008), *Constitution of Kenya*, http://www.justice.
  go.ke/index.php?option=com_content&task=view&id=18&Itemid=94.
Republic of Kenya (2009), *The Harmonized Draft of the Constitution of
  Kenya*, http://www.coekenya.go.ke/index.php?option=com_content&vi
  ew=article&id=113&Itemid=109.
Republic of Slovenia (1991), *Constitution of the Republic of Slovenia*, 23
  December, http://www.unhcr.org/refworld/docid/3ae6b4fc20.html.
Republic of Slovenia (1999), *Aliens Act*, 61/99, 30 July, http://www.unhcr.
  org/refworld/docid/3ae6b59c14.html.
Republic of Ukraine (2001), 'Law "Of citizenship of Ukraine"', No
  2235-III,   18   January,   http://zakon.rada.gov.ua/cgi-bin/laws/main.
  cgi?nreg=2235-14.
Research for Development (2008), *Rights of the Camp-dwelling 'Bihari'
  Community in Bangladesh*, January, http://www.research4development.
  info/caseStudies.asp?ArticleID=50180.
Riigikogu Election Act (of Estonia), 12 June 2002, *State Gazette* I, 57, 355.
Rizzo, H., K. Meyer and Y. Ali (2007), 'Extending Political Rights in The
  Middle East: The Case of Kuwait', *Journal of Political and Military
  Sociology*, **35**(2), 177–97.
Robinson, N. (1955), *Convention Relating to the Status of Stateless
  Persons: Its History and Interpretation*, Geneva: UNHCR.
Sadakat Khan and Others v. The Chief Election Commissioner (of
  Bangladesh), Writ Petition No. 10129, 10 (2007).
Sagna, S. (2009), 'Retour Volontaire et Protection internationale: Le rôle
  du HCR', *Atelier de Réflexion sur le retour des réfugiés*, FONADH,
  IHRDA, HCR, Nouakchott, 12–13 December.
Saldanha, A. (2009), 'Bahrain's Demographic Tensions', Arabist.com,
  http://www.arabisto.com/article.cfm?articleID=756.
Saloojee, A. (2005), 'Social Inclusion, Anti Racism and Democratic
  Citizenship', in T. Richmond and A Saloojee (eds), *Social Inclusion:
  Canadian Perspectives*, Toronto, Ontario: Fernwood Publishing.
Samore, W. (1951), 'Statelessness as a Consequence of the Conflict of
  Nationality Laws', *American Journal of International Law*, **45**(3), 476–94.
Sawyer, C. and P. Turpin, (2005), 'Neither Here Nor There: Temporary
  Admission to the UK', *International Journal of Refugee Law*, **17**, 688–728.
Sen, A. (2001), *Development as Freedom*, Oxford: Oxford University Press.
Sen, S. (1999), 'Stateless Refugees and the Right to Return: Bihari

Refugees of South Asia – Part 1', *International Journal of Refugee Law*, **11**, p (4) 625–45.

Sen, S. (2000), 'Stateless Refugees and the Right to Return: Bihari Refugees of South Asia – Part II', *International Journal of Refugee Law*, 12.

Shah, M.A. (1997), *The Foreign Policy of Pakistan: Ethnic Impacts on Diplomacy, 1971–1994* London: I.B. Taurus.

Shanmugaratnam, N. (1997), *Privatisation of Tea Plantations: The Challenge of Reforming Production Relations*, Colombo, Sri Lanka: Social Scientists Association.

Shaw, J. (2007), *The Transformation of Citizenship in the European Union: Electoral Rights and the Restructuring of Political Space*, Cambridge: Cambridge University Press.

Shevel, O. (2002), 'Crimean Tatars and the Ukrainian State: The Challenge of Politics, the Use of Law, and the Meaning of Rhetoric', Information bulletin, Krymski Studii No. 1 (7).

Shiblak, A. (2006), 'Stateless Palestinians', *Forced Migration Review*, **26**, 8–9.

Shiblak, A. (2009), 'The Palestinian Refugee Issue: A Palestinian Perspective', MENAP, 9 January (London: Chatham House, Royal Institute of International Affairs).

Singo'ei, A.K. (2009), 'Promoting Citizenship in Kenya: The Nubian Case', in B.K. Blitz. and M. Lynch (eds), *Statelessness and the Benefits of Citizenship: A Comparative Study*, pp. 37–49, http://www.udhr60.ch/report/statelessness_paper0609.pdf.

Sing'Oei, K. and A. Hussein (2002), 'Covert Racism: Kibera Clashes. An Audit of Political Manipulation of Citizenship in Kenya and 100 years of Nubian Landlessness', Unpublished manuscript, November.

Smith, G.V., A. Law, A. Wilson, A. Bohr and E. Allworth (1998), *Nation-building in Post-Soviet Borderlands. The Politics of National Identities*, Cambridge: Cambridge University Press.

Sokoloff, C. (2005), *Denial of Citizenship: A Challenge to Human Security*, Report Prepared for the Advisory Board on Human Security with the Support of the Ford Foundation (New York: The Advisory Board on Human Security, http://ochaonline.un.org/ochalinkclick.aspx?link=ocha&docid=1003253.

Sokoloff, C. and R. Lewis (2005), 'Denial of Citizenship: A Challenge to Human Security', European Policy Centre Issue Paper 28, European Policy Centre, Brussels, http://www.epc.eu/TEWN/pdf/724318296_EPC%20Issue%20Paper%2028%20Denial%20of%20Citizenship.pdf.

South Asia Forum for Human Rights (n. d.), 'Bangladesh State and the Refugee Phenomenon', South Asia Forum for Human Rights, http://www.safhr.org/refugee_watch18_4.htm.

Southwick, K. and D. Calabia (2008), 'Bangladesh: Maintain Momentum to Guarantee Citizenship Rights', *Refugees International* September, http://www.refintl.org/policy/field-report/bangladesh-maintain-momentum-gu arantee-citizenship-rights.

Southwick, K. and M. Lynch (2009), *Nationality Rights for All: A Progress Report and Global Survey on Statelessness March*, (Washington, DC: Refugees International), http://www.refintl.org/sites/default/files/RI%20 Stateless%20Report_FINAL_031109.pdf.

Soysal, Y.N. (1994), *Limits of Citizenship: Migrants and Postnational Membership in Europe*, Chicago: University of Chicago Press.

Steen, A. (2006), 'Accessioning Liberal Compliance? Baltic Elites and Ethnic Politics Under New International Conditions', *International Journal on Minority and Group Rights*, **13**, 187–207.

Stevens, J. (2006), 'Prisons of the Stateless', *New Left Review*, **42**, 53–67.

Struharova, B. (1999), 'Disparate Impact: Removing Roma from the Czech Republic', *Roma Rights*, **1**, 47–51.

Swissinfo.ch (2008), 21 October.

Takkenberg, L. (1988), *The Status of Palestinian Refugees in International Law*, Oxford: Clarendon Press.

Tiburcio, C. (2001), *The Human Rights of Aliens Under International and Comparative Law*, The Hague: Kluwer Law International.

Tripartite Agreement of Bangladesh-Pakistan-India, (1974).

Tubb, D. (2006), 'Statelessness and Colombia: Hannah Arendt and the Failure of Human Rights', *Undercurrent*, 3(2), 39–51.

Tyshchenko, Y. (ed.) (2004), *Aktualni pytannya vitchyznyanoi etnopolityky: shlyakhy modernizatsii, vrakhuvannya mizhnarodnoho dosvidu* (*Topical Issues of Domestic Ethnic Policy: Ways of Modernization, Taking into Consideration of International Experience*), Kyiv: Ahenstvo Ukraina.

Tyshchenko, Y., O. Vlasenko, V. Subotenko, N. Belitser. and S. Kadhzametova (2004), *Pravova dopomoha ranishe deportovannym hromadyanam: teorytychni ta praktychni aspekty yak shlyakh do zakonodavchikh zmin* (*Legal Aid for the Formerly Deported Citizens: Theoretical and Practical Aspects as a Way to Legislative Changes*), Kyiv: Ahenstvo Ukraina.

Uehling, G. (2004), 'Evaluation of UNHCR's Programme to Prevent and Reduce Statelessness in Crimea, Ukraine', EPAU/2004/03, March, United Nations High Commissioner For Refugees Evaluation and Policy Analysis Unit (Geneva), http://www.unhcr.org/research/RESEARCH/405ab4c74.pdf.

Uehling, G. (2008), 'Livelihoods of Former Deportees in Ukraine', *Forced Migration Review*, **20**, 19–20.

UN (1949), *A Study of Statelessness*, E/1112, August, New York: United Nations.

UN (2003), *Human Security Now: Protecting and Empowering People*, (New York: United Nations).

UN Committee on Economic Social and Cultural Rights (2008), *Concluding Observations on Kenya's Initial Report*, E/C.12/KEN/1,19 November (Geneva: Office of the High Commissioner for Human Rights), http://sim.law.uu.nl/SIM/CaseLaw/uncom.nsf/804bb175b68baaf7c125667f00 4cb333/4105a1d93c2984cbc12575520048ef41?OpenDocument.

UN Committee on the Elimination of Racial Discrimination (1997), *Concluding Observations of the Committee on the Elimination of Racial Discrimination, Sweden*, A/52/18, (New York: UN Committee of the Elimination Racial Discrimination).

UN Committee on the Elimination of Racial Discrimination (2002), *Concluding Observations of the Committee on the Elimination of Racial Discrimination, Lithuania*, A/57/18, New York: UN Committee on the Elimination of Racial Discrimination.

UN Committee on the Elimination of Racial Discrimination (2004), *United Nations Committee on the Elimination of Racial Discrimination 2004. General Recommendation 30: Discrimination against Non-citizens*, Geneva: Office of the High Commissioner for Human Rights, CERD/C/64/Misc.11/Rev.3.

UN Committee on the Rights of the Child (2005a), *General Comment No. 6: Treatment of Unaccompanied and Separated Children Outside their Country of Origin*, 1 September, (Geneva: UN Committee on the Rights of the Child).

UN Committee on the Rights of the Child (2005b), *Concluding Observations: Iran*, CRC/C/146 (Geneva: UN Committee on the Rights of the Child).

UN General Assembly (1948), *Universal Declaration of Human Rights*, 10 December, New York: UN General Assembly, http://www.unhcr.org/refworld/docid/3ae6b3712c.html.

UN General Assembly (1954), *Convention Relating to the Status of Stateless Persons*, 28 September, United Nations, Treaty Series, Vol. 360, New York: UN General Assembly, p. 117, http://www.unhcr.org/refworld/docid/3ae6b3840.html.

UN General Assembly (1961), *International Convention on the Protection of the Rights of All Migrant Workers and Members of their Families*, 18 December, A/RES/45/158, New York: UN General Assembly, http://www.unhcr.org/refworld/docid/3ae6b3980.html.

UN General Assembly (1965), *International Convention on the Elimination of All Forms of Racial Discrimination*, 21 December, United Nations,

Treaty Series, Vol. 660, (New York: UN General Assembly), p. 195, http://www.unhcr.org/refworld.docid/3ae663940.html.

UN General Assembly (1966a), *International Covenant on Economic, Social and Cultural Rights*, 16 December, United Nations, Treaty Series, Vol. 993, New York: UN General Assembly, p. 3, http://www.unhcr. org/refworld/docid/3ae6b36c0.html.

UN General Assembly (1966b), *International Covenant on Civil and Political Rights*, 16 December, United Nations, Treaty Series, Vol. 999, New York: UN General Assembly, p. 171, http://www.unhcr.org/ refworld/docid/3ae6b3aa0.html.

UN General Assembly (1975), *1961 Convention on the Reduction of Statelessness*, 30 August 1961, United Nations, Treaty Series, Vol. 989, New York: UN General Assembly p. 175, http://www.unhcr.org/ refworld/docid/3ae6b39620.html.

UN General Assembly (1989), Convention on the Rights of the child, 20 November, United Nations, Treaty Series, Vol. 1577 (New York: UN General Assembly), p. 3, http://www.unhcr.org/refworld/ docid/3ae6b38f0.html

UN General Assembly (2007a), *Report Of The Special Rapporteur on the Situation of Human Rights And Fundamental Freedoms Of Indigenous People, Rodolfo Stavenhagen-Mission to Kenya*, A/HRC/4/32/Add.3, 6, 26 February, New York: UN General Assembly, http://www.scribd.com/ doc/2584332/UN-Special-Rapportour-Radolfo-Stavenhagenreport.

UN General Assembly (2007b), *Human Rights Council, Working Group on the Universal Periodic Review–Third Session Geneva, 1–15 December 2008, Summary Prepared by the Office of the High Commissioner for Human Rights, in Accordance with Paragraph 15 (C) of the Annex to Human Rights Council Resolution 5/1–United Arab Emirates*, http://lib. ohchr.org/HRBodies/UPR/Documents/Session3/AE/A_HRC_WG6_3_ ARE_3_United_Arab_Emirates_E.pdf.

UN General Assembly (2008), *Promotion and Protection of All Human Rights, Civil, Political, Economic, Social and Cultural Rights, Including The Right To Development. Report of the Independent Expert on Minority Issues, Gay McDougall*, A/HRC/7/23, 28 February 2008 (New York: Human Rights Council, UN General Assembly, http://www.unhcr.org/ refworld/docid/47d685ea2.html.

UN Human Rights Committee (1986), *CCPR General Comment No. 15: The Position of Aliens under the Covenant*, 11 April, Geneva: United Nations Human Rights Committee.

UN Human Rights Committee (1989), *General Comment No. 18: Non-discrimination*, 10 November, Geneva: United Nations Human Rights Committee.

UN Human Rights Committee (1996a), *General Comment No. 25: The Right to Participate in Public Affairs, Voting Rights and the Right of Equal Access to Public Service*, 12 July, Geneva: United Nations Human Rights Committee.

UN Human Rights Committee (1996b), Concluding Observations: Estonia, A/51/40, Geneva: United Nations Human Rights Committee.

UN Human Rights Committee (1997), *Portugal*, A/52/40, Vol. 1, Geneva: United Nations Human Rights Committee.

UN Human Rights Committee (1999), *General Comment No. 27: Freedom of Movement*, 2 November, Geneva: United Nations Human Rights Committee.

UN Human Rights Committee (2002), *Switzerland*, A/57/40, Vol. 1, Geneva: United Nations Human Rights Committee.

UN Human Rights Council (2008), 'Press Statement of UN Human Rights Council, Conclusion of the Interactive Debate on Reports on Right to Adequate Housing and Minority Issues', 13 March, Geneva: United Nations Human Rights Council, http://www.unhcr.ch/hu ricane/huricane.nsf/0/43480pendocument.

UN Human Rights Council (2009), *Arbitrary Deprivation of Nationality: Report of the Secretary-General*, A/HRC/10/34, 26 January, Geneva: United Nations Human Rights Council, http://www.unhcr.org/refworld/docid/49958be22.html.

UN Office of the High Commissioner for Human Rights (2009), 'The Story of Khalid Hussain', Durban Review Conference, Geneva, 20–24 April, http://www.un.org/durbanreview2009/story27.html.

UNDP (1994), *Human Development Report 1994 – New Dimensions of Human Security*, New York and Oxford: Oxford University Press.

UNDP (2006), *Status of Oralmans in Kazakhstan–Overview*, (Almaty: United Nations Development Programme, http://www.undp.kz/library_of_publications/files/6838-29587.pdf.

UNHCR (1992), *Handbook on Procedures and Criteria for Determining Refugee Status under the 1951 Convention and the 1967 Protocol relating to the Status of Refugees, HCR/IP/Eng/Rev.1, Re-edited January 1992*, Geneva: United Nations High Commissioner for Refugees.

UNHCR (1998), 'Crimean Tatar Activist Receives Nansen Medal', Press Release, 5 October, http://www.unhcr.org/cgi-bin/texis/vtx/search?page =search&docid=3ae6b81840&query=mustafa%20dzhemilev.

UNHCR (2004a), *Final Report Concerning the Questionnaire on Statelessness Pursuant to the Agenda for Protection, March*, Geneva: United Nations High Commissioner for Refugees.

UNHCR (2004b), 'Citizenship for All, Focus On Protection,' (2004), United Nations High Commissioner for Refugees: Colombo, Sri Lanka.

UNHCR (2006), *UNHCR Executive Committee, Conclusion No. 106: Conclusion on Identification, Prevention and Reduction of Statelessness and Protection of Stateless Persons*, Geneva: United Nations High Commissioner for Refugees.

UNHCR (2007), 'The Excluded: The Strange Hidden World of the Stateless', *Refugees Magazine*, 147, September, http://www.unhcr.org/publ/PUBL/46d2e8dc2.pdf.

UNHCR (2008), 'Launch of Voluntary Repatriation for Mauritanian Refugees from Senegal', Press Briefing, 29 January, Geneva: United Nations High Commissioner for Refugees.

UNHCR (2009a), *Climate Change and Statelessness: An Overview*, 15 May, (Geneva: United Nations High Commissioner for Refugees, http://www.unhcr.org/refworld/docid/4a2d189d3.html.

UNHCR (2009b), *Note on the Nationality Status of the Urdu-speaking Community of Bangladesh*, December, Geneva: United Nations High Commissioner for Refugees, http://www.unhcr.org/refworld/docid/4b2b90c32.html.

UNHCR (2009c), Addressing Situations of Statelessness, UNHCR Global Appeal 2009 Update, Geneva: United Nations High Commissioner for Refugees, http://www.unhcr.org/publ/PUBL/4922d4370.pdf.

UNICEF (2008), 'Child Protection From Violence, Exploitation and Abuse', 7 April, http://www.unicef.org/protection/index_birthregistration.html

UNRIAA (1931), *Dickson Car Wheel Co. (USA) v. United Mexican States*, UNRIAA, Vol. IV (Sales No. 1951.V.1), July.

US Department of State (2007), *Country Report on Human Rights Practices 2006, Kuwait*, 6 March, (Washington, DC: United States Department of State).

US Department of State (2009), *Background Note – Bahrain 2009*, Washington, DC: United States Department of State, http://www.state.gov/r/pa/ei/bgn/26414.htm.

United States Supreme Court (1958), *Trop v. Dulles, Secretary of State et al.*, 356 US 86, Washington, DC: United States Supreme Court.

Upchurch, A. (2002), *Modern Child Slavery: The Coercion And Exploitation of Youth Worldwide* (Washington, DC: Youth Advocate Program International, http://www.childtrafficking.com/Docs/yap_international_2002__mod.pdf.

Van Waas, L. (2008), *Nationality Matters: Statelessness Under International Law*, Antwerp: Intersentia.

Vandenabeele, C. (2007), 'Establishing Legal Identity for Inclusive Development: Bangladesh, Cambodia, Nepal', Presentation at Children without a State: A Human Rights Challenge Birth Registration and

Irregular Migration, Kennedy School of Government, Carr Center for Human Rights Policy and Committee on Human Rights Studies, Harvard University, Cambridge, Massachusetts, http://www.adb. org/Documents/Events/2007/Legal-Identity-Inclusive-Development/reg istration-benefits.pdf.

Vandenabeele, C. and C.V. Lao (eds) (2007), *Legal Identity for Inclusive Development*, Manila: Asian Development Bank.

Vetik, R. (1993), 'Ethnic Conflict and Accommodation in Post-communist Estonia', *Journal of Peace Research*, **30**(3), 271–80.

Vetik, R. (2001), 'Democratic Multiculturalism: A New Model of National Integration,' (Mariehamn, Finland: Åland Islands Peace Institute).

Vetik, R. (2002), 'The Cultural and Social Makeup of Estonia', in P. Kolsto (ed.), *National Integration and Violent Conflict in Post-Soviet Societies*, Lanham: Rowman & Littlefield, pp 71–105.

Vetik, R. (2008), 'State Identity and the Cohesiveness of the Society's Public Sphere', in *Integration Monitoring of the Estonian Society 2008*, Integration Foundation and Bureau of Population Minister Tallinn: pp. 164–79.

Vihalemm, T. (2008) 'Language Skill and Attitudes', in *Integration Monitoring of the Estonian Society 2008*, (Integration Foundation and Bureau of Population Minister Tallinn: pp 71–80.

Vivatvaraphol, T. (2009), 'Back to Basics: Determining a Child's Habitual Residence in International Child Abduction Cases Under the Hague Convention', *Fordham Law Review*, May, p. 77, 3325.

Walker, D. (1981), 'Statelessness: Violation or Conduit for Violation of Human Rights?', *Human Rights Quarterly*, **3**(1), 107–108.

Weis, P. (1979), *Nationality and Statelessness in International Law*, Alphen aan den Rijn, the Netherlands: Sijthoff & Noordhoff.

Weissbrodt, D. (2001), *Prevention of Discrimination and Protection of Indigenous Peoples and Minorities: The Rights of Non-citizens, Preliminary report of the Special Rapporteur, Mr. David Weissbrodt, Submitted in Accordance with Sub-Commission Decision 2000/103*, UN Doc. E/CN.4/Sub.2/2001/20/Add.1 (Geneva: Office of the United Nations High Commissioner for Human Rights).

Weissbrodt, D. (2003), *Final Report on the Rights of Non-Citizens*, UN Doc. E/CN.4/Sub.2/2003/23 (Geneva: Office of the United Nations High Commissioner for Human Rights).

Weissbrodt, D. (2008), *The Human Rights of Non-citizens*, Oxford: Oxford University Press.

Weissbrodt, D. and C. Collins (2006), 'The Human Rights of Stateless Persons', *Human Rights Quarterly*, **28**(1), 245–76.

Wertsch, J.V. (2008), 'Collective Memory and Narrative Templates', *Social Research,* **75**(1), 133–156.

Wiegandt, M.H. (1995), 'The Russian Minority in Estonia', *International Journal on Minority and Group Rights*, **3**, 109–43.

Wooding, B. (2008), 'Contesting Dominican Discrimination and Statelessness', *Peace Review*, **20**(3), 366–75.

World Bank (2007), *Sri Lanka Poverty Assessment* (Colombo, Sri Lanka: World Bank).

Wright, W.L. (2009), 'Hannah Arendt and Enemy Combatants: New Implications of Statelessness', paper presented at The Annual Meeting of the The Midwest Political Science Association, Palmer House Hilton, Chicago, Illinois, 02 May, http://www.allacademic.com/meta/p138056_index.html.

Zehra, N. (1992) 'Sindh's Opposition Puts Islamabad in Dilemma', *The Telegraph*, 6 October.

Zorn, J. (2005), 'Ethnic Citizenship in the Slovenian state', *Citizenship Studies*, **9**(2), 135–52.

Zorn, J. (2006), 'Od Izjeme Do Norme: Centri Za Tujce, Pridrževanje In Deportacije', (From exception to norm: centre for aliens, detention and deportation) *Časopis Za Kritiko Znanosti*, **34**(226), 54–73.

Zorn, J. (2007), 'New Borders, New Exclusions', in D. Zaviršek, J. Zorn, L. Richter and S. Žnidarec Demšar (eds), *Ethnicity in Eastern Europe: A Challenge for Social Work Education*, Ljubljana: Fakulteta za socialno delo, pp. 161–77.

Zorn, J. (2008), 'We, the Ethno-citizens of Ethno-democracy: The Formation of Slovene Citizenship', in J. Zorn and U. Lipovec Čebron (eds), *Once upon an Erasure. From Citizens to Illegal Residents in the Republic of Slovenia*, Ljubljana: Študentska založba, pp. 52–69.

Zorn, J. (2009a), 'A Case for Slovene Nationalism: Initial Citizenship Rules and the Erasure', *Nations and Nationalism*, **15**(2), 280–98.

Zorn, J. (2009b), 'Slovenia: Ethnic Exclusion in a Model Accession State', in B. Rechel (ed.), *Minority Rights in Central and Eastern Europe*, Oxford: Routledge, pp. 210–24.

Zorn, J. (2009c), 'The Right to Stay: Challenging the Policy of Detention and Deportation', *European Journal of Social Work*, **12**(2), 247–60.

Zorn, J. and U. Lipovec Čebron (eds) (2008), *Once upon an Erasure from Citizens to Illegal Residents in the Republic of Slovenia*, Ljubljana: Študentska založba.

Index

Printed and bound by CPI Group (UK) Ltd, Croydon, CR0 4YY

16/04/2025

14658487-0001